WHEN BANANA WAS KING

A Jamaican Banana King in Jim Crow America

Leslie Gordon Goffe

Edited by: Martin Henry
Book Design, Layout & Typesetting by: Sanya Dockery
Foreword: Perry Henzell

Published by: LMH Publishing Limited
7 Norman Road,
LOJ Industrial Complex
Building 10
Kingston C.S.O., Jamaica
Tel: 876-938-0005; 938-0712
Fax: 876-759-8752
Email: lmhbookpublishing@cwjamaica.com
Website: www.lmhpublishing.com

Printed in U. S. A.

ISBN13: 978 976 8202 23 9
ISBN10: 976 8202 23 8

For my Mother

Elsie

'a simple stitcher, joiner of things'

Contents

Acknowledgments

'U nprovided with original learning, uninformed in the habits of thinking, unskilled in the arts of composition, I resolved to write a book.' So wrote Edward Gibbons, author of *The Decline and Fall of the Roman Empire*.

I, too, resolved to write a book; one that would not have been possible without the resources of the National Archives of Jamaica, Jamaica's Registrar General's Department, Harlem's Schomburg Institute for Research into Black Culture, the Library of Congress, the National Archives in Washington D.C., the National Archives in London, the British Library, the University of Maryland, College Park, Columbia University libraries, Princeton University libraries, the *Baltimore American* and *Baltimore Sun* newspapers, and *The Gleaner* Company of Jamaica.

I'd like to thank Edward Seaga, former Prime Minister of Jamaica, Perry Henzell, Rachel Manley, Charles H. Johnston, Harold Doley, former US Ambassador to the African Development Bank, and Gordon Shufelt for casting a critical eye over the text in its infancy. I'd also like to thank Jonathan Smith, archivist at Trinity College, Cambridge, Catherine Walker of Napier University, Edinburgh, and the University of California at Berkeley's Regional Oral History Office.

It would not have been possible to put this jigsaw puzzle together without the help of the late Audrey 'Gwennie' Goffe, author of *The Banana Church:*

The Story of St Cyprian's Church, Highgate, St. Mary, Jamaica, W.I., Phillippa Lack, Anthony Lanasa, 'Aussie Andrew', 'jackpancakes', Joyce Ledbetter, Mrs. Keith Mitchell, Margaret-Rose, Tony Goffe, Mrs. Carol Goffe Christie, P. A. Goffe, Keith and Ann Goffe, Sally Henzell, Chris Blackwell, Dickie Jobson, Mary Jane Todd, Paddy Marsh and many others too numerous to mention.

Finally, much love goes out as always to Judy, to Tao, and to Gaia.

Foreword

Over a hundred years ago, at the turn of the 20th century, there was a bunch of Jamaicans who decided to take on the biggest, baddest, hard-core capitalist, multinational corporation operating in the Caribbean and force them to dress back.

At a time when the United Fruit Company was gobbling up entire countries in Central America, universally known as "the banana republics," those Jamaican businessmen not only challenged the mighty UFCo, they won! And not only that, they were black!

At a time when a black man was "no better than a niggah" in the USA, when no non-white could so much as drink from the same tap as a white man, these Jamaicans stayed at the best hotels. At a time when a black man suspected of coming on to a white woman could be lynched in the South, these black Jamaicans took white wives with them when they travelled to the States.

Why? How?

They refused to have themselves defined by racists. They were as self confident in New York in the 1920s as Alexandre Dumas had been as the toast of Paris a hundred years before, or Pushkin had been in Moscow before that. Their self-assurance and their wealth were commanding, and they were treated with respect. American racism held no great sway in Jamaica. These black Jamaicans apparently had no chips on their shoulders, and accordingly the most intelligent white people in the island at the time recognised them as equals. That alone makes this book worth reading, but there is so much else.

They were up, they were down, they fought among themselves as well as with outside competitors, they owned huge properties, and ran steamship companies; they leased docks and warehouses, and controlled a considerable portion of the fruit trade in the USA and England, and they accumulated fortunes of international proportions, but on the other hand they were repeatedly wiped out by hurricanes. World War One virtually shot them down when they were flying highest, and just to prove that they couldn't escape racism entirely, the author's great grandfather landed up in jail, not once but twice.

This story covers a range of characters from the Prince of Wales and future king of England dancing the night away to a direct connection with Bob Marley.

At a time when Jamaica's old enemies in the banana trade have just started their latest battle in the war to wipe out the independent West Indian banana farmer, the example of the pioneers recounted in this book should be an inspiration to our team.

We should not bow, we should fight back, and if we have half the flair and courage of the pioneers a hundred years ago, when banana was king, we'll win again.

Perry Henzell
The Harder They Come
Itopia, St. Ann, Jamaica
October 2005

St Mary's, North Side

Down away South-Westerly, four thousand miles and more away,
Ragged corals ridge the Strand to fret the ceaseless surf;
Over wind-shorn commons there Green Castle looks on Robin's Bay
Moody, empty ruins stare across the tawny turf.

Mile on mile of moving blue that thunders ineffectually;
Jet on jet of dazzling sprays that lash the reefs imperiously;
Boom and hiss of broken waves whose smoke goes up perpetually,
Moaning deep through hidden caves and whispering out mysteriously.

Round the terraced limestone bluff that lifts into the rushing air
Ranks of black pimento-bays to battle with the trade-wind's blow,
Still there walks the ghost of one that ate his heart in exile here,
Don Cristoforo Colon – four hundred shameful years ago.

West and East the watchful headlands questioned an unaltering heaven,
Lilac distances of mountain faint into a sail-less sea:–
Out of those great emptinesses endlessly the sea-wind presses
Where Columbus heard it calling – calling as it calls to me.

You and I were here together – long before the Earth had age –
Loved them and could not forget them – reefs and commons, hills
and skies;

Born not yet of Adam's race, uncumbered of Eve's heritage,
We were happy in this place, when all the world was Paradise...

Sydney Olivier
Governor of Jamaica
1907-1913

In The Beginning

King Banana

"He who trusts in his riches will fall, but the righteous will flourish like a green leaf."
Proverbs11: 28

Though it's hard to believe it now, there was a time when Jamaicans battled Americans for control of the billion-dollar international banana trade. They battled in boardrooms in New York and Kingston and sometimes battled one another with guns and knives on wharves in Baltimore and Port Maria over the tasty, strangely shaped fruit. Most controversial of the banana men back then was a larger than life Jamaican named Alfred Constantine Goffe.

Though he was one of the largest exporters of bananas from Jamaica to the United States, owner of two of Jamaica's earliest hotels and founder of one of the island's first agricultural co-operatives, Goffe's achievements, and exploits – he was arrested in America for allegedly conspiring with the Mafia to commit murder and he was jailed in Jamaica for killing a man – are little remembered today.

"There are two prominent Men in the shipping world today who Jamaica and Jamaicans are bound to respect...A.C. Goffe and Marcus Garvey," Jamaica's *Daily Gleaner* newspaper reported in 1920.

Loved by some and loathed by many more, Goffe, a black man, was a big landowner and banana business millionaire at a time when black people were not long out of slavery. Goffe's mother, Margaret, had been a slave.

A black man in a business dominated by whites, A.C. Goffe and his brothers joined with an Italian-American merchant, Antonio Lanasa, in 1906 to form the Lanasa and Goffe Steamship and Importing Company. The firm, which had offices in Jamaica and the United States, was launched on 4 January 1906 in Baltimore, Maryland.

"*We do certify that the said corporation is formed for the purpose of conducting a General mercantile business and exporting and importing of domestic and foreign fruits and other goods articles and merchandise necessary for navigating the oceans and high seas by steam electricity sail or other ships or vessels and the transporting of goods and passengers thereon,*" the company's papers of incorporation read.

Together Lanasa and Goffe coordinated the growing and purchasing of bananas in Jamaica and the chartering of a fleet of steamships to deliver the fruit to the U.S., and once there the distribution by railway of millions of bunches of bananas to cities across America.

"The company is one of the largest importers of and dealers in foreign fruits, not only in Baltimore, but in the East," the American Journal of Commerce said of Lanasa and Goffe's firm in 1909. The company was a good example, the journal said, of what could be accomplished by "a competent organisation...under the direction of men of ability and progressiveness."

The Lanasa and Goffe firm was an unusual collaboration between black Jamaicans and Italian-Americans. It defied racial prohibitions of the time. The company was incorporated in a ceremony at Baltimore's City Hall, the seat of local government and bastion of the mostly German, Irish, and White Anglo-Saxon Protestant power brokers who ran the Southern seaport city. The august, Renaissance-style building, erected in 1875, stood four storeys high and was capped off by a 260-foot iron dome, its outer facing made of white Maryland marble.

Italians and blacks would have been a rare and unwelcome sight in the grand building. There nonetheless, at 2:30pm on 4 January, 1906, to launch their banana import and shipping company was Antonio Lanasa and A.C. Goffe. Also at the ceremony was Lanasa's father, Michael, two of his brothers, Giovanni and Santo, all directors of the new firm, all outsiders. Though they were not quite so reviled as were black people, Italians, especially the darker-skinned from Sicily and other parts of southern Italy, were regarded as inferiors by fairer-skinned whites from northern Europe. As far as the German, Irish and Anglo-Americans were concerned, Italians, the last of the European immigrants to arrive in America in large numbers, were far beneath them and only one step above blacks in the racial hierarchy.

That a company like Lanasa and Goffe's could be launched at all was cause for celebration. If the incorporation of the new banana firm was celebrated at all, it must've been a brief one. With the ink barely dry on the company's charter, A.C. Goffe and Antonio Lanasa left for New York on 6 January, 1906. The same evening they boarded a passenger and cargo ship for Jamaica. The sea journey aboard the *S.S.Tagus* would normally have taken six days, but the steamer completed the journey in record time – three days, twenty-three hours and twenty minutes. This was an amazing feat. When the ship, owned by the British Royal Mail Steam Packet Company and skippered by a Captain Doughty, set out from New York it was buffeted by a strong gale. This soon passed, though, and fine weather prevailed until the ship arrived two days ahead of schedule at Kingston on January 10.

Aware they'd been part of a very special voyage, the passengers, among them C.J. Ward, owner of one of Jamaica's largest companies, J. Wray and Nephew, cheered the captain and his crew. The island's newspapers, too, celebrated the achievement. The newspaper correspondents wanted to know everything: Had the ship's two unusually tall, thin funnels or its unusually square propeller boss contributed in some way to its speedy arrival in Jamaica from the United States.

The *Tagus'* passengers had to fight their way through the reporters and curious onlookers in order to disembark at Kingston harbour. A.C. Goffe was convinced that at least one of the newspaper correspondents had been dispatched to record the big news he and Lanasa were bringing with them from Baltimore. This wasn't the case. The only thing anyone was interested in was the incredibly swift crossing from New York.

The record-breaking voyage over, Goffe and Lanasa made their way to the railway terminus in Kingston. There they boarded a train to St Mary parish, in northeastern Jamaica. The 40-odd mile journey from Kingston to Albany in St Mary – with stops along the way at Gregory Park, Grange Lane, Spanish Town, Bog Walk, Riversdale, Troja and Richmond – cost Goffe and his business partner around six shillings apiece. Rail was the quickest and most assured way to travel across Jamaica in the early 1900s. Automobiles were here and there around Jamaica, but hadn't yet become a widely used form of transport on the island. Besides, Jamaica's railway, built in 1845, was among the very best in the world, stretching as it did almost from one end of country to the next.

Unfortunately for A.C. Goffe and other citizens of Port Maria, the capital of St Mary parish, the railway did not stretch as far as their town. Though Port Maria was a centre of the island's banana trade, it did not enjoy the same access to the railway that other parts of the country did. Robert Percy Simmonds, the parish's representative in the island's Legislative Council, had tried but failed to convince the government to fund the building of a rail extension from the Albany station to Port Maria, eight miles north. St Mary people were convinced they hadn't won approval for an extension because people in the island's other parishes were jealous of them and the wealth and prosperity bananas had brought them. They were, locals felt, deserving. The facts spoke for themselves. Next to Kingston and St. Andrew, the most densely populated of the island's fourteen parishes, was St Mary. It was clear the area would need better transportation if the banana industry there was to continue to grow.

The town of Port Maria had grown rich off the banana trade. It had a thriving business district, a public general hospital, an almshouse, a court house, an excellent market, two schools, several churches, among them an Anglican, a Baptist and a Moravian. It also, most important of all, had the busiest port in Jamaica.

Located at Port Maria harbour was the building that housed the offices of Messrs Goffe Bros, a banana-purchasing firm begun by A.C. Goffe and his brothers in 1897.

Goffe's father, John, had spent most of his working life at the harbour. He started a large general store there in the 1850s that sold everything from leather saddles from England to exotic foodstuffs from New York. He operated a shipping company at the harbour, too, which his sons took over after their father's death. Apart from the general store and shipping company, A.C. Goffe's parents also left him and his siblings the Lee Wharf, a property with a murky past.

Contained within the Lee Wharf premises was a pier which stretched one hundred feet out into the sea, a three-storied main building made almost entirely of stone, with corrugated zinc roofing. It had several warehouses, as well, which could store anywhere from 1,000 to 1,500 tons of wood and anywhere from 10,000 to 15,000 bunches of bananas. The eastern section of Lee Wharf, which had once served as a headquarters for Port Maria's Young

Women's Christian Association, housed a reception room, four bedrooms, a clubroom, a dining room, a pantry, a bathroom and a spacious verandah that commanded a full view of the Caribbean Sea.

Also contained within the wharf premises was a tennis court and a court for basketball, a new game that had become very popular in Jamaica since James Naismith, a Canadian physical education instructor, invented it fifteen years before in the United States. Few people, though, knew what sinister business had gone on at Lee Wharf. During the days of the slave trade the Lee Wharf had hosted one of St Mary's busiest slave markets. Slave ships docked at Port Maria and Africans brought as chattel aboard them were deposited in holding pens in one of the wharf's buildings. After they'd been fed and watered, their sores cleaned and their bodies greased to make them more attractive for sale, Africans were offered to the highest bidder.

Once a storehouse for human cargo, Lee Wharf became a depository for an entirely different cargo to be bought and sold and make profit on after A.C. Goffe and his brothers set up their banana-purchasing firm, Messrs Goffe Bros, there in 1897. This time it was not black men that were being bought and sold, but black men, the Goffe brothers, doing the buying and selling.

'Dagoes and Niggers'

'I am free of all prejudice. I hate everyone equally.'
W.C. Fields

It was during the spring and summer months that Americans, the principal gobblers of the banana, craved the fruit most for their banana splits, their banana daiquiris and the many other inventive concoctions in which they employed the tasty, strangely shaped fruit. Aggressive exporters who got bananas quickly from the plantations of Jamaica to the dining tables of America could make enormous sums in one brief season.

With this in mind, weeks after they launched their business in January 1906, Lanasa and Goffe arranged for their first load of bananas to be shipped to Baltimore from Jamaica in March 1906. The new company sought, and won, the support of the many smaller growers in Jamaica not under contract to the United Fruit Company, the giant American conglomerate that had gobbled up and absorbed most of the independent companies in the banana trade. Growers were desperate to break the grip of United Fruit, which had achieved its dominance using dubious methods.

"It looks as if the banana war here is about to begin," Jamaica's *Daily Telegraph* newspaper reported on 8 March 1906. The paper was, of course, referring to the launching of Lanasa and Goffe's company and to the launching a short time before of the Atlantic Fruit Company by Joseph Di Giorgio, a business rival of Antonio Lanasa's in Baltimore. "Two new companies have put in their appearance and threatened the United Fruit Company's hold on the banana trade." American Lorenzo Dow Baker, a founder of United Fruit, spoke publicly of his disappointment at the arrival of interlopers in the trade.

"We have got to take charge of every banana that reaches the wharf," Baker told a Jamaican newspaper. "This is for our own safeguard, just to form a nucleus and shut out the element of danger in a crabbed and jibbing market." There is, Baker said, none too convincingly, "no danger of our spreading our tentacles like an octopus and grabbing all the land in sight."

Some of what Baker said was true. He warned, correctly, that enormous changes were occuring in the international banana trade and that these changes would threaten Jamaica's place as the leader of it.

Jamaica had been the largest single producer of bananas since the banana trade's beginnings in the 1870s. But there were signs Cuba, the Dominican Republic and several countries in Central America would soon be in a position to challenge Jamaica's dominance. The only way to guard against this, Baker said, was for Jamaican growers to improve the quality of their bananas and for them to accept lower prices for their fruit. Baker encouraged Jamaicans to abandon what he called their "don't-care way of cutting, carting and handling of fruit." Instead of growing bananas year round, Baker said Jamaicans ought to grow the fruit when it was most in demand in North America. "Quashy," the Captain said, "will grow the fruit when they can because it is the only income they have, but Buckra, boss man, has got to use agricultural common sense."

Though many Jamaicans thought Captain Baker a heroic figure because he had brought banana wealth to the country, others knew better. In 1898, Seward Scott Smith, a former commission agent, began a small banana export company, S.S. Smith. The Port Antonio firm became in a very short time a big success. Port Antonio was also the home of Captain Baker and of his Boston Fruit Company, the forerunner of the United Fruit Company. Baker thought of Port Antonio as 'his town'. After all, a beach had been named there for the Boston Fruit Company. Seward Smith's little company was well run and though it provided no real competition to the Baker company, the Americans were determined to close it down. So in 1900 the Americans offered to buy Smith out. Smith would, United Fruit told him, be allowed to purchase shares in their company at very favourable prices and would eventually become the manager of all of their Jamaican operations. To top all of this off, Smith was promised a salary that would make him the highest paid man in Jamaica. The deal was struck and United Fruit purchased Smith's operations. It dismantled some bits of it and kept other bits intact. Smith, as promised, became assistant manager of United Fruit operations in Port Antonio. But, after only a few months, he was dismissed. Smith took United Fruit to court, suing the firm for the largest amount ever in Jamaican history. Smith won the case, but received much less than he'd hoped for. Though battered by the experience, the Port Antonio banana man returned to the trade, remaining in it, in one form or another, for many years.

This, then, was what was facing Antonio Lanasa and A.C. Goffe as they formed their banana company in 1906. United Fruit had two very different faces: the cuddly, deeply religious Captain Lorenzo Dow Baker on the one side and on the other, its president, Andrew Preston, a hard faced businessmen determined to dominate the banana industry. When asked by a journalist to reflect on his years in the banana trade and how he'd come to fall in love with the fruit, Preston said bluntly: "I saw 'em, I bought 'em, and I sold 'em."

Despite obstacles, Lanasa and Goffe were able to secure markets for their fruit in the United States not controlled by United or Atlantic. They purchased fruit in Jamaica in the open market from small settlers not contracted to the big companies. While United and Atlantic had lucrative agreements with most of the larger banana planters in Jamaica, Lanasa and Goffe became the export company of choice for the small man, the small farmer. In St Mary, the firm's agents purchased fruit at Parochial Beach, Frankfurt Wharf, Highgate Siding, Richmond Railway Station, Bailey's Vale, Lee Wharf, and Salt Gut. In neighbouring Portland parish, the firm purchased bananas at Drapers, Breastworks, Sherwood Forest, Moore Town, St Margaret's Bay, Jumbi Fording, and Nonsuch. In St Ann parish, its agents, were granted licences by the Clerk of Courts to purchase produce at Ocho Rios, Gloster Hill, Dillon Town, Blackstonedge and at White Hall.

Whether because of patriotism or simple self-interest, many Jamaican growers gave their support and sold their fruit to Lanasa and Goffe's upstart company. In St. James, in the western part of Jamaica, banana agents working for the firm appealed to patriotism to convince growers to give them the fruit they needed to make the new firm a success.

"Goffe Bros…are no strangers to you and I," banana agent C.A. Wallace, told growers. "I ask you to give them your support. They are Jamaicans and deserve Jamaica's support." Moved by the appeal, many growers promised to support the new firm whether or not others offered them higher prices.

With banana workers ready to cut and deliver Lanasa and Goffe's maiden shipment of fruit, the firm's leased fruit steamer, *S.S. San Miguel*, set sail from Baltimore on 22 March 1906 for the four day voyage to Jamaica. Minutes into the ship's journey disaster struck.

'FRUIT STEAMER DAMAGED IN A COLLISION…HAD HOLE IN HER SIDE,' read a headline in the *Baltimore Sun* newspaper the next day. Twelve miles out to sea, at 10 pm on March 22, the *San Miguel*, piloted by its German captain, Mueller, collided with a schooner, the *Harry T. Hayward*. The schooner had been ferrying 1,650 tons of phosphate rock from Punta Gorda off the Gulf Coast of Florida to Baltimore. Badly damaged, the stack and deck fixtures dismantled and a large hole above the water line on the port side, the *San Miguel* made its way back to Baltimore harbour. A.C. Goffe was there to see it. He had recently returned to Baltimore from Port Maria to prepare the ship for its maiden journey to Jamaica. Goffe saw his fruit steamer leave and saw it return a short time later, busted and broken. His bid to become a major player in the banana export and shipping trade had been scuppered, it seemed. But, somehow, the *San Miguel* was fixed up and made it to Jamaica only a day behind schedule on 27 March, 1906.

Once it was clear the steamer had overcome its difficulties and would arrive at Port Maria, the frenzied business of getting the fruit from field to wharf began. An army of workers set about the task. There were cutters, carriers, sidemen, truck and cart men. There were receivers, handlers, and washing tank men, whose dangerous job it was to flush out the deadly spiders that sometimes nested amongst the fruit. There were boatmen, stevedores, selectors, inspectors, and tallymen, whom Harry Belafonte made famous in the song, 'Day-O (Banana Boat Song).' Interestingly, the 'Day-O' chant, 'Come Mr. Tallyman, tally me banana,' was said to have been sung originally by workers loading bananas at wharves in St Mary.

The business of cutting bananas and loading them onto a steamer was not an exact science, but it was getting close to it. The carrying capacity of a fruit steamer was known almost to the very last bunch. As a result, just the right amount of bananas could be cut and delivered to the wharves. Port Maria was a very busy seaport. It was the largest and safest of Jamaica's ports after Port Antonio. Six or seven of the largest steamers could load their produce at one time without much difficulty. Lanasa and Goffe's *San Miguel*, which weighed around 3,000 tons and had room for up to 30,000 tightly packed bunches of bananas in its holds, was one of the smaller steamers. On average it took around 200 people, many of them women and children, to load a steamer in Jamaica. To unload it in Baltimore, anywhere from 250 and 400 men were employed. Unloading usually took an entire day to complete. This done, the produce was placed into special ice and salt-laden refrigerator cars of the Baltimore and Ohio Rail Road.

In later years, the produce was loaded into specially adapted railway cars fitted with steam heating during the winter and cooling ventilation during the summer months. A typical cargo usually took up one hundred to one hundred and fifty or so railway cars.

Lanasa and Goffe's produce was dispatched to customers in various parts of America: Delaware, Philadelphia and New York to the north and Washington D.C., Virginia and North Carolina to the south and St. Louis and Chicago in the Midwest. Fruit not dispatched on trains was sold to the thousands of fruit vendors who lined the dock area at Baltimore harbour, eager for the arrival of the banana steamers from Jamaica. These mostly Italian vendors hawked the fruit themselves or sold it to an assortment of retailers in Baltimore and elsewhere in Maryland.

A good deal of Lanasa and Goffe's produce was auctioned off, too, at the Baltimore Fruit Exchange. Though the exchange belonged to their bitter enemy, Joseph Di Giorgio, a rival fruit merchant, as it was the only one in the city, the Jamaican and the Italian had no choice but to use it to win customers for their produce. They believed Di Giorgio charged them a higher than usual commission to handle their fruit. Lanasa and Goffe produce not disposed of in this way was kept in storage at their warehouses on East Pratt Street, adjacent to Baltimore harbour.

Baltimore had one of America's busiest harbours. Only three other U.S. cities handled more export items and handled more import items in 1905 than did Baltimore. Yet despite the harbour's obvious importance to the city, Baltimore's government and its business leaders did little to improve it. The harbour was badly out of date and presented special difficulties for fruit steamers emptying their produce there.

Unlike cities with more developed wharves, a steamer that docked at Baltimore in 1906 had to have its produce unloaded, first of all, onto a barge.

The fruit was then loaded onto railway cars. It was a primitive and time-consuming system that could not be avoided as the railway was at a distance from the harbour. It was not unusual for shipping companies, for whom speed was everything, to threaten to pull their operations out of Baltimore unless improvements were made. To appease shippers, the city did finally make improvements. The water line in the Union, Frederick and Long Street area was, for example, deepened so larger ships could dock there.

What improvements were made in Baltimore occurred, ironically, as a result of the 'Great Fire' of 1904. The fire destroyed 1,500 buildings spread over eighty blocks of the 32- square mile city. More than 2,000 businesses were forced to close and around 35,000 people were left jobless. Damage was put at more than $125 million, or around $2.5 billion today. The fire was believed to have been started by a cigarette dropped down a grating into the basement of a dry goods store. It raged for two days before being brought under control with the help of more than a thousand firefighters. Miraculously, only five people died, all of these as a result of pneumonia contracted battling the flames.

When the blaze seemed to weaken at one point Baltimore's mayor, eager to claim victory, declared to a newspaper reporter that thanks to his actions the blaze had run its course and the city had been saved. He was wrong. It wasn't until the next day, February 8, that firefighters managed to stop the fire at Jones Falls in the east of the city as it approached the 'Little Italy' area. The Lanasa family lived near here and many of their businesses were located in the area. Desperate for divine intervention, residents of Little Italy were said to have gone into the streets praying loudly to St. Anthony of Padua, the patron saint of lost causes, to save their neighborhood. When the blaze stopped a short distance away locals were convinced a miracle had occurred. Since then the Little Italy neighborhood has, so the story goes, held a festival of Thanksgiving each year dedicated to St. Anthony.

"Baltimore has been visited by a catastrophe which is without a parallel in the history of this city," read an editorial in a Baltimore newspaper two days after the fire had been extinguished. "It is a cruel blow to the material interests of Baltimore, but not a crushing one; for the business men of this city, with undaunted spirit, will surely prove themselves equal to the occasion."

The fire defeated, the city turned immediately to rebuilding. Streets were widened and extended and new buildings, made of sturdier stuff, were put up.

Though some businessmen complained, those in the shipping industry welcomed the changes. They were pleased the city decided to purchase the wharf area from the private company that had owned it and set about modernising the docks and building new piers.

By 1905, a year after the fire, Baltimore's decrepit, rundown wharf area had been entirely transformed. Perhaps most important of all, the docks were now in the hands of a city agency not in private hands. In a short time two hundred places of business burnt out by the fire opened again. More than 170 new buildings were put up. A modern sewer system was finally begun in 1906, putting an end to the foul smelling open sewers that had given the city its awful smell. The 'Great Fire,' some Baltimoreans said, was the best thing that ever happened to the city. Soon fruit steamers filled the modern harbour. The increase in the number of banana steamers docking at Baltimore caught the attention of city newspapers.

"The advance this city has taken in the tropical fruit trade in the last few years has been steady," the *Baltimore Sun* reported in March 1906. "Where there was formerly but one or two companies, eight concerns are now engaged in the fruit-importing business." In one week in 1906 almost one and a half million bananas, so much it could have stretched to Chicago 700 miles away and allowed every man, woman, and child in Baltimore to have two fingers of the fruit each, arrived in the city from Jamaica and from Central America.

But with the growth of the banana trade came problems. The City of Baltimore published a report saying the shortage of docking facilities was a "grave matter." Battling one another for those docking facilities was: the United Fruit Company, the Atlantic Fruit Company, The Battaglia Steamship Company, the Italian Fruit Dealer's Association, the Vicari Brothers, the S.Oteri Company, and the Lanasa and Goffe Steamship and Importing Company. All of them had offices in the East Pratt Street area of Baltimore.

East Pratt Street, one of the city of Baltimore's main thoroughfares, was a veritable banana row. There, hardscrabble banana men and hardened wharfingers held sway. Bloody fistfights frequently broke out on the wharves between employees of the rival banana companies. On more than one occasion Baltimore police were called to 'Old Bowly's Wharf' to break up fights between workers of the Lanasa and Goffe company and dock hands working for its arch rival, Joseph Di Giorgio. It was not unusual for guns and switchblades to be drawn by the warring wharf hands. It was impossible for the two banana companies to ignore one another. Lanasa and Goffe's premises were located at 12 and 14 East Pratt Street, just a door away from the offices of the Di Giorgio Fruit Company at 18 and 20 East Pratt Street.

In this cut-throat environment any advantage gained by one or other of the banana companies was bitterly resented by the rest. Joseph Di Giorgio considered himself the 'Banana King' of Baltimore, the Pezzo Novante, the big shot. Though a poor boy from Sicily, Di Giorgio thought of himself as banana royalty. He got a title to go along with his kingly ways in 1904. Italy's King Victor Emmanuel conferred the honor of *Chevalier of The Royal Crown* upon the Sicilian banana man. The self-styled 'Banana King' was now a kind of knight of the Italian realm.

"The King's government could not lose sight of Mr. Joseph Di Giorgio," wrote Italy's Foreign Minister, Pitoni, in a letter sent to Di Giorgio. "Mr. Di Giorgio is deserving of admiration, for with his ability he has made his name illustrious." Joseph Di Giorgio's achievements in the banana trade were an "honour to him," Foreign Minister Pitoni said, " and the land that gave birth to him." Antonio Lanasa and A.C. Goffe received no such princely honours. They had to make do with praise from the media for running an efficient commercial concern. In 1909, their firm was singled out for praise by a leading American business magazine.

"Ample facilities having been provided for the receiving, storage and shipping of invoices of any size, so that no matter what may be desired this company is able to supply it and in the most prompt and satisfactory manner," read a report in the *Journal of Commerce*.

Glowing endorsements aside, Lanasa and Goffe elected to take a cautious approach in its first year in the banana export trade in 1906. While their rivals operated many vessels, the company employed just two steamers between Baltimore and Jamaica. The *San Miguel* arrived one week in Jamaica. The *Oxus*, their second chartered vessel, arrived the next. Lanasa and Goffe had seen too many ambitious, aggressive banana men rise quickly, and fall even quicker. Joseph Di Giorgio had, for example, begun the grandly titled fruit produce company, The Monumental Trading Company in 1890 only to have it collapse less than thirty days later. Lanasa and Goffe were determined not to suffer a similar embarrassing fate.

By the end of 1907, their second year in the export trade, the firm, buoyed by tremendous profits, increased the number of vessels it employed. Each of their steamers was now carrying upwards of 20,000 bunches of bananas each journey. Soon the company claimed it was responsible for exporting a half of the nearly six million bunches exported from St Mary to the United States each year. Though Jamaica's newspapers had not paid as much attention to Lanasa and Goffe's firm as the company would have liked, the Jamaican government delivered a flattering assessment of the firm in a 1907 report.

"During the year the enterprising firm of Messrs Goffe Bros. inaugurated a fruit business between the Island and Baltimore starting with one vessel a week and so successful has their business been that a second steamer has been put on, and it is probable that there will be further developments in the near future," the Jamaican government reported. Indeed, so good was business, the firm begun to explore markets for its produce in American ports besides Baltimore. Tampa, in the west of Florida, seemed an ideal spot. Lanasa went south to explore.

Expanding their operations to a European port was also considered. Goffe, who had connections there, went to London in the spring of 1907. He combined his business trip with a visit to siblings of his living in London. He told his sister, Laura, who was living the leisurely life of a lady of means in the metropolis at Portman Square, about the earthquake that'd destroyed much of Kingston on 10 January, 1907. A.C.'s brother, Ernest, a physician, was curious about the number of dead and how the hospitals had managed to care for the wounded. Rowland, a law student, was interested in the many lawsuits he knew would be filed as a result of the earthquake. All three were surprised to hear that Port Maria, almost 50 miles from Kingston, had been damaged by the quake. There wasn't much damage, but the town's clock tower had developed large cracks and would need some work.

News of Jamaica aside, Rowland talked to A.C. about his recent appointment as a member of the West India Committee, a body that had a murky past as a lobby for sugar planters during slavery, but had recently re-invented itself as a lobby in Britain for West Indian banana planters and exporters. Rowland's appointment was a boon for his family. Lanasa and Goffe now had an insider who could feed them information of value to their business. In

Jamaica, too, they had an insider, of sorts. A few weeks before A.C. arrived in London, his older brother, Robert, got the good news that he'd been elected treasurer of the Port Maria branch of the Jamaica Agricultural Society, a quasi-government body concerned with agricultural policy.

His visit to London over, Goffe headed home to Jamaica. Discussions with distributors in Britain came to nothing so he decided to forget expansion and concentrate on the banana business in America. There was some good news, though. A new Norwegian-made ship with state of the art technology and large holds that Lanasa and Goffe wanted to be the first to charter, had been offered to them by its owners at favourable terms. The deal done, it was decided the ship, in deference to Goffe's partner in Baltimore, would be called the *Antonio Lanasa*. The future looked good, but the shipping business was both a profitable and perilous trade. Trouble was never very far away. While Goffe had been in Britain there'd been a death at the harbour in Port Maria.

A little over a year after a steamer chartered by Lanasa and Goffe, *San Miguel*, was almost sunk on its way from Baltimore to Port Maria, another ship belonging to the company, the *Oxus*, met with disaster. On 11 June, 1907, the father of the *Oxus'* captain, McKenzie, fell overboard and drowned. "SAD ACCIDENT ON A FRUITER, is how The *Daily Gleaner* newspaper reported it. "PORT MARIA FATALITY. Rescued in Water, But It Proved Too Late."

In time, the *Oxus* was dropped by the company. Seamen are a deeply super-stitious breed and the death of Captain McKenzie's father made employing crews to work the *Oxus*, which was named after an ancient Greek waterway, impossible. The ship was returned to its owners. Giving credence to the sea-men's fears, the *Oxus* sank mysteriously at Cape Finistere off the Spanish mainland a year later. The ship's master claimed it had hit a sunken wreck. Others claimed to have heard the chief engineer telling how he would sink the "damned ship" and deposit it at the bottom of the sea where it belonged. A board of inquiry set up to get to the bottom of the mystery concluded, "…the *Oxus* foundered under circumstances of which no adequate explanation has been offered."

The death of Captain McKenzie's father aboard the *Oxus* led to calls for improvements at St Mary's harbours. Ship's captains had long complained that it was a dangerous business entering Port Maria harbour, especially at night. Three years before, in 1904, two banana steamers, the *Ethelred* and the *Schlezwig*, were wrecked coming into Port Maria via Galina Point, the most northerly part of the St Mary coastline. After the two steamers were wrecked, the island's government commissioned a survey of the Galina Point area. Scaffolding was set up and locals were convinced a lighthouse would soon be erected at the Point. But after an initial exploration, the surveyors and workmen were withdrawn.

With Port Maria harbour in the news because of the death there of a ship captain's father, A.C. Goffe's brother, Clarence, a member of St Mary's Parochial Board, called for the Galina lighthouse project to be revived. This letter, written by Clarence with the support of his colleagues on the Board, was sent to Jamaica's governor, Sydney Olivier: "Whereas the importance of Port Maria as a shipping port and chief town of this important parish of St Mary and the centre of the banana growing districts of the island having being brought clearly before the public as shown by the recent report of the Collector General in that the number of steamers visiting this port was only exceeded by the port of Kingston (Kingston 44, Port Maria 40)…Be it hereby resolved – That this Board seeing the necessity for the lighthouse, do convey the substance of this resolution to His Excellency the Governor and ask him to authorize the placing on the estimates of the Legislative Council for the next financial year the funds for the construction of this work, which is of vital importance to this island…"

The death of Captain McKenzie's father and the demands for a lighthouse at Galina Point aside, 1907 was, all in all, a very good year for Lanasa and Goffe. Other Jamaicans had observed their success and wanted to follow them into the export trade. In October 1907, Alfred Vincent de Lisser, a Trelawny businessman, announced he was looking for customers in the United States willing to be a part of a new banana company. Nothing came of it, though. It foundered after only a few weeks.

As for A.C. Goffe, it was time for him to return to Baltimore. His firm's new fruit steamer, the *Antonio Lanasa*, had been delivered to Port Maria. To celebrate the event and show off their new ship, A.C. and his brothers arranged a fancy reception onboard the new steamer. Invitees were told to arrive at the harbour by 4pm on 13 July, 1907 for a sea journey to Annotto Bay, a few miles away. There was lots of food and plenty of dancing aboard. The festivities ended deep into the night. A.C. hoped he had made the kind of splash that would make his friends happy and his enemies envious. He hoped the spectacle would show banana growers that Lanasa and Goffe had plenty of money and would be in the banana business for a very long time.

Unlike the *S.S. Oxus*, the maiden journey of the *S.S. Antonio Lanasa* from Jamaica to the United States went off without hitch. Onboard were A.C. Goffe, his brothers Alec, Cecil, and Cecil's wife, Mildred. In Baltimore Antonio Lanasa and his family received the ship, their name emblazoned on it, with excitement. Five months later, in December, Goffe traveled aboard the steamer again from Port Maria to Baltimore with a nice haul of fruit for the American market: 14,900 bunches of bananas, 14 crates of oranges, 102 crates of grapefruits, and 470 bags of coconuts. The ship, after a trouble-free four-day journey, arrived in Baltimore on December 10.

Interestingly, as A.C. Goffe was arriving in the city from Jamaica, Salvatore Lupo, a member of the fearsome Mafia-like Black Hand gang, was arriving in Baltimore, too, by train from Pittsburgh, Pennsylvania. Goffe waited while a bad-tempered Jamaican ram goat, a surprise gift he was sure Antonio Lanasa would appreciate, was led off the fruit steamer and taken the short distance to his firm's offices at East Pratt Street.

Lupo, whose name means 'Fox', had also come to Baltimore bearing gifts bound to cause the recipient great surprise. Goffe went about his business. Lupo went about his. Before long the two would be brought together in one of the biggest trials the city of Baltimore had ever seen. It had everything: the Mafia, dynamite, U.S. congressmen, U.S. senators – and bananas.

Blowing Up the Banana King

'It's not personal. It's just business.'

Don Vito Corleone

"**B**IG TRIAL, Arrest of Mr. Alfred C. Goffe in Baltimore," shouted a headline from the front page of *The Daily Gleaner* newspaper on 19 January, 1908. "A Startling Charge, said to be connected with Black Hand outrage." The story also made the front page of newspapers in the United States. 'Plot To Murder Told,' *The Washington Post* reported. "Lanasa said he would be Banana King of Baltimore if Di Giorgio was slain." The New York Times, too, covered the story. 'THREE DYNAMITING ARRESTS,' read a headline in the 12 January, 1908 edition of the newspaper. A.C. Goffe, *The New York Times* reported, "is said to have connections occupying prominent places in England and other countries." A week later, on 18 January 1908, the *Times* was still on the story. 'BLEW UP THE BANANA KING,' the paper reported.

Joseph Di Giorgio, the self-proclaimed 'Banana King' of Baltimore, was not slain, though, when seven gangsters from the Black Hand gang, the early Mafia, came calling with dynamite at his grand home at the corner of Westwood Avenue and Tenth Street in the Walbrook section of Baltimore at around midnight on 10 December 1907. The bomb, which was placed at the back of the house, destroyed the toilet, the pantry, and almost completely wrecked the kitchen. It did not, though, kill the inhabitants: Di Giorgio's wife, Amelia, her cousin, Joseph Trombetta, an employee of the Di Giorgio Fruit Co., his wife, Marietta, a sister of Di Giorgio's, their three children, and a Di Giorgio servant.

Though they were all far from the site of the blast some of them, nonetheless, claimed they had been thrown from their beds by the impact. Susan Wolford, the Di Giorgio's African-American cook, said she had been resting in an attic room and had slept undisturbed through the commotion. The only living things in danger from the dynamite, as it turned out, were three parrots whom Mrs. Di Giorgio told police later she found in a room near the site of the explosion speaking, no one knew why, Spanish and French.

The target, Joseph Di Giorgio, was not home nor even in the country at the time of the dynamiting. He'd left the country to conduct some important business in Jamaica and to avoid being subpoenaed by the U.S. Congress in an investigation it was conducting into the United Fruit Company. Di Giorgio was afraid it might be discovered that a majority stake had been bought by United Fruit in his Atlantic Fruit Company in contravention of anti-trust laws. After successfully dodging the subpoena, Di Giorgio headed for Jamaica where he negotiated a five-year contract to purchase the entire produce of one of Jamaica's largest banana estates.

Meanwhile, back at the Di Giorgio home in Baltimore, the police officer whose regular beat this was, Patrolman Hardesty, said he passed the Sicilian's home minutes before the explosion and came back in the same direction minutes after but found no suspects in the area. The first arrests in the case came within days of the bombing during the 'Fisherman's Feast,' a festival put on each year by Italian immigrants in honor of Madonna del Soccorso, a saintly figure they believed protected them from the Devil. But the Madonna had done little to protect them from the murderous Black Hand gangsters who'd preyed on them in Sicily and now preyed on them in America, too. The police weren't much good, either.

Like the police, Hollywood didn't yet take the Black Hand, also known as 'Mano Nera,' seriously. In the 1913 Hollywood film, *The Black Hand*, a woman pretends she is being threatened by members of the gang so she can trick her father into letting her marry the man of her choice. Novelists, too, exploited the public's growing fascination with Italian organised crime. Arthur Benjamin Reeve, a writer of trashy crime fiction titles such as *The Scientific Cracksman* and *The Bacteriological Detective* wrote one of the earliest novels about the criminal syndicate. In his book, *The Black Hand*, Italians victimised by gangsters in New York fight back. They set up a vigilante group called 'The White Hand' to combat the Black Hand menace.

Though fictionalised by Hollywood, the Black Hand remained a very real danger for Italians in 1900s America. The gang was implicated in the deaths of Italians in Connecticut, in New Jersey, in Baltimore and in many other cities across the United States. A 1904 survey of Italians living in New York City showed that nine out of ten of them had been sent a letter by the Black Hand threatening death if money were not furnished.

By 1906, hardly any of the United States' prominent Italian-Americans could say they had not been sent menacing correspondence by the Black Hand. Baltimore's Chief of Detectives, A.J. Pumphrey, was convinced there was a simple answer to the Black Hand problem. "If all rich Italians would," Pumphrey said, "join and determine not to be frightened we could end the trouble."

The authorities might have stopped the trouble had they not allowed Ignazio Saietta, 'The Wolf,' into the United States in 1898. A member of the Black Hand in his hometown of Corleone, in Sicily, Saietta was the first to establish a branch of the criminal gang in the United States. It is from Saietta's Black Hand gang that the American Mafia sprang. Former Black Hand members established the Genovese crime family, which was for many years the largest and most powerful of the American Mafia's 'five families.'

Antonio Lanasa's father, Michael, thought he had left the Black Hand behind in Sicily when he migrated to the United States. He hadn't. In 1906, letters with a Black Hand inscribed on them began arriving at his Baltimore home. The letters demanded he deliver cash to the gang or face death. One was signed, 'The Mafia Association.' A second letter was signed, 'The Head of the Black Hand and Company.' Both demanded $5,000. He contacted the police and they told his wife, Anna, to reply to one of the letters. When a young Italian came to collect, the police were alerted and the man, Ignazio Castalano, was captured after a chase through the streets of Baltimore. Castalano told police he'd been sent from New York by four men whose full names he did not know. He had no idea, he said, the letters he delivered contained threats from the Black Hand. The authorities were not convinced. Castalano was sentenced to seven years in prison. Castalano's accomplice, Rosarto Romeo, told the same story and was also sent to prison.

The Black Hand became so powerful in New York the city's police department set up a special squad to combat it. The squad was made up of detectives who had either been born in Italy or who were fluent in Italian and familiar with Italian culture. The special unit was led by Giuseppe Petrosino, a Sicilian from Palermo, the city in the Italian South where the Black Hand was born and where it was at its most deadly. An Eliot Ness-like figure, Petrosino had some success against the gang before he was gunned down in Palermo in 1909 while pursuing Black Hand fugitives wanted in the United States.

It was to this deadly criminal gang that the seven Italians arrested and charged with conspiracy to murder Joseph Di Giorgio were alleged to belong. Oddly, several of the men had been, at one time or another, employees in one or other of the Lanasa family enterprises. One had also been, interestingly, an employee of Joseph Di Giorgio's.

Believing they would become immune from attack if they put Black Hand members on their payrolls, many Italian businessmen employed the gangsters. Rarely did this give them the protection or peace they hoped for.

The seven men charged with participating in the dynamiting of the Di Giorgio house were: 47-year old Michaelina Russo, a Lanasa employee; 52-year old Joseph Tamburo, a Lanasa employee; 49-year old Cologero Monteleone, a book-keeper and fruit checker for a company owned by Michael Lanasa, Antonio's father's; 31- year old Antonio Battistone, an employee of Joseph Di Giorgio's; 22-year old Joseph Catalano, brother-in-law to Antonio Battistone; 28-year old John Scaletta, a Lanasa employee arrested in Cleveland, and 26-year old Salvatore Lupo, another gangster who somehow, weaseled his way onto Antonio Lanasa's payroll.

Lupo, who was captured by Baltimore detectives in upstate New York near the Canadian border, was the key to the case. A low level member of the Black Hand, Lupo, police said, was so terrified of the criminal organisation that he broke down on a train while being returned to Baltimore and had to be given a sedative. Convinced by the police that they would protect him from the Black Hand, Lupo confessed his part in the bombing conspiracy and cut a deal with the State's Attorney's office. He would receive only 18 months in prison if he agreed to name names.

Baltimore's State's Attorney's office had its own reasons for letting Salvatore Lupo off so lightly. The authorities didn't want the small fish. They wanted the big fish, or in this case the big banana. The State Attorney's office got what it wanted when Lupo told authorities Antonio Lanasa and A.C. Goffe had masterminded the bombing. Lupo claimed he was present at

Lanasa's home when the banana merchant told Goffe: "If we kill Joseph Di Giorgio, I will be the Banana King of Baltimore."

The developments came thick and fast. On 11 January, 1908, a little over a month after the Di Giorgio home was dynamited, the odd couple, 36-year old Antonio Lanasa and 44-year old A.C. Goffe were arrested and charged with conspiring to murder Joseph Di Giorgio and locked-up in Baltimore's Central Police Station.

"I am a British subject and if you lock me up," Goffe threatened Chief of Detectives, Captain A.J. Pumphrey, "I'll have a fleet of English warships in this harbour." Pumphrey told the Jamaican he should do what he had to because to jail he was going. "Have to let them come," Pumphrey said, "for I am going to lock you up."

News of the arrest spread quickly through Baltimore. In the streets of the Italian Quarter — Fawn, Albermarle, South High and Pratt — the talk was of nothing but the arrest of their Sicilian countryman, Lanasa, and his black business partner, Goffe.

"Strangers were regarded suspiciously by groups of Italians who stood on the pavements discussing the arrest of the well known merchant and his partner, Goffe," read one newspaper report. "Conversation was hushed for a moment and then broke forth again, excited, exclamatory..."

The next day, 12 January, 1908, after an uncomfortable night in jail, Lanasa and Goffe were brought to court for a preliminary hearing of the charges against them.

"The usual peace and quiet of the Central Station–house on Sunday was seriously disturbed, was replete with dramatic incidents," the *Baltimore American* newspaper reported. Though the special Sunday morning hearing did not begin until 9 am, the assembly room and the courtroom were filled many hours before. "Italians of all classes and stations in life and from all sections of the city, were," a newspaper reported, "present to the number of 300 inside the police station, with nearly twice as many outside."

Expecting trouble, whether from Black Hand assassins or from Italians angry at the arrest of one of their prominent citizens, Baltimore's Chief of Police, Marshall Farnan, sent dozens of plain clothes officers to mingle with crowds gathering outside the police station. Farnan had reason to be concerned. The Black Hand had murdered a colleague of his, New Orleans' Chief of Police, Daniel Hennessy, only a few years before.

Finally, a few minutes after 9 am, Justice Eugene E. Grannan ordered the prisoners brought into the courtroom. "When the word ran through the crowd of chattering Italians that the case had been called, there was a rush to get into the magistrate's office," the *Baltimore American* reported. "When Antonio Lanasa made his appearance several members of his family stepped up to him and began an animated conversation."

Earlier that morning, before coming into court, Lanasa had protested his innocence to a reporter from his cell at the Central Stationhouse. He had nothing to do with the dynamiting, he declared. It was a wicked plot hatched by Di Giorgio, Lanasa insisted. He told the reporter that he was still shaken by a rough encounter he'd had with Di Giorgio in Jamaica a few months before the bombing. Di Giorgio, Lanasa said, promised he would "get me on the end of an umbrella, and when he closed it he would crush me with it…well, he has succeeded tonight," the distraught Lanasa said. "If they find me guilty, which they can't do, I do not want to serve time, but want to be hanged. This is nothing but jealousy."

The rivalry between the two Italians – the villages where they were born in Sicily were only a few miles apart – was well established. Di Giorgio's associates insisted he was the 'cream of the banana trade' and his Atlantic Fruit Company was second only to the United Fruit Company in importance in the fruit trade. Lanasa and Goffe's firm, Di Giorgio's friends said, had been struggling since it began business in 1906. Lanasa and Goffe associates said the opposite. It was Goffe and Lanasa who were increasingly lapping up the cream and eating it off of Di Giorgio's plate. Lanasa and Goffe, they explained, had recently secured an important banana contract which gave them access to the entire output of a large Jamaican banana plantation which had been until a few weeks ago under contract to Di Giorgio. This, Lanasa and Goffe's friends said, was the reason the Italian and the Jamaican now found themselves defendants in an attempted murder case that could put them in prison, perhaps for life, and mean the collapse of their banana company.

The Daily Telegraph newspaper in Jamaica splashed a headline on 24 January across its front page mentioning the case. "THE ARREST OF MR. GOFFE AT BALTIMORE…Great Sympathy In His Island Home." There is, the *Telegraph* reported, much anxiety here over the arrest of Mr. A.C. Goffe in Baltimore. "The present standing of the Lanasse and Goffe Steamship and

Importing Co.," the paper said, "is largely due to his (A.C. Goffe's) undaunted courage, business-like methods and unflinching perseverance. There is not a man in this community who does not extend to Mr. Goffe the keenest sympathy in the trouble that has come upon him like a whirlwind. All are waiting anxiously to hear further developments."

Lanasa and Goffe, too, were waiting anxiously for further developments. Imprisoned in a Baltimore jail, both men had time to consider how they had ended up in this unhappy situation.

They'd ended up in this predicament, in part, they concluded, because they had dared to become independent exporters in a banana trade dominated by the United Fruit Company and by Di Giorgio's Atlantic Fruit Company. Seeking to be free and independent had put them where they were. They had also ended up in this predicament, they concluded, because they had dared flout racial prohibitions which said blacks and whites should remain separate and apart. The partnership, and friendship, was, by any measure, an unusual one. Not least of all because Lanasa was white and Italian and Goffe was black and Jamaican. Back then the races, in America at least, did not mix. But banana was big business, and the prospect of profits sometimes made for strange bedfellows. Still, despite their troubles, and the fact that they were very different sorts of men, the two's friendship didn't waver.

While A.C. Goffe was widely held to be harsh and demanding, Lanasa, it was said, had a genial and pleasing personality. "He is a man of noble character...naturally devoid of selfishness, ever quiet and unostentatious," the *Tercentenary History of Maryland*, a book marking the 300th anniversary of the founding of the state of Maryland, said of Lanasa: "He is not only held in high confidence and esteem by his many personal friends but his clerks...find in his presence an exhilarating and uplifting influence. They brighten perceptibly when their cheerful and kindly 'boss', is around."

The book also said Lanasa gave valuable assistance to thousands of men in Baltimore and was, too, an active and generous member of the main Roman Catholic Church in the city. The same could not be said of A.C. Goffe. He was not modest by nature, nor in attire. He liked expensive, resplendent outfits, diamond and ruby encrusted rings and a fine walking cane. "He was always shouting," a person who knew him well recalled. "He talked to you at the very top of his voice."

A.C. Goffe and Antonio Lanasa were alike in one way, though. They were both small men: Goffe was five foot six and Lanasa five foot five. Though Lanasa could easily have afforded to travel first class on long journeys home to Sicily, he always traveled second class. Goffe always traveled first class no matter how short the journey. Relatives of Lanasa remember him as being unusually tough on his sons, all of whom joined him in the fruit trade at one time or another. Not all reviews of Goffe were unfavourable. Jamaica's *Daily Telegraph* newspaper said this of him in a 1908 article: "His long association with people of all classes here, has won him the esteem and respect which he richly deserves. He is a popular and energetic man." Not energetic enough, though, to participate much in the civic life of his Jamaican parish, St Mary. Unlike several of his brothers who served at one time or other on the parish's local government body, the Parochial Board, A.C. Goffe did not serve. He said business kept him too often out of the country for public duties. But the truth was he did not serve because he was not at all civic-minded. Siblings of his sat on the board of their town's hospital, its public school, and its loan bank. They also served as Justices of the Peace, and some were volunteers in the local militia.

If A.C. Goffe was involved in good works, at all, these were likely calculated to improve the image of a man many thought a heartless robber baron. It could have been Goffe the American investment banker Henry Clews was speaking of when he said of Daniel Drew, the famously ruthless New York businessman, "He holds the honest people of the world to be a pack of fools." Drew, a model for the so-called 'robber baron' band of capitalists that arose in America in the 1870s and 1880s, made himself fantastically rich and others desperately poor through his financial manipulations and machinations.

Henry Clews also said of Daniel Drew that when the tycoon had been "unusually lucky in his trade of fleecing other men, he settles accounts with his conscience by subscribing toward a new chapel or attending a prayer meeting." A.C. Goffe did the same. He gave generously to the Anglican Church in Port Maria. On one occasion he and his brothers gave the church a memorial prayer desk, an angel lectern made of solid oak, an altar cross, and a dossal cross. To honour his parents, A.C. and his siblings later paid for the costly conversion of the South Transept of the Parish Church into the Goffe Memorial Chapel. It was a grand and gaudy exercise meant to show they had the money to buy anything they wanted and were worthy of worship. They'd had first class seats in their life on earth and believed money would secure first class seats for them in the next life, too. In the chapel A.C. and his siblings commissioned are buried their parents, John Beecham Goffe and his wife, Margaret.

If A.C. Goffe was expecting the Almighty to intervene in his troubles on Earth because of what he'd done for the Church, he was disappointed. Heaven helps those who help themselves and it did not look as though there was much the Jamaican could do to help himself from a cell in Baltimore.

Welcome To Jamrock

Great ambition and conquest without contribution is without significance.
William Hundert

A.C. Goffe and Antonio Lanasa had done business together before they set up the Lanasa and Goffe Steamship and Importing Company in 1906. Five years earlier, in March 1901, Goffe had formed a fruit grower's association in Jamaica. It was St Mary parish's first. To try and interest big planters and small cultivators alike in his fruit co-operative, Goffe set off on a tour of St Mary banana districts. He told growers the nine pennies per bunch the American companies were paying them was much too low. He told them the only way they would get a fair price for their produce, and break the United Fruit Company's grip on the industry, was to join his fruit grower's co-op.

Thus was the St Mary's Fruit Grower's Association, with A.C. Goffe its managing director, formed. Managers were selected, offices leased, and a wharf made ready to greet the fruit steamer Goffe said would come to collect the association's bananas. The association did not, though, own a fruit steamer nor had it secured the lease of one. So the managing director set off for New York to find one.

In New York he hoped to find a banana firm that would agree to partner the St Mary co-op in its venture. If Goffe couldn't find an American partner he was convinced he could, at least, arrange for the sale of the association's fruit himself for a good price. Four months later, Goffe sent a telegram to Port Maria saying he hadn't found a distributor, but had found a ship, the *S.S. Tyr* and had leased it on a short, journey to journey basis. He would, he said, arrive soon in Port Maria aboard the steamer. Banana should, the managing director said, be cut and be ready to load.

"Early Saturday morning last the Office of the St Mary's Fruit Growers Association was besieged by a crowd anxious to catch a glimpse of the managing director who, according to a circular issued on the previous Saturday, invited shareholders to meet on that day to welcome Mr. Goffe," read a report in the *Daily Gleaner*. Cultivators by the hundreds came to Port Maria on the Saturday with their donkeys and drays laden down with bananas to witness the arrival of the *Tyr*. But neither Goffe nor the ship arrived. The fruit steamer had been delayed in Kingston and would not, they were told, arrive in Port Maria for another two days. Though many of those who'd come to town to see the ship went home disappointed, many others camped out, covered themselves in banana trash, and were there to greet the *Tyr* when it finally arrived just after dawn on Monday morning. The fanfare over, the business of loading the ship with bananas and other tropical fruit was begun. By noon the association's manager at Port Maria, Frederick Athelstan Taylor, was able to report that a record number of bunches of bananas had been collected and loaded for delivery to the United States. One more stop was made by the ship at Annotto Bay, another St Mary port. There it collected the produce of other association members before finally leaving for New York on the Tuesday morning with 15,000 bunches of bananas, and A.C. Goffe, onboard.

Without an effective distribution network and unable to afford offices there, Goffe had to employ stevedores to unload the *Tyr* himself and also arrange for the sale of the association's produce, as well. He had said he would be back in Port Maria in a fortnight, but that did not look likely. Two weeks passed and nothing was heard. Shareholders began to wonder if the managing director had run off with their money. The *Gleaner* began, too, to wonder in its pages whether Goffe would ever be seen again. Then a telegram arrived from Goffe saying everything had gone well. The association's produce, he revealed, had been well received and had sold for top dollar.

Things could not go on this way, though, he wrote, because the *Tyr*, an old, slow ship, had almost endangered the whole enterprise. Somehow, though, the produce did arrive in New York ahead of the fruit of rival banana firms and so was able to command the highest possible prices. Goffe said the

Tyr would eventually have to be replaced or the co-op would not last very long. He said he would scout around for a new steamer in New York.

He was inundated with offers from one shipping agent and another. The good ships were too expensive. The bad ships were cheap, but looked like they were about to sink. From slim pickings, Goffe settled on the *S.S. Ask*, a ship the United Fruit Company had used often on its Jamaica run. The *Ask* did well enough. It took the Association's second shipment of fruit – 18,000 bunches – to New York in speedy fashion. Six months after the co-operative began operating the *Daily Gleaner* delivered its judgment of it and of its founder, Goffe.

"There is no getting away from the fact that he knows how to get the settlers together," the *Gleaner* said of Goffe, a little grudgingly. "This was clearly shown when the idea of association struck him. His first move was to get into the midst of the small man and instruct him as to the benefits to be received from co-operation; and certainly it was a lesson that the people at once heeded, and while the result up to the present is not altogether a financial success, it is gratifying to know that the people have yielded to the force of Mr. Goffe's arguments and efforts."

It was not exactly true that the Association had not been a financial success. Before the co-op began operating, United Fruit paid only nine pennies a bunch to growers. The U.S. firm raised its price to one shilling and six pennies a bunch in St Mary as a direct result of the Association's entry into the market. Even if the *Gleaner* didn't think so, small growers certainly thought the Association had been a financial success. But if the Association was to thrive and remain in the market it would have to evolve from what was, in essence, a one-man, one-ship operation.

To put the co-operative on a firm financial footing, A.C. Goffe began, in 1902, a long and determined courtship of Antonio Lanasa, who was then the president of the Italian Fruit and Importing Company of Baltimore. Lanasa had been a well-known figure in the American fruit trade for many years and had been employed for several years as a commission agent for the United Fruit Company, and for its predecessor, the Boston Fruit Company.

Though operating as a commission agent for a firm as large as United Fruit had been very lucrative, Lanasa ended his relationship with the company to begin his own export enterprise, the Italian Fruit and Importing Company.

With support from many of the Italian dealers in tropical fruit in Baltimore, Lanasa's firm was an immediate success. But the collapse of the Baltimore bank, the City Trust and Banking Company, forced the Italian Fruit and Importing Company to suspend business. With most of his money, and the money of his fruit firm, in the bank Lanasa was forced, humiliatingly, to return to selling and distributing United Fruit Company produce on commission.

Had Goffe not pursued him, sending letter after letter to his offices in Baltimore, Lanasa might have remained with the United Fruit Company. Instead, he left the comfort of his arrangement with United, revived his Italian Fruit and Importing Company and set off for Port Maria to meet with A.C. Goffe and the St Mary's Fruit Grower's Association.

A.C. Goffe was convinced the St Mary co-operative could be a big success if Lanasa's firm agreed to handle the shipping, distribution, and marketing of the Association's fruit in the United States. It had taken almost a year for Goffe to convince Lanasa to come to St Mary. On 15 February 1903, Lanasa arrived at Port Antonio aboard the *S.S. Watson* with Martin Paulsen, an Italian Fruit and Importing Company executive. Goffe was there at the harbour to welcome them to Jamrock.

For the next eleven days, Goffe, and the directors of the co-operative, wined and dined the Americans. The two Americans were not strangers to the island. Lanasa visited Jamaica for the first time in the late 1890s. Paulsen first visited in 1872, two years after another American, Captain Lorenzo Dow Baker, purchased the first large shipment of Jamaican bananas and sold them in the United States for three times the amount he had bought them for.

Goffe insisted St Mary plantations were superior to those elsewhere on the island. He pointed to Roslyn, a 528- acre one owned by his family as an example. The estate, situated on a plateau about 300 feet above sea level, was widely regarded as one of the best in the parish. It was well tilled and produced magnificent fruit. The three visited large and small properties owned by members of the St Mary's Fruit Grower's Association.

By the end of the tour, Lanasa and Paulsen were convinced the Association could provide them with between 40,000 and 50,000 bunches of bananas a week, as A.C. Goffe had insisted. Satisfied, the Americans said they would like to ally their Italian Fruit and Importing Company with the Association. All that was left was for Lanasa and Paulsen to be presented to the Association's shareholders and for the co-op to vote 'yea' or 'nay' to partnership.

On 26 February, 1903, at Port Maria Town Hall, the shareholders of the St Mary's Fruit Grower's Association were introduced to Lanasa and Paulsen. Five hundred of the Association's 2,000 shareholders — small settlers and big planters – squeezed into the meeting room. Other co-op members gathered outside the town hall and listened intently to the discussion inside through open windows. On the platform sat Association directors, A.R. DaCosta, Alec Goffe, Cecil Goffe, Horace Goffe, John Goffe, J.T. Atkinson, and A.C. Goffe. DaCosta spoke first. "These men who had come here from America had money, these gentlemen were not going to send their steamers here for fun." Next to speak was Martin Paulsen. He explained that his firm was made up almost entirely of Italian-American fruit dealers and merchants in Baltimore. His firm had been a success, he said, because it knew its market, had an excellent distribution network, and sold only the very best, full figured fruit to a loyal group of wholesalers and retailers. How well organized was his firm?, Paulsen asked rhetorically. He told Association members that should, for example, the steamer carrying their produce arrived in Baltimore at, say, 6 am, it would be unloaded and the produce sold before noon. By 12.30, Paulsen said, a telegraph would be sent to the offices of the Association in Port Maria telling exactly what price its produce had fetched. Paulsen made sure to say kind things about A.C. Goffe, the irrepressible managing director. He wanted the co-op's members, he said, to understand that because Goffe was a Jamaican and a black man, he had encountered many obstacles while busy on Association business in America.

"They did not realise the mountain he had to climb – how he had to contend with the prejudice that was to be found on the one side, and on the other side the powerful corporations laughing at his proposals," Paulsen told the audience. He told them if Jamaica wanted to be successful in the international banana trade it would have to deal with Italians because Italians, he said, controlled the banana trade in the United States. "They had no middle men," Paulsen said. "The St Mary people had organised their association on the same lines…and what they proposed to do was amalgamate the two into one and they would have no fear in the future for their fruit", Paulsen told the audience. He was cheered loudly.

Antonio Lanasa stepped up to the dais. He was brief and to the point. "If you mean business," he told the shareholders, "I will guarantee Italian blood will stick to you. No other nation would do as the Italians would," suggesting that Italians did not share the racist views of other white Americans. Jamaicans would, Lanasa said, get justice and fair treatment from Italians. "There could be no other better combination than this," Lanasa said, closing his speech to loud applause.

Next to speak was Alec Goffe, A.C.'s brother. He recommended the Association purchase $1,000 worth of shares in the Italian Fruit and Importing Company. He said Lanasa's firm had been started with only $100,000 in capital, but predicted it could, in time, be worth as much as $50 million.

"If the people stick to the company it would be the making of themselves and the making of Jamaica," Alec Goffe said. A partnership between the St Mary Fruit Grower's Association and Lanasa's company would be, he told the excited crowd, "a thorn in the side of the United Fruit Company."

The last of the speakers was A.C. Goffe. He soured the happy occasion by launching into a bitter criticism of Jamaican banana growers. "Jamaica was a dead failure in anything she took up because the people did not realise the importance of co-operation," Goffe said. No one was really surprised to hear him say this. He'd said it many times before and it was a widely held belief on the island that Jamaicans were a querulous, bloody minded lot who preferred discord to accord, lacked ambition, and disliked anyone who displayed any desire for improvement. As long as Goffe produced results like this deal between the St Mary's Fruit Grower's Association and the Italian Fruit and Importing Company, banana growers would tolerate him and let him speak as harshly to them as he liked. "I am the first man in the island," Goffe said boastfully, "who taught the peasantry the value of co-operation."

The speeches over, shareholders were asked whether they wanted to enter into a partnership with Antonio Lanasa's company. The result was unanimous. The Jamaicans wanted to partner the Italians in the banana trade. The Americans promised that one of their ships would arrive at Port Maria in the next two weeks. If the growers could produce sufficient fruit to require a ship each week they would send one. If they could produce sufficient fruit to require that a ship be sent twice a week or every day or every hour, Lanasa said, he would send one. Their business in Jamaica concluded, Lanasa and Paulsen left for Baltimore, with Goffe in tow.

Though he had an agreement with Lanasa, A.C. Goffe continued to look for the best possible deal for himself and for the Association. On 10 August 1903, seven months after coming to terms with Lanasa's firm, Goffe set off from Port Maria for Baltimore to meet with Joseph Di Giorgio. Di Giorgio was at the time president of the Di Giorgio Fruit and Steamship Company and a director of the Maryland National Bank. Di Giorgio had been partners with the wealthy Jamaican family, the Verleys. But that arrangement had come to an end and he was in desperate need of a new partner in Jamaica to provide him with the quantity and quality of fruit the Verleys had.

In 1903, Ernest, Leopold, Vincent and Frank Verley, owners of large estates in St. Andrew and St Catherine, incorporated the Verley Fruit Company of Providence, Rhode Island in the United States. The four Verley brothers owned Mona, Papine and Hope estates in St. Andrew and Cumberland and Thetford estates in St Catherine. Their Abbey Court mansion in upper St. Andrew's 'millionaire's row' was one of the island's showpiece properties. The Verley patriarch, Louis, made the family's fortune first in baking with his famous, 'Steam' bread and then in sugar.

In 1878, Louis Verley and a group of Jamaica's wealthiest businessmen and landowners set up the Hartland Fruit Company, one of the first Jamaican companies to begin large-scale cultivation of bananas. The firm was formed, a company circular said, because of the "large and increasing demand for Tropical fruits, especially for banana, and the regular and frequent departure of steamers from Kingston to Great Britain and the United States."

The Hartland Fruit Company purchased 2,251 acres in St Catherine and began fruit cultivation in earnest. Success in this venture led the Verleys to enter the export trade. In the early months of 1903, the Verleys and Di Giorgio became partners. Di Giorgio brought bananas from Cuba to Baltimore and the Verleys brought fruit from Jamaica to New York. They'd set themselves a very difficult task, though. Most of the large banana planters in Jamaica had signed contracts to sell their fruit to the United Fruit Company. When this did not discourage the Verleys and Di Giorgio, United began a bidding war. Banana growers selling their fruit in the open market were offered higher than normal prices to ensure little fruit was available to the Verleys. What banana they were able to purchase came at a very high price and fetched low prices in the United States because United Fruit flooded the US market with lots of cheap produce.

United Fruit could afford, large as it was, to absorb the losses. The Verleys and Di Giorgio, small as they were, could not. Eventually, the Verleys quit the banana export trade, leaving Joseph Di Giorgio to find a new Jamaican partner.

This is why Di Giorgio summoned Goffe to his banana company's headquarters in Baltimore in August 1903 that, as it turned out, was only a few blocks from Antonio Lanasa's offices. Ironically, the day Goffe arrived in Baltimore on 10 August 1903, a massive hurricane hit Jamaica, the most powerful one to strike the island in more than thirty years.

The hurricane was terrible news for Jamaica and for the island's banana industry. News of it brought the talks between Goffe and Di Giorgio to a halt. Goffe had nothing to bargain with. With the banana crop in Jamaica destroyed, Di Giorgio decided instead to look for fruit in Central America. Goffe left Baltimore for Port Maria as soon as he could to survey the damage at home.

"The morning of August 10th, 1903 will never be forgotten in the annals of Jamaica," wrote an eyewitness who saw what the hurricane did to St Mary parish. "When day broke an awful scene of desolation met the eye. The hand of God lay heavy on the land, and what the day before had been smiling fields, and lands that yielded the rich promise that had been expected there lay blank and devastated." Coconut trees that had stood for fifty years were torn up by the roots; every description of vegetation was damaged.

"The houses of the peasantry have, with very few exceptions, been blown down and God only knows how these poor people will manage to exist." The larger houses of the gentry, the eyewitness reported, were also damaged but had, for the most part, remained standing. The gentry's loss was mostly in the destruction of their banana acreage.

"Gone is the work of years. Port Maria as far as can be learn't from eye-witnesses is a barren waste, not a house or a wharf standing and the streets feet deep in sand. Most of the shipping destroyed and everything black with despair. The parish of St Mary is utterly dependent on the fruit trade and now that everything is blown down one is at a loss to conjecture what is going to be done to save the people from starvation."

A.C. Goffe and his brothers weren't starving exactly, but they had suffered big losses.

"These gentlemen have also sustained a further loss of fully £5,000 pound on their Oxford and Roslyn properties," a newspaper correspondent reported. "The houses on these properties having been blown down, and their entire banana cultivation destroyed. They are now partially homeless." They lost their mother, Margaret, too. Born a slave in 1829 in St Mary,

Margaret died of a cerebral embolism on 4 September, 1903, aged 74, at her home, *Grantham*, on the outskirts of the St Mary town of Highgate.

St Mary wasn't the only banana parish devastated by the 1903 hurricane. The parish of Portland, too, took a direct hit. Many important public buildings in Port Antonio, such as the Town Hall, the Titchfield School, and the Public Hospital were very badly damaged.

As in St Mary, in Portland, banana men took a big hit. The Port Antonio homes of banana planters and merchants' David Gideon, E.B. Hopkins, and Charles Edward Johnston were destroyed. Johnston's general store, C.E. Johnston and Co., was damaged and a tavern owned by him in Port Antonio was blown down. The hurricane did, at least, bring people together, according to one eyewitness. "For hours after the wind had ceased merchants, clerks, fruit-dealers, tradesmen, men of all shades walked indiscriminately side by side."

The destruction of the banana crop forced many Jamaican businesses to close, among them the export branch of the banana firm, J.E. Kerr and Company. The firm had been started in Montego Bay in the 1870s by the English expatriate, John Edward Kerr. The firm had been a success almost immediately. It exported large amounts of Jamaican fruit to the United States and to Britain, and in its heyday never shipped less than a million bunches a year to the United States. Though Kerr's export wing - its ships, its warehouses and wharves – was sold off to the American firm, Cuneo & Co, which was owned by the United Fruit Company, it continued to operate under its old name so as not to reveal that it had been taken over by Americans. Kerr's dry goods stores, though, remained in Jamaican hands.

As for the St Mary Fruit Grower's Association, it too had been turned upside down by the 1903 hurricane. Its warehouses and its wharf were destroyed. It looked as if it would either be absorbed by United Fruit or forced out of the banana trade by the Americans. Like a shark, United Fruit began to circle. It offered prices no other company could match and banana growers found it hard to resist, even those who were contracted members of the Association. Many of the co-op's members began selling fruit, 'over the fence', as it was called, to United Fruit they'd agreed to sell to the co-op. Some shareholders compromised; selling part of their produce to United Fruit and the rest to the Association.

By the summer of 1904, Lanasa's company and Goffe's Association began to stall. In financial difficulties, the Italian Fruit and Importing Company was forced to re-organise itself. On 15 July 1904, the stockholders, met in Baltimore at Sonnenberg's Hall. With the firm in turmoil, Antonio Lanasa was forced to step down from the presidency of the company. He was replaced by William Coulbourne, a commission agent and owner of a Baltimore wholesale fruit dealership.

The Italian Fruit and Importing Company's financial problems forced it to seek investors far and wide. That's how Coulbourne, an Irish-American, came to buy a large piece of the company. Antonio Lanasa welcomed him at first, but came to resent him, especially when he displaced him at the head of the fruit firm. Lanasa agreed to take the post of general manager while Coulbourne took the post of president.

A few weeks later, Joseph Di Giorgio approached the firm. Lanasa didn't trust him, but his firm needed investors, especially one that was a director of a Maryland bank. Lanasa and Di Giorgio had been rivals in the fruit trade of Baltimore for more than ten years. But perhaps it was time, Lanasa thought, to put this rivalry behind him. Di Giorgio was preparing, he told Lanasa, to launch a company that would rival the United Fruit Company. He'd convinced many of the leading independent banana firms in Baltimore, he said, to join him in this new enterprise, the Atlantic Fruit Company. Jamaican firms had also agreed to join him, as well, Di Giorgio said. Among them was the Fruit Importing Company, begun by Port Antonio merchant David Gideon.

Di Giorgio offered Lanasa a directorship and a large stockholding in Atlantic Fruit. Lanasa happily accepted. In quick time the sale of the Italian Fruit and Importing Company was agreed. As the St Mary Fruit Grower's Association had stock in the firm – £200 worth — A.C. Goffe's agreement was needed before the deal could be completed. He gave his assent in exchange for a directorship in the new company and for a sizable amount of stock, as well. Goffe and the St Mary Fruit Grower's Association shareholders were jubilant. It wouldn't last.

Di Giorgio's Atlantic Fruit Company was launched in January 1905. The first few weeks went well enough. But by March 1905 it was clear pressure from United Fruit – flooding the markets in New York, Philadelphia, Boston and Baltimore with cheap fruit – was having an effect. Certain his company was going to collapse and he would be driven into bankruptcy, Di Giorgio agreed five months later to sell the controlling share in Atlantic Fruit to the United Fruit Company. The deal was a violation of the United States' anti trust laws and so would have to be kept secret and away from the scrutiny of federal regulators. Before United Fruit would agree to sink money into Di Giorgio's company there were two things that had to happen. Lanasa and Goffe had to go. Lanasa had once been a commission agent for United Fruit in Baltimore and its boss, Andy Preston, never forgave him for starting a rival company, the Italian Fruit and Importing Company. Goffe had to go because the United Fruit Company would not countenance a black man holding a directorship in any company under its control. Though resentful at being dictated to by United Fruit, Di Giorgio happily carried out its orders to dispose of Lanasa and Goffe.

Di Giorgio had never liked his fellow Sicilian, Lanasa, nor Goffe, the haughty Jamaican, anyway. Casting them off would be a pleasure. A telegram was sent to Goffe in Port Maria. Another telegram was sent to Lanasa's office in Baltimore. Both telegrams said the same thing: Thank you and goodbye. Enraged, Goffe took the first available steamer to Baltimore to confront Di Giorgio. The Atlantic Fruit Company boss wouldn't see him.

A.C. Goffe's removal from the Atlantic Fruit Company caused panic in St Mary. The fruit grower's association wondered what would happen to it. Goffe filed a lawsuit for breach of contract against Atlantic. The St Mary Fruit Grower's Association filed a lawsuit against Di Giorgio's firm, as well. It would be many months before the lawsuits would make their way through the legal system into court.

In the meantime, Lanasa and Goffe, left high and dry by Di Giorgio, decided there was a way they could take revenge on him and the United Fruit Company, and enrich themselves at the same time. They would start a banana export and shipping company of their own. Lanasa and Goffe worked furiously throughout the summer of 1905 to put things in place so they could launch in early 1906.

Bit by bit news began to spread in Jamaica that A.C. Goffe was preparing to re-enter the banana trade, this time at the head of his own export company. Many who heard the news scoffed. Goffe hadn't made a success of the St Mary's Fruit Grower's Association, so why should anyone believe he would make a success of this new export company. Goffe and his brothers were out of their depth in matters of international shipping and finance, some said.

Since its beginnings in the 1870s, the international trade in Jamaican bananas had been controlled by American whites, English whites and by Jamaican whites. Before the nay Sayers would believe black Jamaicans like the Goffes had formed an export company capable of competing with the big American companies, they would have to see proof. They got proof when leaflets began circulating in the towns and villages of St. Mary in 1906.

'Dear Sir, – We are starting a line of steamers to run between Jamaica and Baltimore, The Lanasa and Goffe Steamship and Importing Company, Baltimore,' read a circular distributed in Annotto Bay in St Mary. 'We will be buying banana weekly...our first steamer being the *S.S. San Miguel*, and will be followed by the *S.S. Oxus*...We must ask you to give us that support again which you did in the past, as we intend doing a regular weekly and permanent business. Thanking you in advance for your support. We are yours faithfully, GOFFE BROS Per A. Constantine Goffe.'

There was truth in the rumour, after all.

Antonio Lanasa

Rivalry is the life of trade, and the death of the trader.
Elbert Hubbard

Antonio Lanasa's story reads like something out of Horatio Alger. Alger was, of course, the 19th century American writer who produced dozens of inspirational novels which painted romanticised portraits of hardworking, good-hearted street children triumphing against the odds.

Unable to speak English and on his own without family members, 14-year old Antonio Lanasa arrived in the United States in 1884. He taught himself simple English quickly. His father, Michael, his mother, Anna, and his siblings remained behind in Italy, in Termini Imerese, a small town of a few hundred people near the city of Palermo in Sicily. The town was known for its citrus fruit, its olives, and its artichokes. Antonio's father made a living in Termini Imerese as a fruit vendor.

Though Italy finally became a modern nation with a democratic constitution in 1871, little changed in the feudal part of the country where the Lanasa family lived. Life in Sicily, and in other parts of southern Italy, went on pretty much as before: insects destroyed crops and floods washed away the soil from prime agricultural lands, leaving peasants penniless. Peasant families like the Lanasas, too, found themselves oppressed by aristocrats who controlled the land and by criminal networks, like the Black Hand, which ruthlessly exploited them. It was no surprise, then, that millions of Italians, primarily those from the poor, agricultural South, left their homeland to seek opportunity abroad in America and elsewhere.

In the forty years between 1880 and 1920, an estimated four million Italians migrated to the United States. Among them was Antonio Lanasa. After successfully clearing immigration at New York harbour in 1884, he made his way to Cincinnati, Ohio, where he made a living in the fruit trade hawking oranges, apples and pears in the city's wharf district.

Whether because Cincinnati, a Midwestern city that was bitterly cold in the winter, was too harsh for people used to the warmth of the Mediterranean or because there was greater opportunity elsewhere, Antonio left the city after only a year. He moved to Baltimore, a port city near Washington D.C., where a small Italian community – many of them from the region of Italy Antonio Lanasa was from – had settled. He arrived at exactly the right time. Baltimore's Italian population was small, but had big plans. Four years before, in 1880, the Italian community put on its first ever parade. The same year the cornerstone was laid for a new church especially for Italians, the Church of St Leo the Great. Italians were frequently turned away from Catholic churches attended by Irish or Germans or made to sit in the back with African-Americans. So, the Catholic Church in Baltimore decided to build them their own place of worship.

Established in 1789, the city of Baltimore's claim to fame rests almost entirely on the crucial role it played in the war of 1812. American soldiers in the city held off heavy attack from British troops who tried to re-capture their former colony after losing it years before during the American Revolution. That victory became the inspiration for the American national anthem. The anthem apart, Baltimore in the late 1800s was a busy port and was for a time the second largest city in the United States. During this period Baltimore was, too, a centre of shipbuilding. In 1884, when Lanasa arrived in the United States, the population of Baltimore was around 350,000. The immigrant, for-eign-born population of the city numbered just over 56,000. Most of these were German, Russian, and Irish immigrants who'd arrived in the early to mid-1800s. The Italian population was still very small at barely a thousand people, but it would grow rapidly over the next few years and become an eco-nomic and political force in Baltimore.

It was in the Italian Quarter – Fawn, Albemarle, South High and Pratt Streets – that Lanasa, still a teenager, found his niche. He returned to Italy and convinced his family members to come with him to the United States.

Antonio, his father, and his brothers became a familiar sight peddling fruit from baskets on the streets near Baltimore's wharves. A few years after this, after amassing a little capital, he made a breakthrough as an importer of Italian macaroni, olive oil, cheese, and lemons.

But it was as an importer of bananas that he would make his name, and his fortune. By the time Antonio Lanasa was 23-years old he was one of the wealthiest men in Baltimore. The Lanasa empire included: A. Lanasa and Co., M. Lanasa and Co., S. Lanasa and Co., and later the Lanasa and Goffe Steamship and Importing Company.

A success in America, Lanasa did not forget where he came from. In 1893, nine years after he left Italy for America, he returned to Sicily to marry his childhood sweetheart, Giuseppa Sansone. They had eight boys and one girl together in what Italians called 'La 'Merica.'

Joseph Di Giorgio's story was very much like Antonio Lanasa's. Both of their fathers had been lemon farmers. Neither was poor, exactly. Both were from Sicily. Both arrived in the United States as teenagers. Like Lanasa, Di Giorgio became a successful businessman within a few years of arriving in Baltimore. Di Giorgio was born in 1874 in the village of Cefalu, only a few miles from Termini Imerese, Lanasa's hometown. His father, Salvatore Di Giorgio, was a small farmer who belonged to an agricultural collective that exported lemons to the United States.

In 1888, 14-year-old Joseph, or 'Peppino' as he was known, was sent by his father to America. There, in the old Washington market in Baltimore, he set up a shop selling lemons sent to him by his father's fruit collective. He quickly expanded the business, becoming a receiver and general distributor of Sicilian lemons. After five years he tired of the citrus business. He borrowed $5,000, a very large sum in 1893, and went into the fruit retailing business. So successful was Di Giorgio, within a year he paid off the large loan and by age 21 was manager of the grandly titled Monumental Trading Company and a director of a bank in Baltimore.

In 1899, aged 25, Di Giorgio embarked on the business of importing bananas and other fruit from Jamaica. In 1901, he formed the Di Giorgio Fruit & Steamship Company. In very short order he, not Antonio Lanasa, was the 'Banana King' of Baltimore. In January 1905, Di Giorgio launched his most significant enterprise of all, the Atlantic Fruit Company, an importer of tropical fruit. Di Giorgio had been planning this venture for some time.

Joseph Di Giorgio had quite an empire in Baltimore. It included the Baltimore Fruit Exchange, the city's only fruit auction house, the Di Giorgio Fruit & Steamship Company, a handler of domestic and some foreign fruit, the Atlantic Fruit Company, a handler, principally, of tropical fruit. In nearby Washington D.C., Di Giorgio also had interests. There he had his Joseph Di Giorgio and Company, another firm handling tropical fruit. In time Di Giorgio would extend his reach in the fruit business to New York, Chicago, and eventually to California, where his ownership of more than 20,000 acres of land led the *San Francisco Chronicle* to say of him, "Di Giorgio is to farming what Tiffany is to jewelry."

Not a shy or modest man, Di Giorgio named the chartered ships in his fleet after each and every member of his immediate family. There was the *Rosario Di Giorgio*, the *Jolanda Di Giorgio*, the *Salvatore Di Giorgio*, the *Vincenzo Di Giorgio*, the *Concetta Di Giorgio*, the *Marie Di Giorgio*, the *Marietta Di Giorgio*', and, of course, the *Joseph Di Giorgio*.

Knocked off the top spot in the fruit business in Baltimore by Di Giorgio, Lanasa was not happy being the second banana. The rivalry between the two men was intense. One section of Baltimore's Italian community were Lanasa loyalists and the other Di Giorgio devotees. Thousands of Italians in the city – fruit vendors, dock workers, warehouse workers – looked to the two men for employment and Lanasa and Di Giorgio looked to their workers for loyalty in return. The bad feeling between the two men drove both sides to try and out-do one another at every opportunity. They jockeyed for wharf space in Jamaica and battled for dock space in Baltimore, violence flaring between the workers of both companies. So it went on, growing from bad to worse, until Di Giorgio, Lanasa, and Goffe found themselves all in court, the subjects of one of the biggest trials the city of Baltimore had ever seen.

Pezzo Novante

Tutti copevoli, nessuno colpevole.

Anon.

European immigrants arriving in the United States by the millions in the mid-1800s, had, by and large, not encountered people of African descent before and so had no ready antagonism or hostility toward them. They had to be taught to hate them. Nationality and regional differences had been for these new immigrants from Europe their dividing line, not race. As such, many were unfamiliar with the American system of racial discrimination and often violated it. American academic Gordon Shufelt studied the socio-economic status of African Americans and Italians in late 19th and early 20th century Baltimore. He discovered that the two groups had much in common in both their economic conditions and how they were viewed by the white Anglo majority.

"Italians, and especially southern Italians," Gordon Shufelt writes in his book, *Strangers In A Middle Land: Italian Immigrants and Race Relations In Baltimore 1890-1920*, were viewed by northern Europeans as coming from a land dangerously close to the African continent.

"The proximity of southern Italy to Africa was important in the European perception of southern Italians," Shufelt writes. "All parts in Sicily are geographically closer to the North African coast than they are to Rome – a fact that had long been noted in Western Europe. An early 19th century French traveller, for example, commented that Europe ended at Naples...Sicily and all the rest is Africa."

In the American racial pecking order, Italians were not quite white enough. Shufelt says Italians were looked upon as replacements on Southern plantations for African-Americans who'd left the land after slavery. In 1906, in South Carolina, for example, hundreds of Italians were held under peonage conditions at temporary labour camps belonging to the South and Western Railroad Company. Similar conditions existed in other Southern states.

Desperate for labour, European migration to America was encouraged. Migration from southern Europe, the sun-baked, darker half of Europe, was frowned upon, though. Theodore Roosevelt, president of the United States during the biggest influx of Italians into the United States, was not shy about his dislike for southern Italians. He described them, bluntly, as "the least desirable population of Europe."

Roosevelt was not alone in these views. The United States Immigration Commission produced a report in 1900 in which it described southern Italians as a people descended from 'Hamitic' stock or people with 'some traces of an infusion of African blood in certain communities.' Luigi Villari, an Italian historian, counseled his countrymen in a 1903 newspaper article to keep their distance from African-Americans. "Italian feeling rebels on hearing," Villari said, "that our peasants are compared with Asiatics or Negroes." The comparisons made sense. Italians and blacks often worked together on labouring gangs and sometimes formed strong bonds. But just as not all Italians warmed to African-Americans, so not all blacks accepted the newcomers. In 1905, an African-American in New Orleans wrote a stinging letter to the *Colored American* magazine during a deadly yellow fever outbreak insisting Italians were at fault.

"The Italians are a filthy people who care very little for air, less for water," the writer said, "and not at all for soap, and who can and do live contentedly with 15 in a room and one towel as they can with eight."

Despite the racial obstacles, A.C. Goffe, the black Jamaican, and Antonio Lanasa, the Sicilian, formed an effective alliance. Blacks and Italians in Baltimore were less successful. In 1905, the Democratic Party in Maryland, which was at the time the party of segregation, introduced a measure designed at depriving African-Americans of the right to vote. It was a crude effort by the Democrats, the party of the Old South, to rob the Republicans, the party of Abraham Lincoln, of one of their most loyal constituencies.

The Democrats also wanted to block black advancement in the city. In 1890, Harry Sythe Cummings became the first black person elected to a seat on Baltimore City Council. Between 1890 and 1930, six different black Republicans won election to the Baltimore City Council. Though blacks lived a mostly segregated existence there, they nonetheless retained the vote and were able to exercise some influence, however limited, in Baltimore.

"I do not want to be governor of this State unless I am elected by a majority of the white race in Maryland," declared Democrat Arthur P. Gorman campaigning in Maryland. "This is a contest for the supremacy," Gorman said, "of the white race in Maryland." Gorman won. With the state legislature three-fifths Democrat, Gorman decided this was the ideal moment to try and push through an amendment depriving African Americans of the ballot. It was in this hostile racial climate that A.C. Goffe came to Baltimore to start a business. Had the amendment not been poorly drawn and had Italian immigrants not been scared the measure would rob them, too, of the vote it might have passed.

"Common people of all races and tongues ought to stand shoulder to shoulder," a black leader in the anti-amendment campaign said in 1905. Italians and blacks did not exactly stand shoulder to shoulder to defeat the measure, but their opposition was crucial. Republicans were also opposed to the measure. Their campaign, though, was as openly racist as was the Democrats.

"There's no man in the State that hates the darky more than I do," boasted Will Garland, a Republican ward leader. Garland and other Republicans calculated they could not win by appealing to anti-racist feeling. They needed the votes of whites, racist or not. The amendment was overwhelmingly reject-ed. Four years later, in 1909, the Democratic Party tried once again to deprive African-Americans of the vote. This time it made a concerted effort to con-vince Italian immigrants to support it. The measure failed. Had Joseph Trombetta, an employee and brother-in-law of Joseph Di Giorgio's, had his way the disenfranchisement measure would have passed and African Americans would have been deprived of the vote.

"The passage of the amendment will create more interest in the affairs of the government by the foreign born citizens," Trombetta said at a meeting held in Baltimore's 'Little Italy.' "It will show them their superiority over the black man."

One Italian, at least, was not keen to show his superiority over the black man. Antonio Lanasa rejected the measure. He was ahead of his time in business, and in his racial views, his grandson, Anthony said. "You can imagine what it was like in 1908 with the blacks and whites," said Anthony. Like his ancestor, Anthony, who lives in Virginia, about an hour's drive from Baltimore, is in the fruit business. "I think it was almost unbelievable that my grandfather and Freddy Goffe could have done what they did together at the time they did. People didn't mix like that then. But he and Fred were the best of friends. He came to the house, and they stayed best friends all through life as far as I know. It must have been real difficult, though, back then."

A Jamaican in Jim Crow America

'Prejudice not being founded on reason, cannot be removed by argument.'
Samuel Johnson

Finally, the waiting was over. Antonio Lanasa made his way into the court at Baltimore's Central Station House on 11 January, 1908 from his police cell. He was immediately surrounded by his large family, among them Anna, his mother, and his father, Michael. Lanasa was calm, the Baltimore newspapermen attending the court proceeding noted. His business partner was not. Right behind Lanasa was Goffe, bristling with indignation over his night in jail.

"He showed plainly that he had not slept a wink and that the effect of his imprisonment had brought him to grief, chagrin and shame," the *Baltimore American* newspaper said of the Jamaican. "He carried himself erect, and with eyes flashing, he glanced first at the Justice…and then for one brief instant, around the room."

When A.C. Goffe glanced angrily around the courtroom it's likely he didn't recognise the tall, sandy-coloured haired, bespectacled figure dressed in a tweed suit and white waistcoat sitting at the prosecutor's table. His name was Eugene O'Dunne, deputy State's Attorney for Baltimore. O'Dunne, one of the finest young attorneys in the city, had been given the career-making case over the protests of more senior colleagues in the State's Attorney's office. O'Dunne's bosses thought him a fiery, reform-minded Irish-American on a mission to punish wrongdoers in high and low places in Baltimore. He was, they thought, just the man to send a message to the likes of Lanasa, Goffe, and their Black Hand cohorts. Even the celebrated Baltimore author and columnist, H.L. Mencken, had noticed the young prosecutor. Mencken described O'Dunne as having "an Irish frenzy to break heads – a kind of boyish delight in alarming sinners."

It didn't improve Goffe's defence either, that he'd arrived in Baltimore from Jamaica on 10 December, 1907, the very day of the bombing of the Di Giorgio house. If Goffe was innocent, then it was bad luck and an unhappy coincidence that he happened to arrive on that day. If he was guilty, then it was a bad idea to be present in town when the dirty deed was being done. Whatever the case, some ten hours after Goffe arrived in Baltimore from Jamaica, the Di Giorgio mansion, at the stroke of midnight, was dynamited.

If he was going to win his freedom, the Jamaican was going to have to convince the court that he could not have participated in a conspiracy with alleged Black Hand gangsters, all of whom were Italian and spoke no English, as such. As he spoke no Italian and the plotters spoke no English, how, Goffe would have to argue, could they have conspired together without benefit of a common language?

"We expect that our clients are not conspirators," Goffe and Lanasa's lawyer, William Purnell Hall, told the court. Lanasa and Goffe had assembled the best attorneys money could buy. This included the youngest member of the U.S. Congress and the oldest member of the U.S. Senate. "We will prove that they were conspired against," William Purnell Hall told the court. "The conspiracy against them is one of the greatest that has ever been directed against two innocent men."

Outraged at the arrest of A.C. Goffe in America, Jamaica's *Daily Gleaner* newspaper published a stinging, sarcastic condemnation of the U.S. justice system in its pages. The editorial, written by the newspaper's editor, H.G. de Lisser, made fun of the American legal system and the legal lynching that appeared to be taking place in Baltimore.

"News comes by cable to-day that a desperate attempt was made on Thursday to rob an Italian bank doing business in New York," wrote H.G. de Lisser sarcastically. As well as being the *Gleaner* editor, de Lisser was a well-known writer of novels such as *The White Witch of RoseHall*. "A bomb was used by the burglars and the whole of the front portion of the building was destroyed. We have not yet heard that a Jamaican has been arrested on a charge of being a party to the attempted burglary, but we are expecting such news momently. More we are satisfied that when this Jamaican accomplice is arrested, the certain proof of his guilt will be found in fact that he was at least 5,000 miles away from New York on Thursday, and had been for a month."

The *Gleaner* editor admitted he had not taken seriously the news that A.C. Goffe had been arrested in America when he had first heard it. He regretted it, he said, and now wanted to implore Jamaicans to protest the imprisonment of one of their own abroad. "At the present moment, as everybody in this island knows, a Jamaican gentleman of sound commercial standing and good reputation is in custody in America," de Lisser wrote. "In this island the news was at first received with contemptuous amusement, but as Mr. Goffe is still under arrest, we have begun to think his position a very unpleasant, if not serious one…We feel indignant," the *Gleaner* editor wrote, "that Mr. Goffe should be thought to be the accomplice of a rascally gang of Italian murderers."

The view in Jamaica that Goffe was being lynched by the American legal system seemed to have some foundation when it was discovered that Thornton Rollins, foreman of the grand jury investigating whether the Jamaican ought to be indicted was a vice-president of Joseph Di Giorgio's Atlantic Fruit Company. It looked more and more like the Italian and the Jamaican were the unwitting victims of a conspiracy, not the architects of one. Rollins later stepped down from the grand jury, but state prosecutor Eugene O'Dunne remained convinced he had the bombing masterminds in front of him.

"These two are the arch-conspirators," O'Dunne bellowed, pointing across the courtroom at Lanasa and Goffe, "so I understand, and I think it will develop at the hearing that all the others were merely their tools."

One of the state's most important witnesses was Baltimore's Chief of Detectives, A.J. Pumphrey. He claimed he'd gotten word from informants in Pittsburgh, Pennsylvania the day before the Di Giorgio home was dynamited that three Black Hand men were on their way to Baltimore. Pumphrey told the court that he sent two of his best detectives, George Armstrong and William Atkinson, to watch the Lanasa home at 411 Hanover Street and Lanasa's offices on Pratt Street for any unusual activity or unusual visitors. Chief Pumphrey said he stood guard himself near the premises of A. Lanasa and Company on the morning of December 10. There he saw two of the Black

Handers, Salvatore Lupo and John Scaletta, leave the offices of the Lanasa Fruit Company.

As for Salvatore Lupo, the state's chief witness against Lanasa and Goffe, he was keen to put the Jamaican at the very heart of the conspiracy. His written confession, translated from Italian and full of racial expletives, was read before the court by Chief of Detectives, A.J. Pumphrey: "I went down and found that the boat was unloading," Lupo said. "There I met a nigger (Goffe)…then Tony (Lanasa) asked the nigger (Goffe) if he would give $1000 to help out of any trouble, and the nigger (Goffe) said he would give $10,000."

If A.C. Goffe was no more than a 'nigger' to an admitted killer-for-hire like Salvatore Lupo, what must the rest of white Baltimore have thought of this Jamaican in trouble in Jim Crow America?

Before Goffe's troubles began in Baltimore, he enjoyed an unusual amount of freedom in the Southern city for a black man. This was, in part, because he was rich and his shipping business provided employment to hundreds of Baltimoreans. Though he shared the same skin colour and racial ancestry as African-Americans in the city, that's all they appeared to share. Goffe had little contact with black Baltimoreans. They lived behind the veil, a miserable, mostly segregated existence, and Goffe gave them what Zora Neale Hurston described, memorably, as a "first class leaving alone." The Jamaican did, though, number Baltimore's most powerful white citizens, people like Richard Lynch of the Fidelity and Guarantee Trust Company, among his closest friends. While Goffe was able to eat and drink at the best restaurants in Baltimore, African-Americans could not. African-Americans could not stay in the city's hotels, yet whenever the Jamaican was in Baltimore he stayed at the Kelly or at the Eutaw House hotels, both of which had a 'whites only' policy.

Baltimore was the first city in the United States to pass a law making it illegal for blacks and whites to live on the same street. Though the law was later struck down, it was clear 'Jim Crow' segregation was alive and well in Baltimore. The City Council passed hundreds of laws making it illegal for African-Americans to attend the same schools, travel on the same buses, eat at the same restaurants or even urinate in the same public toilets as whites.

It hadn't always been this way. For much of the 19th century Baltimore was viewed as a relatively safe haven for black Americans. Thousands of free blacks, hearing they would receive better treatment there than elsewhere in the South, moved to the city in the pre-Emancipation period. When slavery ended and Maryland did not deny blacks the right to vote as many other states did, thousands more African-Americans moved there. Many of them settled in the East Baltimore area and found work in the booming shipbuilding industry.

Over time, though, the black caulkers and carpenters began to be squeezed out of the shipping industry to make room for immigrants from Europe. To make sure blacks were not closed out of shipbuilding entirely, two African Americans, John Locks, the richest black man in Baltimore, and Isaac Myers, head of the Baltimore Colored Caulker's Union, set up the Chesapeake Marine Railway and Dry Dock Company, a firm which provided teams of workers skilled at building sea faring craft.

Though most African-Americans in Baltimore earned their living as labourers, as caulkers, as carpenters, as barbers, as washerwomen and as hack drivers, a few earned their livings as physicians, attorneys, and as businessmen. Among the best known black Baltimoreans were: Everett Waring, who started the first black bank in Baltimore, Whitfield Winsey, one of the first black doctors in the city, George Lane, the first African-American to run for mayor in the city, and Harry Sythe Cummings, the first African-American to be elected to Baltimore's City Council.

Still, despite some advances, life in Baltimore and elsewhere in the American South was precarious for black people. Between 1900 and 1906, 575 African-Americans were lynched. In March 1906, eight weeks after A.C. Goffe launched the Lanasa and Goffe Steamship and Importing Company in Baltimore, a black man, Edward Watson, was lynched by a white mob in Pocomoke City in Maryland, southeast of Baltimore. Five months after this, whites in Maryland's capital city, Annapolis, lynched another black man, Henry Davis. America had been mostly silent on the subject of lynching until Theodore Roosevelt, president between 1901 and 1909, tackled the subject in his 1906 State of the Union address.

"I call your attention and the attention of the Nation," Roosevelt told Congress, "to the prevalence of crime among us, and above all to the epidemic of lynching and mob violence that springs up, now in one part of our country, now in another." There is but one safe rule in dealing with black men and with white men, Roosevelt said. "It is the same rule that must be applied in dealing with rich men and poor men; that is, to treat each man, whatever his color, his creed, or his social position, with even-handed justice on his real worth as a man."

The lynching did not stop, though. Between 1882 and 1948, more than 4,700 African-Americans were lynched by white mobs.

These conditions stirred some African-Americans to act. In 1904, the Committee of Twelve for the Advancement of the Interest of the Negro Race was formed. In 1905, W.E.B. Du Bois and other black activists attending an historic conference in Niagara, New York called for all distinctions based on race in America to be abolished. In 1909, the National Association for the Advancement of Colored People, the NAACP, was founded. Still, discriminatory laws kept the races in America separate and very much apart.

Jamaica was not like this. Though of course colour prejudice existed there, it was not the institutionalised racial discrimination practiced in the United States. Even the Black Nationalist leader Marcus Garvey acknowledged that Jamaica "had no open race prejudice." Garvey said while it was true that black and white were not equal in Jamaica, the races did not, however "openly antagonize one another" as they did in the United States. W.E.B. Du Bois, the founder of the NAACP, agreed with Garvey. In 1915, he went to Jamaica to give a lecture on how well black people were doing in the United States. He was overwhelmed, however, by what he saw in Jamaica.

"Jamaica is a most amazing island," Du Bois said. "In Jamaica for the first time in my life I lived beyond the color line—not on one side of it, but beyond its end." He was surprised to find that the mayor of Kingston was a man of his own colour and that people of colour played many and varied roles on the island. It was, Du Bois wrote, "a strange sort of luxury to ride on railways where engineers, firemen, conductors and brakemen were black." The island was, he said, facing the world proudly with one great gift, "the gift of racial peace, the utter overturning of the barbaric war of color, with a chance for men to lift themselves regardless of the complexion of their grandfathers." Jamaica was, Du Bois said, "the most marvellous paradox of this paradoxical Western world."

So proud was Jamaica of itself, and desperately in need of labour to replace emancipated slaves who had left the plantations in the 1830s, in the 1840s the country tried to encourage African-American freedmen to migrate there. Behind the campaign to entice African-Americans to the island was Alexander Barclay, Jamaica's Commissioner of Emigration. Barclay published a pamphlet on the subject, 'Remarks on Emigration To Jamaica: Addressed To The Coloured Class in the United States.' The campaign took a literary bent, as well. This poem appeared in the book, A Description and History of the Island of Jamaica by J. Ogilby: *The Yankee will not let you touch/The cap of Freedom, nor so much/ As look on't; can ye hope to bear it? /Come to Jamaica, then, and wear it!*

As for A.C. Goffe, the charmed life he enjoyed in Baltimore came to an abrupt end. Imprisoned, his 'honorary white' status revoked, he was just another black man on the wrong side of the law in the American South. In the same week he was arrested and imprisoned in Baltimore in January 1908, an African-American man suspected of striking a white woman and stealing her bag was attacked by a white mob. 'Angry Mob Beat Negro' a newspaper reported. "The throng was ready to lynch the man, but the arrival of the police saved him." The man was lucky to be left with nothing more serious than scalp wounds, gashes under his eyes, a badly bruised body and internal injuries.

Racism was a way of life in America in 1908. There seemed little chance that a black man like Goffe could receive justice in such a racially hostile climate. If his case did go to trial it was likely a jury of his peers would be a group of white men who had a copy of Thomas Dixon's best-selling 1905 racist novel, *The Clansman*, a celebration of the Ku Klux Klan, by their bedsides.

Another popular piece of reading material among whites in America at the time was *The Effects of Tropical Light on White Men* by U.S. Army surgeon Major Charles Woodruff. The book claimed to have unravelled the age-old mystery of 'why the Negro is black.' Among its conclusions were: "The Negro is really a nocturnal animal, like other black animals of the tropics. Left to himself, he behaves like a cat – inclined to sleep all day, and become lively, energetic and active at night." African-Americans were figures of fun and ridicule. *Sambo and His Funny Noise*, a cartoon featuring a bug-eyed black boy, was one of the *Baltimore Sun's* most popular features. One of the most popular songs in the early 1900s was 'All Coons Look Alike To Me." This song was sung, bizarrely, by an African-American, Ernest Hogan. The shelves of

American stores were filled with products that featured racist images of black people. Among the most popular of these was the *Niggerhead* brand of products: *Niggerhead Ink, Niggerhead Dye*, and *Niggerhead Oysters*. The company even had a special line of toys: The *Niggerhead Cap-Gun* and the *Jolly Nigger Toy Bank*.

The white world was turned upside down, though, in 1908, when the African-American boxer, Jack Johnson, defeated the white American Tommy Burns to become the first black person ever to be heavyweight champion of the world. The myth of white supremacy punctured, a challenger had to be found. Jim Jeffries, an Irish-American, was offered up as 'The Great White Hope.' But he, too, was beaten by the black man, Jack Johnson. Whites were so enraged by Johnson's victory, many marauded through black neighbourhoods attacking defenceless residents. But this didn't diminish African-Americans' joy. William Waring Cuney wrote a poem which showed just how happy blacks were to, at last, get even with whites: *'O my Lord/ What a morning, /O my Lord,/ What a feeling, /When Jack Johnson/ Turned Jim Jeffries'/ Snow-white face/ to the ceiling.'*

A fair and unbiased hearing for A.C. Goffe seemed impossible in such a racially charged environment. But either unaware of the dangers or indifferent to them, Goffe struck a defiant pose at a preliminary court hearing in January 1908, much to the annoyance of the white reporters covering the case.

"He dressed in a gray sack suit and wore patent leather shoes and a maroon tie, knotted with the precision that comes from years of practice," the *Baltimore American* newspaper correspondent reported patronisingly. "His evident mortification at being arraigned as a prisoner was exceeded only by his manifest determination to make a long and bitter fight to get free and make good his stout denials that he had any connection with the dynamiting of Mr. Di Giorgio's residence."

A Mulatto Aristocracy

'If you want to know what God thinks of money, just look at the people he gave it to.'
Dorothy Parker

Strange as A.C. Goffe, a wealthy, boarding school educated black man who neither bowed nor stooped to white authority, must have seemed to Americans, in Jamaica he was far from an oddity.

"Far more of them were freed before the general emancipation," wrote historian Ken Post of Jamaica's free coloured people, the caste from which Goffe sprang. Many were owners of land and small businesses during slavery. "With this head start, they moved after the final emancipation of 1838," Post writes in his book, *Arise Ye Starvelings*, "into capitalist and petty bourgeois enterprise." This was true of Goffe's maternal grandfather, Robert Clemetson, a resident of the rainy, hilly parish of St Mary in northeastern Jamaica.

"Old Maker put himself to a lot of trouble to make that part of the island of Jamaica, for everything there is perfect," wrote the American author Zora Neale Hurston of St Mary. "The sea is the one true celestial blue, and the shore, the promontories, the rocks and the grass are the models for the rest of the world to take pattern after."

It was in St Mary, around 1805, that Robert Clemetson was born, a 'free man of colour.' This freedom didn't amount to much, though. Coloured freedmen – the offspring usually of a white man and an African slave woman – couldn't vote or hold public office and were usually confined to lowly occupations. Though many were granted their freedom by their white fathers, their lives were severely circumscribed. As late as the 1760s, for example, free coloured people were required, humiliatingly, to wear a blue cross on the right shoulder of their clothing to prove they were indeed free. By the time Robert Clemetson was born in the early 1800s, conditions had begun to improve somewhat for the free coloured. Under increasing pressure to end slavery, the British government demanded planters in Jamaica make concessions.

In 1813, the island's House of Assembly passed legislation removing many, but not all, restrictions on freedmen. Restrictions removed, many coloured men became clerks and ships' pilots. It was to the sea that Robert Clemetson and his brother, Richard, turned to make their living. Beyond the navigation and operation of a ship at sea, a ship's pilot was responsible for coordinating the activities of the deck crew, controlling cargo stowage, and the loading and unloading of the ship. It was a well paid, if sometimes dangerous profession. In February 1823 – three years before Robert Clemetson won a job as a pilot for the St Mary and St. George municipalities – ten pirates who'd killed the passengers and crew of several ships were apprehended and executed at Port Royal by the British Navy. In May of the same year, nineteen more pirates were caught and executed off Jamaica's south coast, at Gallows Point. Though it was clear the job of pilot had its dangers, it was a small price to pay for men of colour who'd once been confined to the lowliest of professions.

Still, though Jamaica's free people of colour were granted a raft of new rights and privileges in 1813, they remained little more, really, than second-class citizens on the island. In 1825, John Campbell, a prominent person of colour from St. James, estimated that 22,900 of the free coloured population was "absolutely poor," 5,500 were of "fair circumstances" and only 400 were "rich."

Robert and Richard Clemetson were not among the rich. They were ambitious, though. In 1830, the two, busy with full time jobs as pilots, purchased a sloop – a fore-and-aft rigged boat with one mast and a single jib – from George Tingle, a master mariner from St Ann, and began a small shipping enterprise.

That year, 1830, was a good one for free men of colour like the Clemetson brothers. They won the right to vote and to hold public office. African slaves, though, remained in miserable bondage until full emancipation eight years later.

By the time emancipation arrived in 1838, Robert Clemetson was already a wealthy landowner. Slavery over, his fortunes increased and he was elected in 1838 a member of the vestry, or local government, of St Mary. The high and the mighty of the parish were members of the vestry: the Justices of the Peace, the Custos, or chief official, of the parish, and the Rector of the Church of England. Clemetson and the nine other mostly white vestrymen were responsible for assessing taxes among other things. By 1839, Clemetson had risen to the lofty position of Harbourmaster of the St Mary ports of Oracabessa, Rio Nuevo, and Port Maria. He supervised the comings and goings of commercial shipping at the three ports.

In time, Clemetson became St Mary's Collecting Constable, the chief of the tax collection office, a Justice of the Peace, an Assistant Judge of the Common Court of Pleas, a coroner, and a representative to Jamaica's House of Assembly. A member of what was called the Town or Coloured Party, Clemetson was one of a number of coloured men – among them George William Gordon – elected to the Assembly in the years following Emancipation. With coloureds outnumbering them five to one, whites became very nervous about their control of the colony.

Determined to hold on to power on the island, the whites made a desperate attempt to block the advance of the people of colour. Members of the Country Party, mostly white merchants and planters, passed a measure in 1833 calling for a steep increase in the amount of property a candidate for the Assembly was required to own in order to run for office. This didn't deter the coloured candidates, though, as many were quite wealthy. Robert Clemetson was one of eight coloured representatives elected in 1841 despite the best efforts of the whites of the Country Party. After only a few months in the Assembly, however, during which time he contributed to the passing of at least one piece of legislation, Clemetson's election was voided on a technicality. The same thing happened when he ran again three years later.

"The actions of the Assembly during this period were chaotic," wrote W. Adolphe Roberts in his book, *Jamaica-Portrait of An Island*. Richard Bickell, a Christian minister who lived in Jamaica during the early 1800s, described St Mary and the parish of St George as "the two most barbarous and unenlightened parishes" on the island. Deprived of office, Clemetson probably agreed.

Frustrated by the efforts of white assemblymen to limit the influence of blacks and coloureds in Jamaica's political affairs, Clemetson decided instead to dedicate himself to the business of making as much money as he could. He wheeled and dealed his way into possession of valuable real estate in Port

Maria's business district and wharf area. With many white planters eager to sell their sugar estates and leave Jamaica after Emancipation, former slave plantations were available at bargain basement prices. The 1,244-acre Spring Valley estate in St Mary, for example, had once been valued at £18,000, but was sold in 1842, lock, stock and barrel, for only a £1,000. Between 1832 and 1849, one hundred and forty sugar plantations, amounting to more than 168,000 acres, were abandoned in Jamaica. In St Mary parish alone, twelve estates, amounting to 13,236 acres, were abandoned.

It was during this period that Robert Clemetson was able to purchase several large St Mary plantations, most notable among them, Frontier, an enormous property upon which much of the town of Port Maria, St Mary's capital, was erected. Frontier had once been the scene of a famous slave rebellion. It was there on Easter Monday in 1760 that Tacky, a slave who had once been an African chief, led a revolt that spread across Jamaica. By the time the revolt was done 400 Africans and sixty whites were dead.

A.C. Goffe's father, John, was, like Robert Clemetson, a coloured man of means and influence in St Mary. A wealthy merchant, shipping agent and landowner in the parish, John Goffe's beginnings were quite modest. Born in 1822, Goffe earned his living as a clerk in Kingston as a young man. His family claimed, without positive proof, that he was a descendant of the surveyor John Goffe who drew up the plans in 1692 for the town of Kingston. For some reason, Goffe moved from Kingston to St Mary in the 1840s, a time when many people of colour were escaping from the shadow of the plantation and the domination of white planters in the country parishes to Kingston and to Spanish Town.

In Port Maria, John Goffe found work as a chief clerk to a merchant in agricultural produce. When the owner retired, Goffe bought the business. But it soon foundered and Goffe was forced into bankruptcy. In time he settled his debts, paying twenty shillings in the pound to his creditors. His future looked grim. His luck changed, though, when he made the acquaintance of Margaret Clemetson, the oldest child of Robert Clemetson. Though Goffe hadn't exactly distinguished himself in life so far, he would, nonetheless, have been considered a catch for a coloured family looking for a match for a daughter.

Margaret Clemetson was of marrying age but a suitable prospect had not been found for her. In the Jamaican race and class stakes, Margaret had her pluses and her minuses. On the plus side, she was the daughter of a wealthy man. On the minus side, she was darker-skinned and thus in the colour calculus not as desirable as one of fairer skin. Additionally, she had been born a slave, though she was freed when she was still an infant. Goffe had his pluses and minuses, too. On the plus side, he was light-skinned and so very sought after. On the minus side, Goffe had once failed in business and nothing was known of his pedigree. Just who his parents were and where he had been born and raised was a mystery which remained a perpetual possibility in a world of speculation.

John Beecham Goffe, aged 31, married Margaret Clemetson, aged 24, on 11 August, 1853 in St Mary. The wedding was officiated by Church of England curate J. Davidson at the Holy Trinity Anglican Church in the town of Retreat in western St Mary, near the border with St Ann. This presented some problems. It was customary for a bride to marry in the town where she was born and for the bride and her wedding party to walk together from the family home to church for the service. Wedding ceremonies were usually held at noon and the wedding reception or feast held a short while later at the bride's parent's home.

But, for some reason, John and Margaret chose not to marry at the Anglican church at Haldane Hill a mile or so from Port Maria. A new church was being built in the town, but that would not be ready for another eight years. Anyway, the wedding ceremony at Holy Trinity Anglican church in Retreat over, it was a 20-mile journey to Port Maria for the wedding feast at Frontier, an estate owned by the father of the bride. A grey horse pulled the wedding carriage. A grey horse was considered lucky. It was lucky for the bridegroom. Among the wedding gifts were several valuable bits of real estate from his father-in-law. With this head start, it wasn't long before John Goffe had established himself as a prosperous merchant selling fashionable footwear and clothing from London and tasty foodstuffs from New York.

On 8 August, 1867 a large delivery arrived at Port Maria from New York for John B. Goffe & Co. General Stores on the brig, *Eclipse*. Onboard there were half barrels of ox tongues and pork, water crackers and kegs of New Goshen butter, cases of refined kerosene oil and several cases of Bristol's

Sarsaparilla. Three weeks later the ship, *Talisman*, from Liverpool, brought Regatta shirts, striped jean shirts, brown silk garden umbrellas, Castor Oil pomade and violet hair powder. As well as importing fancy clothes and fine food, John Goffe was also an exporter. On 10 March, 1870 a schooner commissioned by him, the *A.M. Biles*, left Port Maria for Boston "with a general cargo of oranges and cocoanuts" onboard.

John Goffe owned a wharf, pier and several other properties in Port Maria, among them the Kirk Corner Buildings. He also owned three large St Mary plantations, Oxford, Roslyn and Boscobel, and was a part owner with his father-in-law in a plantation called Speculation. Like his father-in-law, John Goffe became a public official. He followed Clemetson's lead and became a vestryman, a churchwarden, a member of St Mary's Municipal Board, and a Justice of the Peace. But even as he became involved in the civic life of the parish, Goffe didn't let it interfere with making money.

His various enterprises multiplied. There was: John B. Goffe & Co., Merchants, Drugs and General Dealers, Lee Wharf and Bonded Stores, and John B. Goffe & Co., a shipping agency. Goffe was also an exporter of a wide range of products, as well. On 18 November 1879, his firm loaded the London-bound ship, *James Thomason*, with sugar, 142 puncheons of rum, 282 bags of pimento, 7 tons of logwood, 3 tons of fustic, 23,910 coconuts, and one cask of beeswax.

"A proud and self-sufficient mulatto aristocracy that had been building up and propagating its kind, generation after generation" is how the Jamaican author Claude McKay described the coloured people of Jamaica. The British writer Anthony Trollope, after a visit to Jamaica in the 1850s, wrote the book, *The West Indies and the Spanish Main.* In it Trollope betrays both his admiration, and his contempt for the island's coloured people. "They do make money, and enjoy it. They practice as statesmen, as lawyers, as doctors in the colony," Trollope observed grudgingly. "They are by no means humble in their gait, and their want of meekness sets their white neighbours against them. They are always proclaiming by their voice and look that they are as good as the white man."

Many of the people of colour did, indeed, think themselves as good as any white man. They could also, though, be as bad. Like whites, many free coloured and free black people owned slaves. Indeed, records show that in

1826, twelve years before the end of slavery, free coloured and free black people owned more than 50,000 of Jamaica's 310,000 slaves.

The Clemetsons made sure they had their share. In 1828, Robert Clemetson appears in the *Jamaica Almanack* as the owner in St Mary of a single slave, who would have been worth exactly forty-four pounds, fifteen shillings and two and a quarter pennies. Clemetson's mother, his brother Richard, and a sister all owned slaves, too. Robert Clemetson's slave was believed to be a quadroon woman – someone three quarters white and one quarter black – named Eliza Ayton.

Clemetson's property, Ayton, fell pregnant by her master and had their child, Margaret, in 1829. Margaret like her mother, Eliza, was born a slave. Either they were liberated at Emancipation in 1838 or Clemetson purchased their freedom. It is not known which.

There was no fairy tale ending. Clemetson didn't marry Ayton. In 1833, his prospects improving, Clemetson married Elizabeth Ellison, the daughter of James Ellison, a wealthy coloured man from St George, a parish to the east of St Mary. Ellison was a shipping man who served as St George's Harbourmaster, Waiter and Searcher, and Surveyor and Admeasurer of Shipping and as a magistrate. Ellison and Clemetson married in January 1833 at the parish church in St. Andrew. They produced nine children together. Margaret, Clemetson's child with his slave Eliza, married John Beecham Goffe in 1853. They produced nine children in the marriage, the fourth of which they called Alfred.

Born in comfort and splendour in St Mary's parish on 30 December, 1863, all appeared well in Alfred Constantine Goffe's world. His large extended family group – which included the Clemetsons of Frontier, Union Hill, and Mount Zion estates, the Taylors of Speculation, the Culletons of Friendship Estate, the Campbells of Williams Park Estate, the Marshes of Warwick Castle, and others – were all members of the local plantocracy, who wielded a great deal of power in their northeastern Jamaican parish.

"The Goffe family of St Mary, with the Walkers, the Phillpotts, the Clemetsons, the Constantines, the DeLissers, the Vernons, and, of course, the Pringles are, I think, probably the oldest inhabitants of this attractive North Coast banana area," wrote a columnist in a Jamaican journal.

Though John Goffe had become a wealthy man about town in Port Maria by the 1860s, some older citizens of the parish considered him part of the nouveau riche, the newly rich, the recently arrived, who could be found here and there around the island. Goffe wanted his brood to gain sophistication quickly so he sent his three oldest sons off to be educated at English public schools.

John Goffe had no education to speak of, but he had a way about him that convinced many otherwise. Sure he could read and write and knew enough arithmetic to know whether his books balanced or not. But what style, sophistication and knowledge he had of the arts, the sciences, and finance he picked up along the way of life, not at a fancy prep school or English university. Try as wealthy coloured men like him did, rarely, if ever, did they win the respect or regard of whites.

Being richer than a white man or better educated than one, the English author Anthony Trollope made clear, was not enough to win a white man's approval. In *The West Indies and the Spanish Main* Trollope mourns the end of the slave system. He complains that former slaves are wandering the island idle and unwilling to work and that white planters are squandering what little they have left on high living and entertainment. Trollope's harshest judgment, though, was reserved for Jamaica's coloured people. He accuses them of trying, and failing, to hide their African ancestry.

"Such denial is never allowed," Trollope wrote. "The crisp hair, the sallow skin, the known family history, the thick lip of the old remembered granddam, a certain languor in the eye; all or some, or perhaps but one of these tells the tale. But the tale is told, and the life-struggle is made always, and always in vain."

The Goffes couldn't hide their roots; they were too obvious and not easily obscured. What they could do was cultivate those roots at an English boarding school. So it was off to school in Britain. The *Daily Gleaner* newspaper of 26 March, 1868 announced the departure from Annotto Bay in St Mary of 9-year old Robert Horatio Goffe and 13- year old John Beecham Goffe Jnr.

"Passengers sailed in the Barque *Chebucto*, from Annotto Bay, for London – Masters J.B. and R.H. Goffe, of Port Maria." Two years later, on 9 July 1870, another of John Goffe's sons, 11- year old Cecil, set sail on the barque *Eliza Hunter* to join his siblings at school in England.

The Britain the Goffe boys found themselves in was in the midst of great social transformation. Benjamin Disraeli, a man of Jewish ancestry, became Prime Minister in 1868. Only eight out of a hundred boys attended school beyond the age of ten in 1868. Those who were able to attend school at all went to one of the so-called 'ragged' schools where poor children were provided with a free, basic education of reading, writing and arithmetic.

In 1870, while the Goffe brothers were at Wesleyan College in Taunton, Somerset, the British government approved legislation guaranteeing primary school education to all. The next year trades unions were made legal. In 1872, the Public Health Act was passed and health authorities, charged with improving the generally poor physical condition of most Britons, were set up. This period, too, was one of relative peace for the British. There were few foreign military adventures and so the period became known as a time of 'splendid isolation.'

Life must have been very isolating and far from splendid for John, Robert and Cecil Goffe in Taunton, Somerset. It must have felt to them as though they were the only black people in Britain, tucked away as they were in south-west England. There were, in fact, many thousands of black people living in Britain at the time. Africans first visited Britain during Roman times, records show. By the mid 1700s, around 20,000 black people. When the three Jamaican boys arrived in Britain in 1868 the most well known black person in the country was Mary Seacole, a Jamaican nurse who had won fame as the 'Black Florence Nightingale' during the Crimean War. Beloved, she settled in London and wrote a memoir of her exploits called, *Wonderful Adventures of Mrs. Seacole in Many Lands.*

By the time A.C. Goffe and his younger brothers – Alec, Ernest, Clarence and Rowland – were ready to go off to school, Jamaica was preferred over Britain. They were sent not to Wesleyan in Somerset or Framlingham in Suffolk but to the Jamaican prep school, Maryvilla at 37 Duke Street in Kingston.

"FIRST CLASS EDUCATION. The completest in Jamaica. The healthiest and nicest situation in Jamaica. Excellent Masters. Come and See." Run by Father Xavier Jaeckel, a German born Jesuit priest considered the best headmaster in Jamaica, Maryvilla boarders paid £24 per school year. Alec Goffe did well there. In the annual prize giving for 1879, he snagged awards for his work in Greek and in Algebra. A.C., meanwhile, was attending York Castle, a boarding school in the

highlands of St Ann parish. He arrived there in 1877, aged 14, a year after the school opened.

"Wesleyan High School, ST. ANN. Situation Picturesque and Healthy," reads an advert for York Castle in the Jamaican newspaper, *The Budget. "Educational Course liberal, including Matriculation Class for London University. Domestic arrangements home-like. Terms moderate."* Though A.C. didn't win any awards for his academic work there, he was a good athlete and was included in the school's First Eleven cricket team. In March 1879, in the first of the twice-yearly cricket matches between York Castle and rival St Ann boarding school, Walton, which later became Jamaica College, 16-year-old A.C. and his partner, F.W. Guiselin, opened the batting. York Castle won the match by 18 runs. In the 1880s, Alec, Ernest, Clarence and Rowland joined A.C. at York Castle. The school's hundred or so boys – white, coloured, and black mix easily.

"From St Mary came the Goffes," wrote the attorney and author Ansell Hart in his memoirs of his school days at York Castle. "I heard tell of the eldest "Samson" Goffe; and I knew at York Castle as Master, Ferdinand Charles MacTavish ("quashie Gilbert") and as Boy, Roly Poly, who knew the name and history of every English Prime Minister, wore on Sundays a morning coat, and later qualified as barrister in England. C.H. Clemetson Goffe was a well known solicitor of Port Maria, and Freddie, a famous Banana Agent, who when imprisoned unlawfully in America for imaginary complicity with the Italian Black Hand, threatened to have a British gun boat thundering at Boston Harbour."

York Castle was located 2,000 feet above sea level between the town of Claremont and the Pedro River in St Ann parish. The school was run by the evangelical Protestant denomination, the Wesleyans. The boys there were among the brightest on the island. In the fourteen years between 1881 and 1895, York Castle boys outdid their rivals at Jamaica College and Potsdam College, later Munro College, to win the island's highest academic award, the Jamaica Scholarship, eight times.

In the annual prize giving at York Castle for 1883, 16-year-old Ernest Goffe, a fifth former, won an award for Math and his younger brother, Clarence, won awards for French and Scripture. Three years later, in 1886, Ernest won prizes for Math, Science, English, French, and a special medal for Book-Keeping. Rowland, the youngest of the brothers, a third former, won prizes for Scripture and for English. Seventeen-year-old Clarence snagged a special certificate for 'Good Conduct.' The Latin motto of York Castrians, as the schoolboys call themselves, is *'Nil Sine Magno Labore'* or 'Nothing Without Great Labour.' Though York Castle shut down in 1906, the school was remembered fondly in several memoirs by one old boy or other.

"Those were the days when the York Castle school was in being, and the Goffes were then the leading cricketers of the parish," wrote old York Castrian J. Luther Saunders in his history of St Mary's Middlesex Cricket Club, which was based at Palmer's Park, Port Maria. "They were," Saunders said of A.C. and his cricketing brothers, "so powerful that the ground was found much too small, and the Church as well the Court-house in close proximity suffered heavily as a result of broken glasses – windows."

While many of the boys at York Castle were preparing for life as scholars and clerics, A.C. Goffe was preparing to earn his keep in trade. By the time he returned home to Port Maria aged 18 in 1881, St Mary was a changed place.

Harbours that had lay almost empty were now filled with American schooners of one sort or another. They were loading Jamaican bananas and logwood for export to the United States. St Mary land that had once been used to grow sugar cane was now being used for the cultivation of bananas. In St Mary, George Solomon and A.L. DaCosta were among the first to begin extensive banana cultivation. Sir John Pringle, St Mary's largest landowner, began cultivation soon after Solomon and DaCosta. A humble government medical officer when he arrived in Jamaica from Britain in the 1870s, marriage to Amy Zillah Levy, daughter of the wealthy Jamaican Jewish businessman, Isaac Levy, put thousands of acres of fertile lands in St Mary into John Pringle's hands. Pringle used his good fortune wisely. He put the Agualta Vale, Chovey, Coleraine, Greenside, Brimmer Hall, Cape Clear and Nonsuch estates into banana. In a short time, Pringle had more than 5,000 acres in banana stretching from St Mary parish to the parish of St. James in western Jamaica.

Whatever contempt Jamaica's big planters once felt for the banana, long the food of Jamaica's peasants, was forgotten as the enormous sums they made from the poor man's food began rolling in. The demand for Jamaican bananas was such that schooners chartered by American companies jammed Jamaican harbours. Schooners chartered by the Frank Brothers, Henry

Brothers, Clarke & Co, and Warner & Merritt could all be seen in one Jamaican harbour or another. Captain Lorenzo Dow Baker's company alone owned more than 13,000 acres of Jamaica's best banana lands.

The future seemed obvious to A.C. Goffe. With two large plantations, a wharf, wharf side buildings, a retail and agricultural produce store and other realty in their possession, his family was well placed to take advantage of this new, international interest in the banana. But banana would have to wait, at least, for awhile.

Goffe's father had been ailing for several years. He'd contracted malaria, a disease that thrived in St Mary's rainy, humid conditions. Bananas brought good and bad to parishes like St Mary. With large-scale banana cultivation came prosperity, but it also led to a rise in the cases of malaria. John Beecham Goffe died, a victim of Fever, on 17 October 1882.

"With regret we record the death of J. B. Goffe, Esq., of Port Maria, who died at his residence on Tuesday night at 11:30 o'clock," reads an obituary. *"Mr. Goffe has been a merchant in St Mary's for over a quarter of a century, where he has commanded the respect of all classes of the community. To his bereaved widow and family we offer our deepest sympathy."*

After a period of mourning, John Goffe's general store, shipping agency and wharf opened once again for business. Life went on pretty much as it had before. In January 1884, though, St Mary got a fright. Rumours abounded that the parish's landless were plotting the murder of rich whites and coloureds. The panic began on 27 January, 1884, when the manager of J.E. Kerr's General Store in Port Maria, a white man, claimed a black man told him "Africans were fed up" with how poorly they were treated by the white and coloured people of the parish and so were going to come down from the hills and cut them down. To anyone who'd attended the recent meeting at the Town Hall, where many of the parish's residents complained bitterly about not having land or work, the threats seemed credible. The terrified clerk told the Custos of the parish and the Inspector of Police what he'd heard.

"Wait little. Ooono soon see. Gayle people (the poor, mountainous district to the west of Port Maria) going rise," the clerk reported. "If you value you life and your children, go hide for in a few days Gayle people going to come down and kill all the brown men and the white men..." No one took it seriously until the police claimed a salesman at John Goffe's General Store remembered selling "a numerous quantity of cutlasses." On hearing this, the gentry shut themselves onto their estates and posted guards outside. As it turned out, a large number of cutlasses – fifteen to be exact – had been sold, but not for the purpose of slaughtering the parish's high and mighty. The cutlasses had been purchased for workers employed to clear a large plantation outside Port Maria.

The excitement over, the great and the good of St Mary went back to life as usual. As for A.C. Goffe, he was still trying to figure out what to do with himself. At first he assisted his brother John, and mother, Margaret, with the management of the family's businesses. He proved himself to be a hard-headed, capable businessman, fond of wheeling and dealing. Conversely, though, A.C. was also fond of the life of the sportsman. That's the life his uncles, David and Abraham Clemetson, lived. Landed gentry, they bred and raced thorough-bred horses for pleasure not for profit. Their Clemetson's Stables in Port Maria and Frontier Race Course — erected on several acres of David's 1,200 acre estate — were favourites of the sporting set.

"Mr. Clemetson was loudly cheered when his mare was brought in to weigh," the *Gleaner* reported from the Kingston Races in December 1893. In one race, *The Maiden Pony Purse*, David Clemetson's *Clarice* went head to head with his nephew A.C. Goffe's mount, *Clio*. It was a close race, but Mr. Townsend's mare, *Surprise*, beat out Goffe's mare by a half-length for the 16 sovereigns prize money. The next year, 1894, at the St Ann's Bay races at Drax Hall in St Ann parish, Goffe's filly, *Dione*, won him £60 in the *Two Year Old Stakes* and a £40 purse in the *Untried Stakes*. Later that same year he had success at the Kingston Races with his two-year-old, *Euclid*. Three of his brothers – Clarence, Cecil, and Alec – came with him to the capital city for the event. They all, somehow, managed to secure rooms at Kingston's grand Myrtle Bank Hotel though the hotel was widely known to adhere to a 'whites only' policy.

"A black lady of culture and wealth with her children was denied admission to a public children's party at the Myrtle Bank Hotel in Kingston," wrote Ansell Hart, the Jamaican attorney and writer. "It was difficult to decide which was the more surprised party, the hotel manager at the lady's naiveté in seeking admission or the lady at the denial."

A.C. Goffe's mounts – *Candy*, *Clio*, *Dione* and *Rosedrop* – did well at the Kingston Races. Not well enough, though, to stop him returning to the export trade. Jamaican bananas and logwood were earning large sums for exporters. With this in mind, Goffe left for the United States in 1893 to seek outlets for logwood, a small, thorny tree that produces haematoxylin, an all-purpose textile dye. Logwood grew in abundance in Jamaica. He arrived in Boston on October 30 and after clearing immigration and customs, where he declared he was a merchant and was in possession of two bits of luggage, set off on a tour of several American cities, among them New York and Philadelphia. Though bananas brought a good price, logwood brought an even better price at the time.

"Positively the most profitable crop in Jamaica in 1897 was logwood, a self sown weed of pastures, the export of which rose steadily as that of sugar declined, until in 1893-94 its value exceeded that of either sugar or coffee," wrote Sydney Olivier, a Governor of Jamaica. During these years A.C. Goffe and his brothers exported hundreds of tons of logwood to the United States and to the United Kingdom. In March 1896, alone, they shipped more than 500 tons of logwood roots to Falmouth, in Britain. By 1897, the logwood market had bottomed out so Goffe and his brothers put all their money and energies into bananas. They started a banana purchasing company called Messrs Goffe Bros. and bought all the bananas they could get their hands on. In a short time their firm was shipping thousands of bunches each week to the United States. On 13 February, 1899, for example, a ship leased by Messrs Goffe Bros., the *Jamaica*, arrived in Newport News in Virginia from Port Maria with 18,800 bunches of bananas onboard.

A.C. Goffe and his siblings almost missed the banana boat. Though their father had exported the fruit to the United States, the sons did not, at first, have the same confidence in it. Shortly after their father's death in 1882 they, foolishly, agreed to lease the family's Port Maria wharf to the American banana pioneer, Captain Lorenzo Dow Baker. Baker's firm, the Boston Fruit Company, had its headquarters in the parish of Portland, but wanted to expand its business into St Mary, a parish Baker believed had great promise. A.C. Goffe and his brothers handled some shipments of coconuts and of oranges, but little or no bananas at the time. They got their wharf back from Captain Baker and went into the banana buying business in earnest.

It wasn't long before St Mary was Jamaica's premier banana parish. Holdings in the parish that'd been worth between two and five pounds an acre were within a few years worth forty times as much.

Though A.C. Goffe and his siblings were all, to a greater or lesser degree, shareholders in their family firm, only A.C., John and Clarence were really employed in the business of the firm on a full time basis. John gave up his seat on St Mary parish's Parochial Board, the local government body, in order to concentrate on the banana business. Clarence Charles Ferdinand MacTavish Goffe kept his seat on the board, but was often not able to attend meetings there because he was elsewhere on family business.

Cecil Herbert Clemetson Goffe, a Port Maria lawyer, had also held a seat on the Parochial Board. He gave up his seat on the board to attend to his legal practice and to act as his family's attorney. Educated in Britain, Cecil returned to Jamaica in 1882 after 14 years away in Britain. He'd never really given serious thought to staying there or to settling in Kingston though he opened law offices there after being admitted to practice law in Jamaica in 1883.

As well as practicing law, Cecil, eager for business, set himself up as an agent in Kingston for a British insurance company. *'Mr. C. H. C. Goffe, of 11 Duke Street, has recently been appointed Agent of the City of London Fire Insurance Company, and advertises that he is ready for business,'* read an 1883 advert for his company. Cecil remained in business in Kingston for a very short time. Though the money a solicitor could earn practicing the law in the capital was considerably more than he could earn elsewhere on the island and the sort of legal work an attorney was likely to be retained to handle was likely to be more glamourous than the land disputes that were the bread and butter of a country solicitor's practice, it was to his country roots in St Mary that Cecil returned. He was soon a popular and well-respected attorney in Port Maria, known for his booming, sonorous voice.

"I can recall…Lawyer Goffe of St Mary, whose normal tones shook the 'what-nots' on your tables and rattled the cups and saucers," a longtime St Mary resident remembered fondly. "When he really got into stride…generally in court at Port Maria…people as far away as the bridge or the wharves paused to listen."

One of Cecil's most interesting cases in St Mary concerned, predictably, a land dispute. Two of the parish's largest landowners, Henry James of Rockmore Pen and Leopold George Silvera of Idle Wild, took a long running conflict over a wayward boar to the local courts. Penkeepers, who recognised that this could be an important test case, turned out in large numbers. James charged that Silvera had illegally castrated a Berkshire boar belonging to him. Silvera said the animal had illegally trespassed on his property, destroying cocoa and other of his produce. The constabulary had failed to act, Silvera said, so he decided he should take the law into his own hands and castrate the beast, once and for all. Cecil, Henry James' solicitor, argued that while Silvera was within his rights to kill the boar he caught trespassing on his land, he was not, however, within his rights when he castrated the animal. The judge ruled in James' favour, granting him three pounds for himself and two pounds two shillings for his solicitor. Cecil rarely lost a land case. He built himself a rich practice in St Mary as the 'planter's attorney.'

Robert Horatio Goffe, everyone called him 'Horace', had, like Cecil, been educated in Britain. After completing his studies there he returned to Jamaica in the 1870s. Before long, though, he set sail for the Far East, working on and off there as a ship's engineer. The death of his father brought him home to Jamaica in 1882. He didn't remain in the parish very long. Seeking independence and distance from the stifling influence of his widowed mother, Margaret, who controlled every aspect of her large brood's lives, Horace moved to a home in the Golden Spring district of St Andrew parish, about 40 miles from Port Maria. He took a job in Kingston as an engineer with the island's railway. His mother had wanted him to remain in St Mary and join her and his siblings in their mercantile business or in large-scale banana cultivation on two plantations owned by the family – Roslyn Penn and Oxford Penn.

In February 1876, John Beecham Goffe Snr. bought Roslyn Penn from an English family who'd tried but failed as sugar planters and had left the estate encumbered, laden down with debt. As a result, Goffe was able to purchase it at a very reasonable price. Roslyn had been a very profitable sugar estate during the days of slavery, 40 years before. The estate had around a hundred African slaves on it. Among them were Congo Cale, Nago Grace, Smart, and Eboe Jack. As was the case on many of Jamaica's old estates in the 1870s, Roslyn's sugar cane stems were pulled up and replaced with banana suckers.

Growing banana proved a sound, sensible investment. The fruit had become particularly popular with the citizens of Jamaica's neighbour to the north. So popular was banana imported from Jamaica, Americans attending the 1876 Centennial Exposition of American Independence in Philadelphia paid the exorbitant price of ten cents for a single banana wrapped in tin foil. Pricey though it was, the Jamaican banana won many devoted fans in the United States.

The popularity of the banana established, George Stiebel, a well-known black Jamaican entrepreneur, got together with a group of the island's wealthiest businessmen to set up the Hartlands Fruit Company, the first Jamaican firm to grow large amounts of bananas for export. They purchased a 2,251-acre estate in the parish of St Catherine to grow fruit; mostly banana but some coconut as well.

Like Stiebel, A.C. Goffe's father, John, had success with bananas. The crop he planted on his estate, Roslyn, proved so successful that in July 1882 Margaret Goffe – her husband was gravely ill with malarial fever – purchased from its English owner, Sarah Ann Taylor, Oxford Penn for £800. To the north of the estate sat the Tryall plantation, to the south were both Preston and Langley plantations and to the east the well known Brimmer Hall.

Oxford Penn came replete with dwelling houses, mills, mill houses, curing houses, and still houses, all from its days as a sugar estate. Also on Oxford were several wagons, carriages, cattle, mules, mares, asses and other livestock.

In 1884, two years after her husband's death, Margaret Goffe continued her aggressive acquisition of property in Port Maria. She expanded further the family's property holdings at the town's seafront and in its business district. She bought the property of the town's blacksmith, Matthew Nelson, on Main Street. She expanded the family's sea-front property, Lee Wharf. It sat between land owned by Joseph Parodie to the east and the Ray family to the west. Through her machinations, Margaret Goffe managed to purchase almost a full acre of Port Maria's seafront – a pier, a wharf, the Kirk Corner buildings and more. She had, it had been said, dominated her late husband, her sons, and expected to dominate the good people of Port Maria, as well.

Horace Goffe didn't want to be dominated by his mother. Though a shareholder in his family's various enterprises, Horace wanted nothing to do with the day-to-day workings of the banana trade. That's why he moved to St Andrew parish and took up a job as an engineer in Kingston. The job wasn't rewarding, though. When time allowed, he traveled to the United States, spending time on the East Coast. Though he was offended by the racist treatment meted out to him and others who looked like him in the United States, he was excited by what he heard there about steel tycoons like Andrew Carnegie. Horace returned to Jamaica convinced money was to be made not in bananas, but in iron ore and other minerals. He quit his job at the railway and returned to St Mary, where he bought the 706-acre eastern St Mary estate, Job's Hill, named after the long suffering Job of the Old Testament.

The property, which Horace bought for £200 from Anna Eliza Mc Laren, an absentee English landowner from Sandown in Britain, had been known as a coffee plantation. Trained as an engineer in Britain, Horace had Job's Hill surveyed and was convinced the property was rich in copper ore, tin ore, iron ore, lead and other minerals. It was the first that locals in the Job's Hill area had heard that metals might be in the dirt of the estate. The parishes of St Catherine and Manchester had been known to have metal rich dirt, but not St Mary. If Horace Goffe had hoped to become a metal millionaire, things didn't pan out that way. It would take the patience of Job, and the money of a richer man than he, to make a success of this barren land. After a few years fruitlessly prospecting at Job's Hill, Horace sold up and reluctantly joined his brothers in the banana business in Port Maria.

Alexander Davidson Goffe, or Alec, resigned from a good job as an assistant Superintendent of Roads in the Public Works Department in the parish of St Thomas to join his brothers in the banana business. The truth was, life as a government bureaucrat was deadly dull. The only excitement he experienced in his time in St Thomas occurred in the town of Bath a few days before he quit his post in the Public Works Department. Bath was home to a popular mineral spring and the second oldest botanical gardens in the western hemisphere. On the night of 28 June, 1897, E.B. Crawford's shop caught fire and burned down. Crawford's shop couldn't be saved, so Bath's residents, among them Alec Goffe, jumped into action to save the town. The 32-year-old positioned himself on the roof of a building next to the burnt shop and, according to the *Gleaner*, set about saving the town of Bath from being consumed by flames.

"Great credit is due to Mr. Goffe of the Public Works Department," the *Gleaner* wrote, "who got on the roofs of the buildings, and through whose untiring efforts (although the heat was excessive) managed by pouring water on the portions of the roof opposed to the fire, to save the buildings, which had ignited two or three times. In fact, if the adjoining buildings had taken fire nothing would have saved the lower portion of the town of Bath including the Post Office and the Savings Bank, Mrs. Duffy's lodging and Dr Bartlett's and the Revd. Cornwall's residence."

The excitement over, Alec left his job in St Thomas and returned home to St Mary and the banana business. Though he declared he was ready to dedicate himself entirely to the banana trade, his commitment didn't last long. A social butterfly who loved the whirl of local politics and loved the recognition an elected public official received, Alec was elected to St Mary's Parochial Board in 1898. Within a few years he was vice-chairman of the body. Soon he was being talked of as the man most likely to become St Mary's representative to the island's Legislative Council when Robert Percy Simmonds, an English expatriate who'd held the seat for years, finally stepped down.

Ernest George Leopold Goffe, who became a physician, left Jamaica aged 22 for Britain in 1889 to study medicine at University College Hospital, London. A keen sportsman, he was games champion at his London medical school. During the Great War he worked at the North Eastern Fever hospital in Tottenham, in north London. His work brought him into contact with the harsher side of English life, not the idealised portrait of Great Britain most colonials were raised on in the far-away West Indies. He became a member of the socialist Fabian Society and took up permanent residence in Britain, visiting Jamaica only a handful of times thereafter. Laura Emmeline Margaret Goffe, a sister, joined Ernest in Britain, as did his brother, Rowland Parkinson Goffe who was later admitted a member of the Honourable Society of Gray's Inn.

"I believe him to be a gentleman of respectability, and a proper person to be admitted a student of the Honourable Society of Gray's Inn with a view to being called to the Bar," reads a certificate sent to Gray's Inn in support of Rowland Goffe's application for acceptance to the bar by Samuel Constantine Burke, an attorney and son of the distinguished coloured Jamaican attorney and politician of the same name. The elder Constantine Burke, educated at Harrow and Cambridge, was an important figure in island politics and is best remembered for the role he played during the Morant Bay Rebellion in 1865. Rowland's father had been a close friend of the elder Constantine Burke.

Goffe gave his fourth son, Alfred, the middle name Constantine to honour the politician's entry into the Assembly in 1863 and his child's birth the same year. After qualifying as a barrister in 1908, Rowland practiced at the English Bar for six years until July 1914. When Britain declared war on Germany in August 1914 he went to work for the British government. In 1919, a year after the end of the First World War, he left for Nova Scotia, on Canada's eastern coast. He went there to strike out on his own, away from the influence of his older brothers. He didn't strike it rich as he hoped. He invested heavily in a gold mine in Nova Scotia and even put good money into a patent for the development of a revolutionary reversible rubber shoe heel, an enterprise he fully expected to make him fantastically rich and the envy of his siblings back in Jamaica. He'd have been better off staying in Jamaica, and investing in bananas, 'green gold.'

Captain Baker

"Bananas are worth exactly what you can get for them"

Captain Lorenzo Dow Baker

The banana, or to give it its Latin name, *Musa sapientum*, had not always flourished nor enjoyed kingly treatment in the Caribbean. For much of its life in the region, where it was said to have been brought in 1516 from the Canary Islands by a Friar, Tomas de Berlanga, this delectable fruit was regarded as an oddity and ignored. In India, where it was said to have originated, the banana was known as the 'fruit of wise men' because philosophers and visionaries feasted on it. By contrast, in Jamaica the banana was grown by some, oddly, only for the shade its enormous leaves could provide from the sun, not for the tasty, tender fruit itself. Africans brought to the Caribbean as slaves knew its value, though. It was a staple of their diet. There were, it was said, several hundred varieties of the banana worldwide. Jamaica, alone, was said to have at one time more than twenty-seven varieties. Americans have long been among the fruit's biggest fans. At one time they ate more than twenty-four pounds of imported bananas per person each year.

With the banana growing in popularity in the United States, American textbooks began offering instruction on how to prepare, serve, and eat the fruit. The banana, the American '*Domestic Cyclopaedia of Practical Information*' explained, ought to be "brought to the table as dessert and proves universally acceptable... [Bananas are] eaten raw, either alone or cut in slices with sugar and cream, or wine and orange juice. They are also roasted, fried or boiled, and are made into fritters, preserves, and marmalades." Americans were the banana's biggest fans. Before banana, the American diet was principally composed of meat, grain and potatoes. Though apples, pears and other citrus fruit were widely available in the United States, Americans preferred the tropical taste of Jamaican bananas.

Exactly when the first load of bananas was imported to the United States no one really knows. Some say the first load arrived in New England as early as 1690, and was enjoyed there by Puritan settlers. Others say the first load arrived in 1804 from Cuba. Most, though, point to records showing a delivery of bananas at New York harbour on 6 June 1843. This load of around 300 bunches was brought to the United States by the New York commission agent, John Pearsall. A couple of years later Pearsall brought two more loads of bananas to New York.

There's some evidence, too, of schooners loaded with Caribbean bananas brought to the United States via the southern port of New Orleans during the American Civil War by Italian immigrants, Salvatore Oteri and D. Cifalu. By 1864, another immigrant, German born Carl Augustus Frank, emerged as the first 'Banana King' of sorts. Frank worked as a ship's steward and discovered on journeys between New York City and Panama, the banana's potential. He brought a small load – six dozen bunches – with him aboard ship and made a 1,000 per cent profit on his investment in New York. The next year, 1865, Frank quit his ship's steward job and went into the banana business with his brother, Otto. They set up the New York firm of Frank Brothers.

Hearing tell of the wonderful, strangely shaped fruit, an American sea captain, George Busch went to Jamaica in 1866 in search of the banana. He found it in St Mary. There, at Oracabessa, a port town a few miles west of Port Maria, Busch loaded 500 bunches of bananas. Next he travelled eastward along Jamaica's north coast to Port Antonio in the parish of Portland. There he loaded more fruit. The fruit Busch took with him to the United States turned a tidy profit and he was soon back in Jamaica for more. But Busch wasn't a good businessman. Though he had some early success marketing the fruit and making purchases for American firms, he lost large sums of money in the banana trade.

The banana's true export potential was not realised until the arrival in Jamaica in 1870 of another American sea captain, Lorenzo Dow Baker. It was said Baker, who was born in 1840 in Massachusetts, read the Good Book every day and lead his ship's crew in worship whether they wanted to or not. A tall, imposing man with a voice like a foghorn, Baker began his working life aged 14 as a simple seaman paid not in dollars and cents but in fish. By age 23, though, Baker had become a part owner in a 30-ton mackerel ship. It was said Baker "provisioned and rigged his ships and personally inspected every man, cargo ton, pork side, biscuit, or hawser coil that went aboard." By 1870, aged only 30, Baker was the sole owner of an 85-ton, three masted schooner called, *Telegraph*.

On 20 April, 1870, Lorenzo Dow Baker set off on the *Telegraph* from Boston to Venezuela on a voyage that would make or break him. Onboard the *Telegraph* was a party of ten gold prospectors and about four tons of machinery. Baker had been contracted to take the group and the machinery to Ciudad Bolivar, 300 miles up the Orinoco River in Venezuela. He was putting his ship, which was not in the best shape after years of being battered by hurricanes, at great risk. But the money Baker was offered for his services – $8,500 in gold – was too much to turn down. Though the weather was treacherous, the *Telegraph* made it to its destination safely.

Afterward Baker set out for Jamaica to fix leaks on his schooner. He put in at Port Antonio for ten days. There he collected bamboo, bales of ginger and allspice. Baker noticed a bunch of bananas wrapped in straw at the harbour. He haggled, so the story goes, with the owner and ended up buying the bunch and 159 more bunches to take with him to the United States. The 160 bunches of bananas he bought in Jamaica at around twenty cents a bunch sold in Jersey City for around two dollars a bunch, making the sea captain a nice profit.

Baker set off for Jamaica again a few months later. He spent several stormy weeks at sea before finally arriving in Port Antonio. His vessel was in such bad shape he had to spend a month in Jamaica repairing it. This time Baker decided to commit himself entirely to the banana trade and make Jamaica his base. His ship fixed, the American left with a large load of bananas and other fruit. He arrived in Boston on 28 May 1871 with the first large cargo of bananas, 400 bunches, ever sold in Boston. The fruit was an immediate hit even though some Bostonians described bananas as 'monkey food.' Adverts promoting the tropical delicacy began appearing on Boston billboards: "Fine Tasteful Yellow Banana Fruit on Direct Import from The Antilles."

With the fruit's potential obvious, Lorenzo Baker moved his operations to Jamaica in 1887. His wife, two-year old son, and four associates from Boston, among them his barrister brother-in-law, his bookkeeper, and a neighbour went with him. There, in Port Antonio, Baker acted both as agent for banana speculators and on his own account as an exporter of the fruit.

By the end of 1887 Baker had convinced several Jamaican planters to sign contracts to deliver more than 2,000 acres of bananas to him for export. He also purchased thousands of acres of prime land himself and began the first large-scale cultivation and exportation of the fruit from the island. He made several trips a year from his base in Port Antonio with bunches of bananas aboard his 120-ton schooner, the *Eunice P. Newcomb.*

Success with these small deliveries led Baker to form the L.D. Baker Company. Later he began the Standard Steam Navigation Company which, ironically, used only sailboats. The old sailing boat captain resisted new fangled steamboats as long as he could. By the late 1880s mariners accepted three-masted, wooden schooners were a thing of the past. Iron, steam driven ships were the thing of the future. In 1877, Salvatore Oteri, the New Orleans 'Banana King,' became the first banana man to make a big investment in a steamship. He bought the first steam-propelled vessel used exclusively for shipping bananas, the *E.B. Ward.* But a few months after it was launched, it vanished at sea. Despite this disaster the number of steamships employed in the banana export trade increased. Schooners carried up to 2,000 bunches each journey. The new, purpose built fruit steamers could carry as many as 12,000 bunches. Soon steamers were carrying up to 20,000 bunches of bananas and travelling between Jamaica and Boston in half the time ships once had.

After this, in 1885, Lorenzo Dow Baker with businessman, Andrew Preston, and Jesse H. Freeman began the Boston Fruit Company, merging it with the L.D. Baker Company. The new company quickly became the biggest tropical farm and shipping company in the world. In 1899, these and other companies became the United Fruit Company.

"Steam has brought the tropics to our doors and made the banana, only a few years ago a luxury, one of the commonest of fruits," wrote a correspondent in an 1896 edition of *Harper's Weekly*, a popular magazine. "Its tender shoots are cooked as greens; its stalk yields a valuable fibre which is woven into textile fabrics, twisted into rope, and manufactured into paper…it is the most productive of the fruits of the earth."

Jamaica's good fortune was to be at the centre of the international trade in bananas. "What is to stop this lovely and fertile island from turning its soil into an unending golden stream?" Lorenzo Dow Baker asked in an interview. "The peasant has only to stick a sucker into the ground and in a few months he is provided not only with food for himself and the wife and his piccaninnies…This is not the case with coffee, or sugar, or pimento or anything else at all, except banana."

It took some Jamaicans much longer to recognise the banana's value. Many of the island's white planters, those whose families had earned enormous sums from the sugar trade, showed scorn for the banana. In his book, *Jamaica, The Blessed Island*, Sydney Olivier, Governor of Jamaica between 1907 and 1913, wrote of the contempt Jamaica's sugar plantocracy held for banana cultivators.

"When I first knew Jamaica, banana-growing was still despised as a 'backwoods nigger business'," Olivier wrote. "Old time sugar planters would have disdained to handle, or, if tempted by undeniable prospects of profits, would have thought an apology was required."

But money is the great leveler. Soon the high and the mighty, tempted by the enormous sums being made in the banana trade put aside their pride to get rich in the billion-dollar business. Among those of the old white planter class who put aside their disdain for the 'old backwoods nigger business' was the legislator and planter George Solomon, Colonel C.J. Ward, owner of the J.Wray and Nephew company, and Louis Verley, owner of the Mona estate in St. Andrew. These members of Jamaica's social and business elite were among the first Jamaicans to enter large-scale cultivation of the fruit in the 1870s.

So impressive were the profits earned from banana cultivation in Jamaica, speculators from many countries determined to make their fortunes began to descend upon the island. *The Times* of London did its best to discourage Englishmen intent on quick and easy profits in Jamaica.

"Banana growing is undoubtedly a very risky business," *The Times* wrote. "Its profits are great when realised, but a violent north wind, such as occasionally blows in Jamaica, may destroy the whole growth of a year in a single night. There is no guarding against these 'blows' as they are called, and no anticipating them. The planter must take his chance. The wind bloweth when and where it listeth, and it may ruin one planter's crop, and leave another unscathed."

The Times had to concede, though, that "the profits, when realised, are very great…Jamaica is no El Dorado, it is no place where a man can plant his capital in the ground and then sit down and wait for it to grow. Tropical agriculture is not a trade to be learnt in a day." It certainly could not. A serious planter had to make sure he had a skilled team working for him and all the appropriate tools such as: banana forks, banana gouges, elwell hoes, disinfectant fungol, hurricane lanterns, bass brooms, cane bills, Kentucky axes, red drench, gaseous fluids, chaff cutters, and galvanized cart lanterns.

With bananas a big hit, Lorenzo Dow Baker, and businessman Andrew Woodbury Preston, who started his working life as a produce dealer's handy boy, began the Boston Fruit Company in 1887 with $200,000 and two ships. The growth in the availability of speedy, purpose-built steamships transformed the trade. Schooners, their huge sails fluttering in the wind, proved a haphazard, unpredictable and unreliable way of transporting bananas. Bananas begin to ripen twenty-four hours after they are cut. If the sea's wind were with a banana schooner its cargo would arrive in the United States from Jamaica and make it to market without damage. If the winds were against a schooner, a valuable cargo would ripen and rot aboard ship. Technology rescued the banana. The later development of specially designed railway refrigeration cars, too, made delivering the delicate fruit intact easier.

Emboldened by the development of the steamship and the refrigerated railway car, dozens of American entrepreneurs entered the banana trade in 1890. Few fortunes were made that year, though. Competition was fierce and no sooner had a company entered the trade than it had been forced out. Among those who went belly up and bankrupt in 1890 was the Henry Bros. They ran a weekly service from Jamaica to Baltimore. J.E. Bell and Co, A.B. Bulack and J.M. Ceballos also went bankrupt. Many of these firms were left high and dry when ships carrying their produce either sank or were damaged by hurricanes. Between 1885 and 1890, one in seven American ships carrying bananas from the Caribbean and Central America were lost to storm or to fire at sea.

The companies which managed to survive this tumultuous period ultimately prospered. In 1890, banana imports to the United States rose to 12.5 million bunches, up three and a half million bunches on the previous year. In 1890, New Orleans was the number one port for bananas in the United States, taking in 3,688,000 bunches. New York was next with 3 million bunches, two-thirds of them coming from Jamaica. Third was Boston, with 1.6 million bunches. Philadelphia had 1.5 million. Baltimore was the smallest of the major U.S. banana ports at only 629,000 bunches of bananas in 1890.

By 1896, Lorenzo Dow Baker and Andrew Preston's Boston Fruit Company was a big success. It shipped more than four million bunches of bananas, six million coconuts and large quantities of pimento, coffee, and cocoa to the United States from Jamaica each year. The Boston Fruit Company employed 2,000 people, owned 50,000 acres, twelve steamers and had purchased Jamaica's railway from its government. When the Jamaica railway was built in 1845 it was one of the very few in the world. The sale of the railway caused a political storm. William Baggett Gray, Jamaica's respected Crown Solicitor, was forced out of office after he claimed the Attorney General had taken a bribe from the Boston Fruit Company to use his influence to convince the Jamaican government to sell the railway to the Americans. The Boston Fruit Company didn't keep the railway very long. By 1900, it'd been sold back to the government after incurring heavy losses for the American firm. Never profitable, the railway operated for many years at an annual deficit of close to £300,000.

As the twentieth century approached it seemed the days of the small, independent banana firm was over. In 1898, there had been more than 114 banana export companies of one sort or another lugging fruit from the Caribbean and Central America to the United States. Within a few years there were barely a handful. In March 1899, Lorenzo Dow Baker, Andrew Preston, Minor Keith and other American businessmen formed the United Fruit Company. To form the company, the United Fruit Company gobbled up seven of its chief rivals in the trade. The company became immediately the dominant presence in the world's banana trade.

Key to its growth in Central America was Minor Keith, owner of the Tropical Trading and Transport Company. Keith, the so-called 'uncrowned King of Central America', had recently completed construction of a major railroad in Costa Rica which linked the capital, San Jose, to the country's Atlantic Coast. However, when the railroad did not prove as profitable as expected, Minor Keith began to purchase virgin forest in order to plant bananas. Soon railroad construction took a back seat to his banana business as Keith began extensive banana cultivation in Central America using mostly Jamaican migrant labour.

By 1885, Keith's Tropical Trading and Transport Company exported more than 20,000 tons of bananas a year from Costa Rica. By 1910, Keith, Baker and Preston's United Fruit Company controlled hundreds of thousands acres of banana lands in Central America and Jamaica. In time, the United Fruit Company would become so powerful and influential, the U.S. government would help topple governments in Central America, so-called 'Banana Republics', to protect United Fruit's interests.

The Sticky Fingers of Time

A lie told often enough becomes the truth.

Vladimir Lenin

In court in Baltimore facing life in prison or worse if found guilty of attempting to murder Joseph Di Giorgio, A.C. Goffe seemed not to appreciate how serious a predicament he was in. Angry at his arrest, Goffe expressed his outrage by trying to antagonise the white prosecutors and white policemen. This was a very dangerous thing for a black man to do in a city in the American South in the early part of the twentieth century. The Jamaican planter was convinced that as he was not a black American no harm could come to him. Waiting to be brought to court on the morning of 12 January 1908 for a preliminary hearing to decide whether he would be indicted on charges of conspiracy to murder, Goffe, from his cell in Baltimore's Central Police Station, bared his soul to a newspaper reporter.

"This is the worst thing that could happen to me," he complained, "and if money and influence will do any good I certainly can bring it to bear." True enough, Goffe had the money. Whether he enjoyed much influence outside of Jamaica was another matter. Hoping to influence the press at any rate, Goffe told the *Baltimore American* newspaper that his family members held positions of importance in Jamaica and in Britain.

"They are well thought of and hold places of prominence in the land of the British government." He also told the reporter: "I have nine brothers." It was an interesting admission, one that would not have pleased his late mother.

A.C. Goffe's father, John, was a virile man. He fathered three daughters in St. Mary parish - Caroline, Alice and Maria — before marrying A.C.'s mother in 1853. Five years into his marriage, John had an extra-marital affair which produced a daughter called Thomasina. There was little a wife could do at the time to protest a husband's adultery. Under the law, a husband could obtain a divorce because of his wife's adultery, but a wife could only do so if her husband's infidelity was coupled with, say, proof of cruelty or of desertion. Apart from the three children he fathered before he married Margaret Clemetson and the nine children he had with her, John Goffe fathered two other children, Albert Edward Goffe, born in 1866 and Alexander Constantine Goffe, born in 1870. It was these two half brothers that A.C. Goffe was referring to when he told the *Baltimore American* newspaper reporter he had "nine brothers."

Though the evidence is scant, John Goffe may have had one last child, Thomas J. Goffe. Alfred's brothers, Clarence and Alec, appear to have been closely acquainted with Thomas. When asked by Baltimore immigration officers on a visit to the city in March 1913 to name a responsible person of standing in Jamaica who could verify their identity, Alec and Clarence told the officials to contact their brother, "Thomas J. Goffe."

A.C. Goffe's family history – who was a full brother or sister or who was a half sister or brother – held no interest for A.J. Pumphrey or Eugene O'Dunne. All Pumphrey, Baltimore's Chief of Detectives, and O'Dunne, the assistant State's Attorney, wanted to know was whether the Jamaican was guilty of attempting to kill Joseph Di Giorgio. Frustrated his pedigree hadn't impressed the Americans, the Jamaican decided to threaten them with dire consequences if he was not immediately set free.

"The entire British government will be brought into my case," Goffe promised, "and international complications are sure to follow." Complications did follow. Pompous as he must have sounded, the British government did come to its colonial subject's aid. This telegram was dispatched to the Right Honourable James Bryce, the British Ambassador to the United States in Washington by the Governor of Jamaica, Sydney Olivier:

'It is reported in newspapers here that A.C. Goffe under arrest at Baltimore for conspiracy to murder. Goffe well known businessman of this island and the charge against person named, on the face of it, grossly preposterous.
If your Excellency applied to, please give assistance to him in your power, Olivier.'

Ambassador James Bryce was a well-regarded figure in the United States. He'd written a popular history of the country-*The American Commonwealth*. It wouldn't hurt Goffe's cause to have him as a friend. Bryce put the British Consul in Baltimore, Gilbert Fraser, on the case. Fraser had held several consular positions in the United States and was a keen observer of goings on in the shipping and shipbuilding world. He went to visit Goffe at the Baltimore police station. Bryce said later he was surprised to discover the imprisoned Jamaican was not only "one of the foremost men in the banana exporting business of Jamaica" but a member of the Polo Club of London.

Gilbert Fraser appointed George Dobbin Penniman, a prominent Maryland lawyer and a group of other top attorneys to represent Goffe. Penniman was reputed to be a fine orator and courtroom performer. But it was going to take more than fine words from Penniman, or protests from the British government, or threats from A.C. Goffe, to convince the American authorities to drop the case. The only way Goffe was going to avoid another night in jail, or indeed a lifetime in prison, was to come up with the $10,000 bail that had been set by Justice Eugene Grannan. Goffe offered $5,000. The judge refused. While the Jamaican was trying to find ways to come up with the large sum at short notice, Antonio Lanasa's 80-year old mother, Anna, was brought to the court to stand surety for her son. Her entrance into the courtroom was reported as high drama in newspapers.

"So old and feeble was she that when she arrived at the Station-house she had to be carried very carefully into the courtroom from the carriage," the *Baltimore American* newspaper reported. "The moment she caught sight of her son she raised both hands aloft, while tears ran down her cheek, and her frame shook with heart-breaking sobs, and offered a prayer to heaven for the welfare of the man who was arraigned."

Baltimore's tabloid newspapers, which dredged up scandal and sensation wherever they could find it, made the most of the story. "She looked questioningly at Antonio Lanasa," one tabloid said of Anna Lanasa, "as if asking him to repeat to her his declaration of innocence. The son responded and raising his right hand told her that he was all right and she had nothing to fear."

Fed up with the melodrama, Justice Grannan called for an end to "the religious gestures." Grannan told Lanasa's family that either they should put up his bail or he would be returned to jail. Lanasa's bail was paid and he was released from custody. Things did not go quite so easily for Goffe. He told the court he had several influential men – Richard Lynch of the Fidelity and Guaranty Trust Company of Baltimore, Stafford of the Empire Coal Company, and Whemer of the Pittsburgh Milling Company – ready to stand surety for him, but needed more time to arrange this. The judge refused. It began to look as though Goffe was not going to be able to get someone to stand bail for him, at all. Justice Grannan waited awhile, and then suddenly ordered that Goffe be returned to his cell. Despondent, the Jamaican broke down.

"Instantly he lost all his proud bearing and his bold front," the *Baltimore American* newspaper reported with glee. "The mere thought of going to jail was too much for his proud spirit and he broke down entirely. Goffe laid his head on the iron railing and wept hard at the thought of once more going behind bars. His whole frame shook with sobs, and as his weeping proceeded it gathered force, and in less than two minutes he was hysterical."

Without men of influence on hand to help free him, Goffe was ordered returned to jail. Before he could be taken to the cells, a voice from the other side of the court was heard. Lanasa's mother had put up her home at 2225 East Baltimore Street as surety for the release of her son. Now Mrs. Lanasa said she would stand surety, too, for 'Fedy', her son's black business partner. Anna and her husband, Michael, agreed to put up as collateral five properties owned by her family in Baltimore. The court accepted. The bail was paid. Goffe and Lanasa were freed. Both men would, though, have to return to court the next week, on 18 January. Freed from jail, Lanasa returned to his home at 411 Hanover Street in Baltimore. Goffe returned to the Eutaw House Hotel, a 'whites only' establishment. The hotel's owners, Messrs. Herbert and O'Brien, turned a blind eye, though, in order to accommodate the black man from Jamaica.

A week after they were granted bail, Lanasa and Goffe returned to court on the afternoon of 18 January, 1908. Attorneys for the two men were confident, they said, their clients would not be indicted, at all, as the State's Attorney's office had not come up with the key witnesses that it said it would. Consequently, the proceedings were postponed. The Italian and the Jamaican were ordered to pay bond of $2,000 apiece. This time there was no high drama, no tears from the Jamaican, and no octogenarian mother. This time the influential friends Goffe had boasted of stood up for him and stood his bail. The legal dance went on.

Finally, ten days later, on 28 January, 1908, there was good news for Goffe, and bad news for Lanasa. The case against Goffe was dismissed by the grand jury. Its investigation had not produced evidence the Jamaican conspired to kill Joseph Di Giorgio. The news was not as good for Antonio Lanasa. The court found reason to proceed in a case against him. The question now for Goffe was should he remain in Baltimore to support his friend and business partner or should he leave the United States as quickly as he could? After all, had it not been for Lanasa's mother, Goffe would have spent many hard days and nights in jail. All the same, Goffe chose to leave Baltimore as quickly as he could. Before leaving for Jamaica, a letter was sent to him by one of his attorneys, William Purnell Hall. Hall congratulated the Jamaican on winning his freedom and told him he should return to Jamaica as soon as he could so that he could let his countrymen know how poorly he'd been handled in America.

"I think it is best for you to go home and let your people know how badly you have been treated," Purnell Hall's letter to Goffe said. "I wish I could go with you to tell them in person what you have suffered."

The Return of The Native

The best journey is the journey home.

Anon.

Unable to prove that A.C. Goffe participated in a conspiracy to murder Joseph Di Giorgio, Maryland's State's Attorney's office dismissed the charges against the Jamaican on 29 January, 1908. Free to leave the jurisdiction of Baltimore for the first time in almost a month, Goffe quickly made plans to leave for home on the weekend. On the afternoon of 1 February 1908 in New York City, a free man at last, Goffe boarded the Hamburg-American shipping line's steamer, *S.S. Prinz Auguste Wilhelm*, which was bound for Port Antonio on Jamaica's north side. Hearing that Goffe was free and that he would soon be back home in Jamaica, the island's *Daily Gleaner* newspaper published a rousing editorial in tribute to him entitled, 'The Jamaican in Difficulties.'

" 'I am a British citizen, and as such cannot be left unbefriended.' That is the thought of the Britisher in a strange land." The editorial was written by *Gleaner* editor, Herbert George de Lisser. "It would be a disgraceful thing if a Britisher were to be rescued from the consequences of his own criminal or disrespectful acts," de Lisser conceded. He knew, though, de Lisser said, that this Jamaican was not guilty. "In Mr. Goffe's case…he knew he was innocent…for the man is a countryman of ours, and there is something in the feeling of a common nationality which stirs in the breast when life or liberty of a fellow countryman is at stake in a foreign land. We congratulate Mr. Goffe."

Jamaica's other daily newspaper, The *Daily Telegraph*, also celebrated Goffe's release in its pages. "The Goffe family are well known and highly esteemed in all parts of the island," the paper wrote. "They possess large interests in Jamaica."

By the time the *Daily Gleaner* and the *Daily Telegraph* hit newsstands on February 1, Goffe was already aboard the *S.S.Prinz Auguste Wilhelm* with fifty nine other passengers, most of them American tourists who'd paid $75 for the cruise, plus room at the Titchfield Hotel, the Boston Fruit Company's property in Port Antonio. For most of the white Americans aboard the ship, visiting Jamaica would likely be the first time they ever found themselves a racial minority. To soothe the racist feelings of tourists like these, shipping firms often required black travellers like A.C. Goffe to stay out of the staterooms, the air-conditioned social rooms, and off the promenade decks when whites, especially American ones, were out and about. Unable to bear the indignity, black people travelling first class on steamers often preferred to have their meals in their cabins and see the entire journey out there.

Whatever their colour, the passengers were all in the same boat when bad weather came. The Prinz Auguste Wilhelm's Captain, Brammer, had predicted the weather would be calm all the way to Jamaica, but a short while into the journey Brammer warned the passengers that rough weather – mighty winds and choppy seas – was on its way and might be with them all the way to the Caribbean. As predicted, the first two days were very rough indeed and all but the crew stayed fixed to their cabins. By the third day, however, the rough weather calmed. Favourable winds and smooth seas lasted the final four days of the journey until the ship arrived on 6 February 1908, at around noon, in Port Antonio. By late afternoon A.C. Goffe was back home in St Mary. There to greet him at the Albany railway station were family members and friends, and the press.

"Mr. A. Goffe arrived at Port Maria this morning from Baltimore via Port Antonio," the *Daily Telegraph* said. "He was well received by his relatives and a wide circle of friends. He looks the picture of health."

The Jamaica papers made what they could of the Jamaican's misfortune abroad. He emerged, the papers said, unbowed, unbroken and unscathed by his experience in America. It was good, Goffe told people, to be home again, safe among his countrymen, no longer a minority, a lone dark face among white ones. He was, for a time, the toast of the island. Tales of his trials abroad, reported in the pages of *The Gleaner*, the *Telegraph*, the *Jamaica Times* and the *Jamaica Tribune* newspapers, made A.C. Goffe a celebrity of a kind. He stood up to the racist Americans, people said, and lived to tell the tale.

The Jamaican had, locals told one another, been a success in 'Jim Crow' America and the Americans could not abide it and wanted to knock down what he had built up. How could their countryman have conspired with Italians to commit murder when he didn't speak Italian and the Italians didn't speak English, Jamaicans wanted to know. Others wanted to know what would happen to the Lanasa and Goffe firm and the thousands of Jamaican banana workers who depended on the company for employment. Not everyone in Jamaica was sympathetic to Goffe, of course. Those that worked for rival banana companies or who'd been badly treated by him or his brothers were convinced the St Mary planter was just the sort of ruthless businessman who could have plotted with gangsters to kill Joseph Di Giorgio.

The chatter about his ordeal on everyone's lips, Goffe decided to exploit the interest in his case to drum up business for his company. His firm was, Goffe told banana growers, in the banana export trade for the long run and was, he said, the best alternative small growers had to the big American firms. His notoriety won him an invitation to meet with the island's governor, Sydney Olivier, in Kingston on 10 February 1908.

It had been Governor Olivier's quick intervention – sending dispatches off to the British Ambassador at Washington, to the British Consul at Baltimore and to American government officials – that likely saved Goffe in America. From the start Olivier did his best to make clear to the Americans that the black man in their midst was a British subject and so would receive the full protection of the British government. Olivier made sure the British Ambassador to the United States and the British Consul in Baltimore went quickly to Goffe's aid. Olivier's decision to involve himself in Goffe's troubles was not entirely altruistic. No friend of the United States, Olivier was a vocal opponent of American expansionist policies that had recently taken the United States into Latin America and deep into the Caribbean.

Sydney Haldane Olivier was a most unusual sort of British civil servant. A Fabian socialist, he was one of the best governors Jamaica ever had. Olivier completed his first book, *White Capital, Coloured Labour*, a fierce indictment of racism, capitalist exploitation and British colonialism, the year before he became Governor of Jamaica in 1907. Before becoming governer, Olivier served for a brief time as Jamaica's Colonial Secretary. Though his outspoken attachment to Socialism upset some in Jamaica, many, nonetheless, attended a series of lectures given by him on the subject in 1901 at the Institute of Jamaica. Some in the audience were outraged when Olivier, the son of an Anglican minister, said Socialism had been inspired by the doctrine of Jesus of Nazareth. Though some opposed it, Olivier was, nonetheless, appointed Governor of Jamaica in 1907.

Though critical of Britain's role in the Caribbean, Olivier, reserved a special fury for the United States. The United States military had recently led incursions into Cuba, the Dominican Republic, the Philippines, and encouraged the breakaway of Panama from Colombia so the U.S. could erect the Canal there in the new country. As bad as European colonialism was, Olivier argued, American imperialism was much worse.

Since Sydney Olivier's birth in 1859, the United States had grown from a minor power into a major military force capable of warning Britain and other European powers to stay out of what it called its 'backyard' in Latin America and the Caribbean. America had grown in influence in Jamaica while Britain had declined badly.

The island's British colonial rulers seemed to have little interest in the country's fate once sugar was no longer king. With the beginning of the banana trade in the 1870s, and Jamaica's central place in it, Americans expanded their interests in the island with little opposition from Britain. Americans purchased thousands of acres of the island's most fertile land and purchased Jamaica's British built railway system as well. The British elite, though it had done little to help Jamaica reconstruct its economy in the post-Emancipation era, bitterly resented American expansion.

"There are few things in the West Indies which is being accomplished so silently and at the same time, so thoroughly as the 'Americanising of Jamaica,'" read an article in a 1906 edition of the *Trinidad Mirror* newspaper. "The whole of the banana trade is nearly in the hands of our cousins in the Great Republic." This was true. Nearly seventy per cent of Jamaica's import and export trade was in American hands. "There are few in these parts today who fail to read the signs of the times and to realise that the day when Jamaica

WHEN BANANA WAS KING

will be handed over to the tender mercies of the United States is sure to come." When this day comes, the *Trinidad Mirror* article said, the other islands of the Caribbean should expect to go the way of Jamaica and to share her fate. "It is not, we fear, a pleasant prospect; but probably this generation will not witness the eventuality. It will be for those who will come after us to shift their allegiances away from the old flag to the masterful nation which is dominating these seas."

The American president, Theodore Roosevelt, had, the *Trinidad Mirror* said, told his countrymen in a 1906 speech that Britain would give the United States a 'free hand in Jamaica' if it wanted to expand its economic interests there. In the same speech, Roosevelt, the *Trinidad Mirror* newspaper said, cynically condemned lynching in the United States in order to improve his image at home in the United States and to improve America's image in the Caribbean. "Great Britain, it seems," the *Mirror* said, "feels half ashamed of her willingness to give up these islands to the United States."

The American newspaper, *New York World*, as much as confirmed that Britain had struck some sort of deal with the United States in a report it published in 1905. "If the Government at Washington were to say to the people of Great Britain, 'Hand over your West Indies and we will look after them,' the thing would be done in a twinkling of an eye," wrote the *New York World's* Jamaican correspondent. "The West Indian colonists, white and colored, both wish and hope that before long Britain will hand us over to the land of the Stars and Stripes." Proof of this, Americans suggested, could be found in the large number of Jamaicans migrating to the United States. Thousands of Jamaicans began settling in the United States in the late 1890s. By the 1900s, Boston, Philadelphia, and New York had sizable communities.

"Though they thus decline to be assimilated, they esteem American institutions and form an excellent element in any community in which they settle," New York's *Sunday Sun* newspaper said of West Indians. Though they suffered the same ill treatment African-Americans did, as they were able to earn more money there than at home they kept coming.

"Usually they come to this country poor," the *Sunday Sun* said. "Many a young man arrives at Boston or New York from Jamaica with five or six dollars in his pocket and not the slightest notion of what he is going to do or where he is going to look for a job." West Indians will, the paper said, throw up a good job in Barbados, Jamaica or Antigua and spend almost their last cent buying first class steamship tickets and land in America with a wife and a family, but neither money nor prospects. "Yet somehow or other," the paper said, "they always make good."

Even if they did not always make good abroad, these immigrants often did better than they would have at home. P.W. Wilson, the New York correspondent for the *London Daily News*, said Britain ought to be ashamed that conditions were so bad at home for black Jamaicans that they were willing to brave racism in the United States in order to have a chance at success.

"The American Negro has grievances, but there are 25,000 West Indians alone who prefer New York to the treatment they receive under the British flag," Wilson wrote in the *London Daily News*. "They admitted that in America there was in practice a bar of race. But in Jamaica, they said, it is worse. Society is graded by colour." Black Jamaicans whom Wilson spoke to told him they had no chance at decent employment because people with lighter skin than them got all the best jobs. "The mulatto is selected, not by merit, but by complexion, and the black man is kept at common labour. "I am black," one of the Jamaican immigrants the reporter interviewed told him, "but already I employ fourteen people making rag dolls for children to play with. And why shouldn't I have done this in Jamaica?"

Whatever the case, Governor Olivier, like many others in the English elite, was fearful of American intentions in the West Indies. He chafed at American expansion in Jamaica, believing it had been achieved not through fierce competition and fair play but, as Olivier described it, ' by dirty tricks.'

"It soon became apparent that American promoters were determined to establish a trade monopoly by means of which they could dictate prices to Island producers, regardless of selling prices abroad," Olivier wrote in 'Banana War', a chapter from his book, *Jamaica, The Blessed Island*. "All efforts at competition were resolutely crushed." The methods used to destroy competition were, Olivier complained, the raising temporarily of banana prices to Jamaican growers so as to place the purchase of the fruit beyond the means of competitors and at the same time the cutting of prices in the United States so as to defeat competitors when they attempted to sell their fruit in the centres of distribution in Boston, New York, Philadelphia, or Baltimore. Lanasa and Goffe's firm had battled against just this sort of thing.

"The dagoes and the niggers," Olivier wrote in *Jamaica: The Blessed Island*, as if referring to Lanasa and Goffe's difficulties, "the so called hundred per cent Americans calculated, had now been put in their places."

After his travails abroad, A.C. Goffe was pleased to have been invited to the governor's residence in Kingston for an audience with Sydney Olivier. What the two men, the island's chief administrator, and one of its most colourful businessmen, talked about is anybody's guess. Goffe's treatment while in captivity in the United States, the health of his business and the banana trade and whether Goffe would soon return to the United States, all these must have been questions that Olivier asked of the St Mary planter at King's House.

The meeting at the governor's residence over, Goffe was ferried by horse and buggy to the Kingston railway station to await a train home to St Mary. He was followed to the terminus by a correspondent of the *Daily Gleaner* newspaper. He told the reporter his arrest in Baltimore had been part of an elaborate conspiracy designed to scare Jamaicans away from the lucrative export and shipping trade.

"The whole thing has been a deep-laid plot," Goffe told the reporter. "It is not a matter of yesterday or today, but a plot that had been under consideration for years and it has been caused simply on account of the fruit growers of this island having to do with the fruit business on the other side of the water. It is against the wish of the men in the fruit business in America," he said, "or, at any rate, certain parts of America, that any Jamaican grower should have anything to do with the export business," he insisted. "The desire all the time is to bust any recognised combination of Jamaica growers out of the business."

Goffe was not shy about promoting himself, either. "The men in America are aware that owing to my experience and thorough knowledge of the whole business, at both ends, a knowledge which I have gained after twenty years experience, it is almost a matter of impossibility, with my present connections, as commanding a certain number of people interested in the company in this end and in the other end, for them to get me out of the business."

He wasn't finished. "Furthermore, I challenge any man in Jamaica to say anything otherwise than that I am capable and competent to judge the condition of the trade at both ends." And as for his arrest and imprisonment damaging his company, Goffe said quite the opposite was true. He claimed the publicity from his arrest and imprisonment would help, not hinder his business.

"Very prominent businessmen in America told me that this incident has been the best advertisement that could be given my company," A.C. Goffe told the *Daily Gleaner*, "and I find that on my return to Jamaica that all those with whom I have talked are of the same opinion. My friends tell me that if I had spent $250,000 I could not have had a better advertisement for my business," he said. "I believe that we are going to get overwhelming support."

The train approaching the railway station, the St Mary planter told the reporter he would not remain in Jamaica long and was making plans to return to the United States. "It is my intention to go back to the United States in a short time on the business of the company. I can assure the people of Jamaica that we will have a steady service of steamers," Goffe said, explaining that the *S.S.Banes*, the *Beacon*, the *Oxus*, the *Brighton*, the recently chartered *Uller*, and of course, the *Antonio Lanasa*, would make weekly trips to Jamaica to collect produce. "I ask them for a continuance of their support which they have been giving us for the past three years," Goffe ended.

Back To Baltimore

'Whomever looks for the truth deserves punishment for finding it'

Anon

When A.C. Goffe returned to Baltimore in March 1908 after a month in Jamaica, Antonio Lanasa was free on bail awaiting the start of his trial in the Di Giorgio bombing case. While Lanasa and his family were pre-occupied with preparations for the trial, Goffe began plotting ways of repairing the Lanasa and Goffe Steamship and Importing Company's reputation. Since January 1908 the names 'Lanasa' and 'Goffe' had become synonymous in Baltimore with the Mafia and murder, not the banana trade. Goffe was determined to improve his ailing company's reputation. Hearing that the *Baltimore American* newspaper was planning a special supplement on the city's fruit and shipping industry, the Jamaican took out a large advert in the special section.

The ad sat at the top of the page, overshadowing a smaller one further down the page belonging to Joseph Di Giorgio's Atlantic Fruit Company. It was a small but satisfying victory for Goffe over Di Giorgio. Not so satisfying, was the news that his firm's ship the *S.S. Antonio Lanasa* had run aground off of North Carolina on its way to Baltimore from Port Maria. The ship was rescued, but the entire cargo of bananas and coconuts onboard had to be tossed overboard. Goffe didn't tell Lanasa. He had enough on his mind.

Antonio Lanasa's trial at Baltimore City Criminal Court began on 30 March, 1908, four months after the Di Giorgio home was bombed. Such was the concern about safety at the trial, Baltimore's police department decided extraordinary precautions needed to be taken to ensure the safety of the defendant, the witnesses, the judge and prosecutors from possible Black Hand retribution. An armed guard was placed in the corridor outside the courtroom. Only those with the highest authorisation were allowed access to the building. No one was permitted to enter the court who did not have a special permit from the State's Attorney's office or a summons to appear as a witness in the case.

Goffe made daily visits to the court to observe the proceedings and to offer moral support to his business partner. At the court, too, were many members of Antonio Lanasa's large family: his wife, Giuseppa, his father, Michael, and his brothers. Lanasa employees, Lanasa friends, and Lanasa enemies also attended the trial in great numbers. There from time to time in the courtroom was Joseph Di Giorgio. The injured party, Di Giorgio was keen to see harsh justice meted out to his rival. The trial was expected to drag on for at least a month as more than fifty witnesses were scheduled to be brought in from Pittsburgh, from Buffalo, and from Philadelphia.

The deputy State's Attorney, Eugene O'Dunne, opened the case in dramatic fashion. "This is not wholly a Black Hand case nor is it wholly a case of trade rivalry," O'Dunne said. "We will attempt to show that it is a cross between the two." To make its case, the prosecution produced letters sent by the Black Hand to Italians in several American cities. It produced one sent to the offices of a company owned by Joseph Di Giorgio. "The Black Hand is the hand of God. We request, no we command, you to send $10,000. What has happened to others will happen to you. Your life is in our hands."

When nothing was heard from Di Giorgio, the Black Hand sent him another letter. "Dear Mr. Di Giorgio – We have sent you a command which you until now have paid no attention to…You have read the newspaper and you know what we are capable of doing with a refusal on your part. Therefore do not lose any more time to send what we have written, if you do not want bad things to happen to you as to many others…THE BLACK HAND."

It was a strong beginning for the prosecution. The following days did not go as well.

A few days into the proceedings, the State's Attorney brought Salvatore Lupo, its star witness to the stand. Lupo, an admitted member of the Black Hand, had been given a light sentence for his part in the dynamiting of the

Di Giorgio home in exchange for his testimony against the man he said was the ringleader of the conspiracy – Antonio Lanasa. Lupo told the prosecution that he had encountered Lanasa first in Pittsburgh. Lanasa, Lupo said, gave Philippi Rei, Lupo's boss in the Black Hand gang, a piece of paper with Di Giorgio's address on it and asked Rei to send Lupo to Baltimore to do the job, to dynamite the Di Giorgio home.

It was compelling stuff. But under questioning from Lanasa's attorneys, a flustered Lupo cracked and began recanting his story. Speaking in Italian, Lupo told the court through a translator that his confession of guilt had been "whipped" out of him by Captain of Detectives, A.J. Pumphrey and Detective William Atkinson. Lupo said his head had been badly swollen as a result. Realising he'd cornered Lupo, Lanasa's attorney, Thomas Hayes, a former mayor of Baltimore, put the pressure on.

Lupo, the *Baltimore American* newspaper said, struck out angrily at the former mayor: "To Mr. Hayes' questions Lupo had been shouting replies, reeling off the Italian with great rapidity, while he gesticulated vehemently and pounded the rail of the witness box or slapped his clenched right fist into the palm of his left hand, or shook his finger at the former mayor."

Its case weakened by Lupo's testimony, the prosecution called Charles Thalheimer, chief marine clerk at Baltimore's Custom-house. Thalheimer produced a ship's log showing the *S.S. Antonio Lanasa* had arrived from Jamaica on December 10, 1907. A.C. Goffe was on board. Antonio Lanasa had been in Jamaica, too, in December. He had returned to Baltimore on December 3.

Lieutenant Casey, an officer in the Bertillon Bureau, the Baltimore Police's statistics department, was called to the stand. He presented pictures of Di Giorgio's dynamited house with detailed measurements of its proportions.

Next was Susan Wolford, an African-American woman employed as the Di Giorgio cook. When detectives first interviewed her she said she had heard nothing and had slept undisturbed through the commotion. On the stand, Wolford changed her story. She claimed she heard a noise at the back of the Di Giorgio house on the night it was dynamited, but had thought nothing of it because it had been a very windy night.

The prosecution called John Creamer, manager of the Western Union Company's main telegraph office in Baltimore. He was asked to produce a telegram sent by Antonio Lanasa to a man named Rufelda Giordana in

McKeesport, Pennsylvania in April 1907. Creamer said Western Union rules prevented him from discussing the contents of a telegram unless the sender, or the recipient, gave permission. In a surprise, Lanasa's attorney, Thomas Hayes, said his client had no objection to the dispatch being read before the court. But when pressed, the Western Union man said the cable was no longer available. It was, he said, company policy to destroy all copies of telegrams six months or older.

Convinced the telegram would not incriminate Lanasa, his attorney said they had a copy and would make it available to the court at a later date. The Western Union manager was then asked about a telegram Lanasa sent to a 'L. Scaletta' on 6 December, 1907. Scaletta was the father of John Scaletta, one of the Black Hand gangsters who received a lighter sentence in exchange for his testimony against Lanasa. The Scaletta telegram, written in Italian, was produced and read in court: "L. Scaletta, 821 Woodland Avenue, Cleveland: "Received letters. On account of business leave this evening for Pittsburg. If you can come, come to find me, A. Lanasa."

Next to take the stand was Joseph Di Giorgio. Interestingly, Di Giorgio said he encountered Antonio Lanasa in Baltimore shortly after the dynamiting of his home. He told him off for associating with gangsters.

"You nurse these people," Di Giorgio said referring to the Black Hand. "You sell bananas to them. You keep them in your employ, you actually christened the baby of one of them in your house."

What, the deputy State's Attorney asked Di Giorgio, did Lanasa say in reply. "He couldn't say anything. He knew it was true." Asked how he was lucky enough not to be at his home when it was bombed, Di Giorgio confessed that he had been trying to avoid being summonsed by the US Congress to testify in an investigation of United Fruit. Di Giorgio also said he had not been at his home when it was bombed because he had gone to Jamaica to close a deal for the entire produce of a large banana plantation. Lanasa and Goffe, Di Giorgio sniffed, had tried to secure the banana contract but had been rebuffed.

After lunch Di Giorgio was called to the stand once again; this time to face questioning from Lanasa's lawyers. William Purnell Hall asked him if it was true that a Sicilian of his acquaintance had offered to kill Antonio Lanasa for him. "Any man who said that is a liar," Di Giorgio responded.

The next day, Antonio Lanasa was called to the stand. Gilbert Dobbin Penniman, a Lanasa attorney, believed putting his client on the stand to plead his innocence, 'the innocent man's defence,' would help convince the jury his client was, indeed, an innocent man. Lanasa said he was a poor boy from Italy who had made good in America. He talked of how he met Goffe and how they had set about doing business together and how Di Giorgio had broken his promise to include him and the Jamaican in the Atlantic Fruit Company.

On April 24, A.C. Goffe was called to the stand. "He walked to the stand with a quick, energetic step and gave his testimony in a voice clear and emphatic and in excellent English, with the English accent that made banana sound like 'bahnahnahs'," the *Baltimore American* reported, making fun of Goffe. "He is a bright-faced Jamaican. He was dressed in a well-fitting suit of gray checked goods, that set off a well knit figure and a light soft hat and carried his gloves in his hands in approved style."

The prosecutor, Albert Owens, asked Goffe if he remembered on what day it was he last ate dinner at Lanasa's home and if he recalled who else had been present. Nothing incriminating was revealed so Owens asked Goffe about the banana business and why it was he, Lanasa and Di Giorgio were confirmed enemies.

Goffe explained that he was the assistant general manager of the Lanasa and Goffe Steamship and Importing Company, head of the banana purchasing firm of Messrs. Goffe Bros, and founder of the St Mary Fruit Growers Association. The Association had been, Goffe explained, a co-operative of between 1,500 and 2,000 banana growers in his home parish of St Mary in Jamaica. The Jamaican told the court St Mary was the most important of Jamaica's banana growing parishes and that his firm could furnish from 40,000 to 50,000 bunches of bananas a week.

In a bid to antagonise the Jamaican, prosecutor Owens contradicted Goffe. He said St Mary was not the most important banana area in Jamaica and the St Mary Fruit Grower's Association was a flimsy organisation inferior to the St Catherine Fruit Pool, a co-op under the control of Joseph Di Giorgio.

Flustered by Owens' charge, Goffe insisted "the banana from St Mary are generally considered better than the others." The St Catherine Pool, he said, could only provide 12,000 to 15,000 bunches of bananas a week. He'd been offered St Catherine bananas but had always refused to handle them. "Isn't it the case," Owens asked Goffe, "that the St Catherine banana fetch a higher price?" "No," Goffe said emphatically. But this was just posturing. It was widely accepted in Jamaica that bananas produced from St Catherine's Rio Cobre irrigation system were the best all-round bananas, sweeter, firmer, hardier than any other. Rio Cobre bananas fetched up to three pennies per bunch more than did St Mary banana. Next, Albert Owens asked Goffe why it was there was such bad blood between businessmen in the banana industry. Goffe warmed to the subject. This gave him the opportunity to give his version of how Joseph Di Giorgio's Atlantic Fruit Company came into being. He and Lanasa, Goffe told the court, had been the unwitting victims of double-dealing at the hands of a dishonourable Di Giorgio. Both he and Lanasa had, he said, been promised they would become directors of the Atlantic Fruit Company but, both were abandoned after a few months association with the company.

Finally, the cross-examination was over. The prosecution had no more questions for Goffe. He left the witness stand, though not with as quick or as energetic a step as he had ascended it almost an hour before. It was hard to tell whether he'd helped or hindered Lanasa's case. He'd been forthright with the prosecutor about the rivalries in the banana business. If Lanasa did go to prison it wasn't, Goffe thought to himself, because of anything he said that he shouldn't have.

Lanasa's attorney, William Purnell Hall, couldn't say the same thing. Three weeks into the trial, Purnell Hall made a spirited, but awkward defence of his client. "We have not proved our client innocent," Purnell Hall boldly declared. "We don't have to prove his innocence. Though he be dumb he cannot be found guilty under the law unless the state proves him guilty," the attorney told the court. "He comes into court wrapped in the panoply of innocence, and he cannot be held as guilty until the State Attorney has punctured it by proof beyond a reasonable doubt."

William Purnell Hall did a better job when he attacked the testimony of Salvatore Lupo and Joseph Tamburo, two of the Black Hand gangsters. Lupo and Tamburo claimed they were paid by Lanasa and Goffe to plant a bomb at Di Giorgio's home.

"The testimony of Lupo and Tamburo is false in every material respect," Purnell Hall said. "These two self-confessed criminals were the ones who lit the bomb, who perpetrated the infamous and cowardly crime of attempting the lives of Mrs. Di Giorgio and her innocent children, and it is on this point that I shall base practically all I have to say, for they are now trying to shift the responsibility to the shoulders of Antonio Lanasa."

The prosecution wasn't to be outdone, though. Pacing up and down outside the jury box, State's Attorney Albert Owens asked several pointed questions in his closing statement: "Was Lanasa in Pittsburgh on December 7? If he was, he is guilty, Owens said. "Lanasa received a telephone message from Buffalo when Lupo was arrested asking for money to defray the cost of an attorney and in his defence Lanasa admits that he had such a talk. If he had such a talk," Owens went on, "he is guilty!" Lupo and Tamburo, Owens said, both had dinner at Antonio Lanasa's house on 11 December, 1907, the day after Di Giorgio's home was bombed.

There was more. "If Mr. Lanasa is not a Black Hand man," Owens asked, "why is he a friend of Salvatore Lupo?" Why, Owens demanded, had Lanasa consorted with known mobsters such as Chevalier Lakoso and Philipi Rei? Rei, a feared Black Hand gangster, had been killed in Pittsburgh days before by a man he tried to extort money from.

How, State's Attorney Owens wanted to know, was it Antonio Lanasa, a respectable banana merchant, had agreed to be godfather to the child of a notorious Mafiosi, Vito Laduca. Laduca was killed in Sicily in 1908 trying to shoot a man who'd informed on the Black Hand gang. It wasn't looking good for Antonio Lanasa.

At the close of the State's Attorney's remarks the jury retired to consider its verdict. Four hours and ten minutes later, at 5.15 pm, the jury came in. Interestingly, the judge presiding over the Lanasa case was J. Henry Stockbridge, the same justice who had presided over the signing of the papers incorporating the Lanasa and Goffe Steamship and Importing Company in Baltimore in 1906.

"As Lanasa stood up and faced the jury there was a look of anxiety about his eyes and he paled slightly," the *Baltimore American* newspaper observed. "As the verdict was announced he flushed but stood firmly on his feet and looked steadily at the jury until told to be seated." 'Guilty on the third count,' the jury foreman, Miller, said firmly. 'Not Guilty on the other six counts.' The courtroom was silent. The jury had taken almost five hours to bring the verdict in and none, including Antonio Lanasa, seemed sure exactly what the judgment meant.

The verdict was good news, and bad news. Though Lanasa was found guilty of the lesser charge of conspiracy to destroy the property of Joseph Di Giorgio, he would still have to serve ten years in prison. Had he been convicted of conspiracy to kill Di Giorgio, he would have been sent to prison for life.

Lanasa was stunned. He turned to a nearby reporter. "I didn't expect it, for I am not guilty. I hope I may die if I ever talked to Lupo. I'm going to fight this thing to the end." Lanasa attorney Gilbert Dobbin Penniman, asked the court for suspension of sentence pending a motion for a new trial. The judge agreed to release Lanasa into his family's custody at a bail of $8,000.

Home from jail, Lanasa kept a low profile while the Supreme Bench of Baltimore pondered whether to grant him a new trial. The next day the news-papers had their say.

"It is high time that those natives of foreign lands who bring their old time feuds and vendettas and criminal societies to this country should be brought to understand that they cannot kill and burn and dynamite without running the risk of paying the penalty." This hostile climate would, Lanasa believed, make it impossible for him to get a new trial. Two days after Lanasa was released on bail, his chief attorney, former mayor of Baltimore, Thomas Hayes, filed a motion in criminal court to have the judgment against his client thrown out. Hayes decided it would be best to abandon a motion for a new trial. Baltimore's legal community viewed Lanasa's sentence as unusually severe as he had only been convicted of a common law offence. It had been many years since a punishment of more than two years had been imposed for such an offence.

"No greater miscarriage of justice could have possibly occurred than for a jury," Hayes said, "by an evident silly and foolish compromise to connect Mr. Lanasa of the trifling charge of injuring and destroying the property of Mr. Di Giorgio and acquitting him on every count that relates to the doings of the Black Hand."

The court cases came thick and fast. Days after Lanasa was convicted on April 22, Joseph Tamburo, one of the seven alleged Black Hand gangsters indicted in the case, was found not guilty of all charges. Tamburo's testimony helped convict Lanasa.

Strangely, a few days after his acquittal, Tamburo, a former driver for one of the Lanasa family enterprises, had a devastating stroke which left him paralysed.

Lanasa's supporters said it was divine intervention and God's Judgment. Salvatore Lupo was sentenced to only fifteen months in prison for his part in planting dynamite at the back of the Di Giorgio home. The three months he'd already spent in prison were subtracted from his sentence. Among the handful of people in the court on April 28 for Lupo's sentencing was Di Giorgio. The conviction and sentencing of both Lupo and Lanasa, all in the same week, must have given Di Giorgio great satisfaction. After Lupo's sentencing, Di Giorgio made his way the short distance from Baltimore City Criminal Court to the nearby City Hall for an important meeting. There, awaiting him in the mayor's reception room was an old enemy- A.C. Goffe.

The old enemies were face to face again. Both had come to City Hall hoping the Board of Estimates, which was responsible for formulating and executing the fiscal policy of the city and deciding its rules and regulations, would grant their application for increased space on a newly developed pier at Baltimore harbour. "The question of dock facilities," the *Baltimore Sun* newspaper reported, "is a grave matter."

Lanasa and Goffe both complained, as did Joseph Di Giorgio, that their operations had outgrown the pier space allotted to them. Both companies wanted access to Pier No. 2 so their steamships, they said, could be quickly and easily unloaded on arrival in Baltimore. There were eleven piers, nine of them open and two covered. There were two grain elevators and two coal piers.

The Board of Estimates considered the merits of each case and was ready to deliver its ruling. It was not the first time the board had to adjudicate between Lanasa and Goffe and another shipping firm. There had been friction between the Italian-Jamaican firm and the Merchants and Miners Transportation Company, a shipping concern which operated between Baltimore, Boston and Virginia. When ships of both firms were docked in Baltimore harbour it became impossible for one or other of them to transfer their cargo to railroad barges without causing a blockage.

To witness the conditions for himself, Baltimore's mayor, James Preston, paid a visit to the wharves with members of the Board of Estimates. He saw 27,000 bunches of bananas unloaded from one of Lanasa and Goffe's ships, the *S.S.Katie*. The City ruled against the Merchants and Miners Transportation Company and for Lanasa and Goffe. Settling the conflict between Lanasa and Goffe and Di Giorgio was going to be much more tricky. A ruling by the

Board of Estimates would not, under normal circumstances, have warranted much newspaper coverage. The bombing trial changed all of that. In the full glare of the media, the Board had to determine just who, Lanasa and Goffe or Di Giorgio, ought to be granted the much sought after space on Pier No. 2.

Determined to out-do one another, both Goffe and Di Giorgio arrived hours before the appointed time for the Board of Estimates meeting. They sat directly across from one another in the mayor's reception room, glowering at one another hatefully. The meeting was finally called to order and the two banana rivals went immediately to war. Goffe accused Di Giorgio of attempting to sway the Board against him. Di Giorgio accused Goffe, darkly, of employing 'some element' to influence the proceedings.

"Indeed, so spirited became the word battle between these two that several times during the meeting it looked as if they would come to blows," the *Baltimore Sun* reported. "The argument reached its highest point when Goffe, gesticulating wildly, said there have been times when knives and revolvers were drawn on 'Old Bowly's Wharf' between representatives of the two fruit companies," the *Baltimore Sun* reported.

The Board of Estimates was more convinced than ever that decisive action had to be taken if murder was not to be committed. This warfare on the wharves was, the Board worried, making the conduct of commerce at the harbour, hazardous. Both Lanasa and Goffe's and Di Giorgio's enterprises had become important to Baltimore's economy, providing as they did work to thousands of Baltimoreans. The city did not want to lose either of them but it was clear whoever lost the ruling might pack up their business and take it to a friendlier harbour in Philadelphia, say, or even New York. The Board of Estimates decision was ready. It came in two parts. The City Solicitor, Bruce, decided the two companies should not be allotted space anywhere near one another. This made both of them happy.

"Yes, I don't want to be near these people," Di Giorgio said loudly. "I should like to get as far away from them as possible." Goffe, too, was pleased with the ruling. "The feeling is the same with us he said, waving his ring encircled fingers in the direction of his rival's glowering face," the *Baltimore American* reported.

Di Giorgio was not quite as happy with the second portion of the judgment. To his surprise, the Board ruled against him and in the black man's favour. It decided Lanasa and Goffe's firm had 'priority of claim' over new pier space. It allotted them 275 feet at the southeast corner of Pier Number Two. Lanasa and Goffe's produce would now have access to the harbour's most modern facilities and have the best spot for unloading fruit from its steamships and loading its fruit quickly and efficiently on refrigerated railway cars. Though the Board of Estimates ruling did not favour Di Giorgio, he did receive a consolation – the entire west side of Pier 2, apart from a 190-foot section occupied by John D. Rockefeller's Standard Oil Company.

The defeat over Pier No. 2 was humbling for Di Giorgio. His failure to get what he wanted would lead, ultimately, to him leaving Baltimore.

For Lanasa and Goffe revenge was sweet. Though it didn't make up for being imprisoned or for Antonio Lanasa being sentenced to ten years in prison, it was for Goffe a victory, however small, against Di Giorgio, his arch enemy.

To get even, a few years later, Di Giorgio managed to purchase a significant amount of Lanasa and Goffe Steamship and Importing Company stock from Sir John Pringle, owner of some of Jamaica's largest banana plantations. In a deal that troubled Lanasa and Goffe, Pringle transferred the stock over to Joseph Di Giorgio. The remaining nine tenths of stock in the company remained in the hands of Lanasa, his father, Michael, and in the hands of A.C. Goffe and his brothers.

As for Antonio Lanasa, he remained free on bail while his case went to the Court of Appeals. In September 1908, strange news arrived. Michaelina Russo, one of the Black Hand gang arrested for allegedly trying to kill Di Giorgio, was taken to hospital with chest pains. He later died of a heart attack. Russo was the fourth member of the gang to die under strange circumstances.

In January 1909, a year after Lanasa was first arrested and charged with conspiring to murder Di Giorgio, Maryland's State's Attorney's office, unable to make a case against him, dismissed the charges and set him free. But no sooner had the charges been dismissed against him than new charges were brought against Lanasa in connection with the bombing and death of a banana merchant in another US city. Lanasa was charged with being the organiser of an attack on the offices of the Battaglia Bros., a Pittsburgh banana export company. As in Baltimore, the charges against Lanasa were ultimately dismissed.

Though it didn't make up for the damage to his business and reputation, Lanasa was happy when in February 1910, a state senator in Maryland introduced a bill demanding Lanasa's record be sealed and the fruit merchant be reimbursed the thousands of dollars he spent on attorneys. Even more satisfying to Lanasa was news that Salvatore Lupo, the Black Hand gangster, had been sentenced to 20 years in prison in Canada for extorting money from an Italian businessman there.

It wasn't long before Lanasa and Goffe were back in business. In May 1910, the firm branched out beyond Baltimore. It opened an office in Tampa, in Florida. "We have been looking for some time for a southern port," Lanasa told newspapers, "which would suit our purposes." The company's plan was to ship one or two cargoes of fruit from Honduras in Central America to Tampa each week.

Though Lanasa and Goffe were busy with the fruit trade again, they hadn't forgotten, or forgiven, those that'd implicated them in the Di Giorgio bombing. Later in 1910, A.C. Goffe instructed his attorney in Baltimore, Thomas C. Weeks, to file a lawsuit for malicious and false prosecution against Chief of Detectives, A.J. Pumphrey. Also included in the suit was Joseph Di Giorgio, and his brother, Rosario. The suit said that as a result of the false and malicious prosecution, Goffe had lost a lot of money and many important business contacts were scared away. Goffe also filed suit against his former attorney, George Dobbin Penniman, for £2,400. The suit was later withdrawn without explanation.

The Middle Ages

Green Gold Days

What ah country, what ah people, Lord!

Miss Lou

Unlike many other crops, the banana was a fruit any planter could have success with, or so it was widely believed. By 1912, Jamaicans had planted more than 82,000 acres of their country in the fruit. Approximately two hundred bunches were produced on each of these acres. Bananas were a cost-effective, labour-intensive, year-round crop that was more productive per acre than just about any other fruit or vegetable. One acre planted in banana could produce 17,000 pounds of the fruit each year, the *Fruit Trade Journal*, an American magazine reckoned. This was more than one and one-third times as much as an acre of corn, two and one-third times as much as oats, almost three times as much as wheat or potatoes, and four times as much as rye.

A banana grower could produce bananas from as little as ten to fifteen cents a bunch and expect to fetch twice as much as that when they were sold. At a cost of around ten to twenty dollars per acre per year, the net profit was around fifty dollars an acre in most regions of the world.

A banana plant takes around eight months to bear fruit. First, land has to be cleared and prepared for cultivation. Once this is done, banana suckers are dropped into deep holes which sit about ten or eleven feet apart in rows at around fifteen feet intervals. After a few weeks, the suckers begin to rise from out of the ground. Grass that grows up around the sucker is usually burnt and more dirt and manure placed around the sucker. Soon leaves will begin to show themselves. Several months later, usually four or five, the banana stem will begin to shoot outward. The bananas grow on this stem. The bunches are cut when they are one-half to three-quarters matured. Ready to be cut, banana bunches are graded by the number of hands contained in each. A bunch with seven hands or more is judged a 'first.' One with six hands is a 'second,' and a bunch of five is judged a 'third.' Bunches with less than five on them are not usually saleable.

Growers of most other fruit or vegetable begin their growing process at a set time each year and reap what they sow at a set time. Bananas, like the Jamaicans who grow it, defy such regimentation. Growers planted the fruit so that month after a month, week after week, a ready and steady supply was always at hand. The smartest growers, though, planted so bananas were ready for the months when it fetched the most in American marketplaces.

Sugar had been king in Jamaica, but banana had now ousted it. Sugar had been the foundation of Jamaica's slave economy, but banana had become the foundation of its free economy. Banana parishes like St Mary, with their rainy climates and rich black soil, had now eclipsed the old sugar parishes. Unlike sugar, which required hundreds, if not thousands of acres, and costly machinery, banana could be grown as easily on a few acres as it could on a large estate. All bananas needed, so it was said, was a sharp cutlass and willing workers.

Banana was, somehow, more democratic than sugar. Prior to 1910, fully a third of all holdings in Jamaica were smallholdings of less than twenty acres. True, the big man, with his hundreds and his thousands of acres of banana lands was growing rich off the fruit, but the small man, with his twenty and ten acres and less, wasn't doing badly, either. The banana business was big and getting bigger all the time. A year-round crop with no harvest season as such, bananas seemed to promise unlimited profits for producers and endless employment for workers.

In 1867, the total value of all fruit exported from Jamaica amounted to barely a thousand dollars. By 1889, the value of fruit exports had risen to around half a million dollars. In 1895, it was close to 750,000 dollars. By 1935, the total value of banana exports from Jamaica had jumped to $3 million.

By 1900, the banana had become Jamaica's most important export crop, earning more than three times the amount sugar did. By 1911, the banana industry employed twice as many Jamaicans as did the sugar industry. For the fifty years between 1876 and 1929, Jamaica was the world's largest producer and exporter of banana.

"During the past decade the pioneers in St Mary have demonstrated that from the very summit of the hills to the deepest glades, from the undulating folds of the upland hills to the flat clays of the coastal region, there is hardly an acre of land that cannot be made to produce good banana," wrote William Fawcett in his 1912 book, *The Banana*.

Free of the ugly association of sugar, with its slave past, the banana was a twentieth century product for a twentieth century people. "We called them 'Green Gold Days,'" said longtime St Mary resident Paddy Marsh of the days when the banana brought prosperity to the parish. "In those times people had not long come out of slavery and the sugar period. No one was working and when prosperity came back it was a big thrill to everybody."

No one was more thrilled by the banana boom than the big landowners. H.G de Lisser, editor of the *Daily Gleaner* expressed his delight in his newspaper. "I can tell you that there is scarcely a man with any money in Jamaica who is not in some way connected with the banana trade," de Lisser wrote. "Not the planters only, but lawyers, doctors, merchants and government officials have shares in banana companies or banana properties." It wasn't just the high and mighty, the white and the brown, those in the synagogues or those seated in Anglican pews that had money invested in banana. The black, the poor, and the New Church people invested in banana, as well, de Lisser wrote.

"You think you are dealing with a Seventh Day Adventist and you find behind him are banana. You talk to a journalist and his aspirations are all bananaward. Those who have nothing to do with banana are largely those who have nothing," the editor of *The Gleaner* wrote.

H.G. de Lisser was right. Everyone in Jamaica had a hand in bananas in one way or another. No part of the island had a greater hand in the banana trade than did St Mary. Land there once worth very little, had, since the advent of the banana, come to be worth a lot. In 1888, before the fruit's export potential was fully realised, an acre of prime land in many parts of Jamaica cost little more than two to five pounds per acre and sometimes as little as one pound per acre. Within a few years, prime banana land in St Mary was selling for as much as 40 pounds per acre.

By 1920, only the capital, Kingston, had land valued higher than St Mary. Between 1920 and 1930, prices continued to rise. In a decade, land prices in the parish rose by more than 30 per cent. Between 1920 and 1930, Kingston's population rose by 16 per cent and its land holdings increased in value by only five per cent. St Mary's population, by contrast, rose by 19 per cent and its land holdings rose in value by nearly 21 per cent, more than any other parish.

St Mary, naturally enough, enjoyed its status as Jamaica's premier banana parish. It had, after all, been one of the island's most neglected parishes. Banana, the 'green gold,' changed all of that.

"A suckling pig cost 2 shillings in Vere, 4 shillings in Kingston and 6 shillings in St Mary," wrote Ansell Hart, the Jamaican attorney and author. "St Mary drank more Champagne in the Banana days," Hart pointed out, "than all the other parishes."

Banana brought prosperity and pushed up the price of everything. Whatever the market could bear, that is what landowners and businesses charged. Wharf space was at a premium and could hardly be had at any price. General stores, stocked with all the items necessary for banana cultivation, opened one after another, gouging customers where they could. St Mary's population grew rapidly, as well. Jamaicans had traveled to Costa Rica to build the railroad, to Panama to build the Canal and to Cuba to cut sugar cane. Now they were 'migrating' to St Mary and other banana parishes to tend banana. They came from nearby St Ann, Jamaica's 'garden' parish. They came from the highlands of Manchester, from the flatlands of St Elizabeth and from faraway Westmoreland to harvest banana. Locals complained they were being overrun by outsiders. High officials in the parish, like St Mary's Resident Magistrate, I.R. Reece, agreed with them. Reece was outspoken in his belief that rising crime in the parish was the fault of strangers from elsewhere in Jamaica. "There is no parish in the island in which the people are more law-abiding than in St Mary," I. R. Reece said at the 1904 trial of a man from outside St Mary caught stealing bananas near Port Maria. "The parish is subject to influx of people from other parishes and suffers considerably from this cause. People who cannot make a living in their own parishes come to St Mary, and if a review were made it would be found that a good deal over fifty per cent of the pilfering and other offences committed here are done by people from elsewhere." Resident Magistrate Reece called upon St Mary people to "keep their eyes open and look out for bad characters from other parishes, and send them back."

So wealthy did banana parishes like St Mary become, some suggested residents had been corrupted by their good fortune. The representative in the island's Legislative Council for the parish of St Catherine, an area with a lot of bananas, felt the need to apologise to residents of St Elizabeth, an area with few bananas, while on a visit there to speak before a citizen's association. The politician told members of South St Elizabeth's Citizen's Association those who had no bananas had no cause to envy those who had. Those blessed with the fruit were, he said, an accursed lot.

"There was a tendency of the people in parishes like St Elizabeth to think that they were unfortunately placed," St Catherine's representative to the Legislative Council said. He could, he said, "tell them that in a sense banana, so much spoken of as the saviour of the country, were a curse." Family life had been damaged by banana prosperity, he went on. Bananas had, he said, encouraged young people to leave home too soon, eager to abandon their elders and greedy to earn their own banana riches. *Gleaner* editor, de Lisser, thought this was foolishness and said so in his paper.

"If this fruit is ruining us financially and morally," de Lisser wrote. "If it is a curse instead of a blessing, if it is an evil instead of a good, then of all people we are the most hopeless in that we persist in developing it steadily to a greater and greater extent." The effect of the banana on Jamaica's moral deterioration, de Lisser said sarcastically, would never be an effective argument against the cultivation of the fruit. "When then are we going to abandon the banana?" *The Gleaner* editor asked, "and what shall we substitute for it?" He as much as called the member from St Catherine an ass for claiming corruption came from prosperity. "If what the member for St Catherine says about the detrimental influence of the banana on family life be true, the Churches should unite in a crusade against the dangerous perennial."

Few residents of the banana parishes thought the fruit a dangerous perennial. During sugar's heyday, parishes like St Mary, with relatively few sugar estates, found themselves on the fringes of the island's economy. Most of the island's main sugar estates were located in St Catherine, Clarendon, and in

Westmoreland. In the 1891-92 *Handbook of Jamaica*, for example, only six sugar estates are listed as in operation in the whole of St Mary: C.L. Walker's Ballard's Valley, S. Superansingh's Dover, T. Emslie's Gray's Inn, and Orange Hill and Trinity both owned by Sir John Pringle. By the time the 1900 *Handbook of Jamaica* was published, only one sugar estate, owned by T. Emslie, was listed in all of St Mary. In 1900, fifty banana estates were listed in the parish. Ten years later, this number had risen to sixty.

Banana was king in St Mary, and life there was designed around its planting, its harvesting and the shipping of the fruit abroad. On 'banana day,' no one involved in the trade slept till the steamships with the 'green gold' on them were loaded and had left Jamaican waters. A writer from the American magazine, *Harper's Weekly*, watched as Jamaicans busied themselves on a 'banana day.'

"From all points the banana stream continually to the ports of shipment. From the company's plantations and from private estates where the fruit is grown for export they come in specially constructed wagons. From distant points along the coast, where purchasing agencies are established for the convenience of the small grower and the peasant proprietor, they are sent by sea in great whaleboats," the *Harper's Weekly* writer wrote. Down the shallow rivers from far in the interior the green bunches, he wrote, come floating on bamboo rafts and over the mountain trails on muleback bananas are carried. "It is a common sight on the country roads to see whole families of Negroes filing into the towns, paterfamilias in the lead, with a six or seven 'hand' bunch on his head, followed by the mother of the family, with high tucked skirt and a bunch of equal proportions perched aloft, and on down to the dirty, ragged little pickaniny…Down to the company's wharves they all go, where the bunches are paid for and are stowed away in airy warehouses awaiting shipment."

Once the fruit was loaded and out of Jamaican waters it was time for the cutter and the carrier, who were at the bottom of the banana hierarchy, the selector, the inspector, and the timekeeper, who were in the middle, and the big man, the planter and the exporter, who were at the top of the food chain, to eat, drink and be merry. There was Daniel Finzi's '*Old Jamaica Rum*', S.V. Duran's *El Caribbean* cigars, MacKinlay and Co's Old Scotch whiskey, *Charley's Kola* and other aerated waters, too. Taverns, bars and eating-places were plentiful in St Mary during the 'green gold' days. The most popular of the parish's meeting places and watering holes between 1915 and 1920 was Loila Maude Parodie's tavern in Port Maria, A. E. Nix's tavern in Annotto Bay, and C. S Goodison's tavern in Richmond. In later years, it was Dick Belnavis's 'Mannings Tavern' and the 'TMT Bar,' owned by Messrs. Townend, Magnus and Tinling, hence 'TMT.' In these places banana men, high and low, ate and drank and talked of their adventures on 'banana day.'

While many claimed credit for the revival of St Mary's fortunes, among them the national government in Kingston and the Imperial government far across the seas in London, it was really the initiative and enterprise of local people that gave life once again to the moribund parish.

"The Goffes, along with the Clemetsons, they literally ruled Port Maria," said Paddy Marsh, a longtime resident of Oracabessa, a port town in St Mary. "When the Goffes started to hold court, man, you could hear them anywhere. They were forceful personalities. People didn't mind that they dominated things."

Though A.C. Goffe and his family were among the largest landholders in St Mary, their holdings paled in comparison with banana acreage owned by Scottish expatriate Sir John Pringle, or by members of the Lindo family, or by members of the de Lisser family. But while Pringle, de Lisser, and Lindo and others had extensive interests in the parish and elsewhere on the island, the Goffes concentrated their business interests almost entirely in and around St Mary. The Goffes grew banana on thousands of acres of prime land owned by the family, loaded their produce at wharves owned by them and onto ships owned by them, too.

"In the sugar days they hated the boss; sure, but not in banana days, no," said Paddy Marsh. "People were almost glad that there were people like the Goffes around."

A.C. Goffe and his family were not, of course, the first Jamaicans to enter the banana export trade. John Edward Kerr, founder of the J.E. Kerr Company of Montego Bay, began exporting Jamaican banana and other fruit to the United States as early as the 1870s. But Kerr was an Englishman, not a Jamaican. A former midshipman in the Royal Navy, Kerr moved to Jamaica in the 1850s and began his shipping and produce company there.

Samuel Shephard and James Bell, two Port Antonio businessmen, followed Kerr into the banana trade in 1878, setting up the Portland Co-operative Fruit

Company. A few years later David Sampson Gideon, a Port Antonio merchant and legislator, set up the Jamaica Co-operative Fruit and Trading Company and began, in 1887, shipping banana, oranges, limes and coconuts to America.

Gideon, too, was not technically a Jamaican. Though he spent most of his life in Jamaica, Gideon had been born in New York. He began his professional life in Kingston. He operated a well-known dry goods business at 25 King Street. In 1893, Gideon joined forces with Charles DeMercado, a founder of the firm of Lascelles DeMercado & Co. Joining them in the venture was Charles Edward Johnston, a banana merchant and owner of a chain of dry goods stores.

What distinguished A.C. Goffe and his brothers from the other early entrants into the Jamaican banana export trade was they were Jamaican born and bred, and were black, not white, or 'nearly white' as most of their Jamaican competitors were.

Don't Trust The Trusts

No idol more debasing than the worship of money

Andrew Carnegie

Though A.C. Goffe and Antonio Lanasa were embroiled in an attempted murder trial in Baltimore for much of 1908, their steamship and importing Company somehow managed to remain afloat. Though the United Fruit Company had taken over the Atlantic Fruit Company, and as a result controlled more than 70 per cent of the international banana trade, Americans' seemingly insatiable desire for bananas meant there was still room in the market for an independent firm like Lanasa and Goffe's.

As for Joseph Di Giorgio, he was making money, too. But he was, by 1910, chafing under restrictions United Fruit had placed upon him after it bought a majority stake in his company in 1905. Di Giorgio's company was thriving but he resented his subservient position, dictated to as he was by a board of directors United Fruit had installed to run Atlantic.

With the hefty profits his company had amassed, he convinced United to sell his firm back to him. United didn't need much convincing. Government regulators were getting closer to discovering United and Atlantic had become, in violation of anti-trust laws, one company instead of two.

Di Giorgio got his company back but was soon in trouble. Short of operating cash, Di Giorgio had to find new financing and re-organise Atlantic. He returned to the banana trade a year later. But before Di Giorgio had a chance to celebrate the launch of his new firm he was called before the U.S. Congress to answer questions about the role of trusts and combinations in the international banana trade.

Congress wanted to know why it was that before United Fruit was formed in 1899 there had been more than twenty independent banana firms, and since then only four independent firms remained. These firms were Atlantic Fruit, the Cuneo Fruit Company, The Battaglia Bros Company, and Lanasa and Goffe. Congress wanted to know whether United had come to dominate the banana trade by breaking US anti trust laws.

It wasn't the first time an investigation into the United Fruit Company had been attempted. In 1908, the US Senate began an investigation, led by Senator Johnson of Alabama, to discover whether United Fruit was operating in restraint of free trade in the United States. Senator Johnson said there was no doubt it was. "This trust has not hesitated," Johnson said, "to throw overboard its cargoes when necessary to maintain prices and it has given away fruit when necessary to destroy competition."

Information was collected but nothing was done. Those who wanted to see the United Fruit Company exposed and punished, hoped the 1913 investigation would succeed. The first to be called before the congressional committee in January 1913 was United Fruit Company boss, Andrew Preston. He had to be subpoenaed by the House Committee on Merchant Marine and Fisheries before he would attend the hearing.

Andrew Woodbury Preston was born in Massachusetts, in Beverley Farms near Boston in 1846. A farmer's son, he took a job with a Boston commission agent by the name of Seaverns and Co. at the age of 20. He worked as a janitor, a clerk, a shed handler and fruit sorter before being promoted to a buyer and seller of fruit. An employee of Seaverns and Co. for five years, Preston went into business for himself as a sideline, buying and selling produce his firm was not interested in.

It was Preston's good luck to be at Boston harbour on the July morning in 1871 when Captain Lorenzo Dow Baker arrived from Jamaica with the first significant load of Jamaican bananas ever brought to Boston. Andrew Preston's employers declined to purchase any of Captain Baker's exotic fruit. Preston decided to buy part of the cargo on his own account. He made a nice profit. Seaverns and Co. soon changed its mind about bananas and told Preston to buy as much as he could get from Baker.

Preston eventually quit the Seavern's company and joined with Baker in setting up the first important banana firm, the Boston Fruit Company. Boston Fruit and other companies were later absorbed into the United Fruit Company. Preston had an array of titles: President of the United Fruit Company, president of the First National Bank of Boston, president of the U.S. Smelting, Refining and Mining Company, and president of the First National Corporation of Boston. It's no wonder Boston was known as 'Andy Preston's town.'

A big man in Boston, and a big man in the banana trade, the US congressmen who called Andrew Preston to appear before them in 1913 were determined to show him he was a little man in Washington. The committee's investigation into the banana trade was an exhaustive one. On 27 January 1913, Andrew Preston was called to testify. The chairman of the proceedings was Joshua W. Alexander, U.S. representative from Missouri. Determined to get the upper hand, Preston didn't wait to be probed and prodded by the assembled congressmen. Instead, he quickly launched into a long defence of his company and its practices.

"*It has been the policy of this company to keep itself free from all alliances, combinations, and contracts with other transportation companies,*" Andrew Preston insisted unconvincingly. He explained that United Fruit had 81 vessels, that 68 per cent of its business was in banana, and that it employed 37,000 people in the Caribbean and in Central America. The United Fruit Company had, Preston said, constructed sewerage and drainage systems, installed water supplies, and established hospital services and constructed sanitary homes in Jamaica and Central America.

Done with his presentation, committee chairman Joshua Alexander asked Preston about the birth of his company and how many companies had been absorbed to create it. Before Preston could answer, the congressman intervened. He recited a long list of firms gobbled up by United: The Boston Fruit Company, the American Fruit Company, The Banes Fruit Company, the Dominican Fruit Company, the Fruit Despatch Company, the Quaker City Fruit Company, the Samana Fruit Company, and the Buckman Fruit Company.

"*Just tell us please what was left after the United Fruit Co had absorbed these other concerns trading into Boston?*" Alexander asked Preston. Was it not true, Alexander asked, that United Fruit had purchased 51 per cent of the stock of its main rival in the banana trade, the Atlantic Fruit Company in 1905 and had sought to hide this by hurriedly selling the stock in 1910?

Chairman: *"Can you tell the committee why you disposed of the stock in that concern?"* Preston: *"We sold it to the president of the concern. It was rather difficult to harmonise his methods of doing business with our own."*

Asked why United acquired Atlantic stock in the first place, Preston said, innocently, *"...We acquired it first, rather to keep them from insolvency."*

The Chairman, not convinced, retorted: *"Did you have any such fraternal interest in them as to want to keep them from insolvency."* Preston responded: *"We could see that if, their liabilities were such, a great deal of harm could be done in the Tropics, which would injure the name of the fruit company in those countries and we believed that we could induce those people to conduct their business in a way that would result in their making a fair return on the capital, and we are pleased to say it did."*

Not satisfied, Congressman Alexander persisted. *"They were in active competition with you and hurting your business. Was that not the reason you took them over?"* Preston responded: *"No sir."*

"Chair: Just to support their credit?" Preston responded: *"Support their credit and support the good name of the fruit business, in its broadest sense. It was a benefit to the people in the Tropics to whom they were indebted."*

Chairman again: *"Was there any suggestion that in taking control of that company you were violating the Sherman Anti-Trust law?"* Preston: *'There was none."*

Chairman: *"And that was not the reason you gave up the control?"* Preston: *"Absolutely not."*

Chairman: *"At the time that you took over the majority stock of the Atlantic Fruit Co, as you said, on account of their bad financial, is it true that they were reduced to that condition by the war you had made on them?"* Preston: *"I think not."*

Chairman: *"That it was a merciless system of competition against the Atlantic Co that finally reduced them to the necessity of selling a majority of their stock to you and that it was held by you until in after years, Mr. Di Giorgio, if that is his name, finally managed to get back a majority of the stock, and since then he has been struggling against this same fierce competition on the part of the United Fruit Co."* Preston: *"That is an absolutely false statement in every respect."*

Chairman: *"What other company besides the United Fruit Co imports into Baltimore?"* Preston: *"There is the Atlantic Fruit Co and the Lanassa, Goffe Co"*

Chairman: *"Is it just a selling company or is it a transportation company, as well?"*

Preston: "*It is a company that charters its own ships, buys its fruit in the Tropics, brings them to Baltimore, and sells them in the Baltimore market for general distribution.*"

Chairman Alexander then asked Andrew Preston if United Fruit held stock or other investment in the Lanasa and Goffe Steamship and Importing Company. "*None whatever.*"

Chairman: "*Either by ownership or control, directly or indirectly?*" Preston: "*It has absolutely no ownership or interest whatever today in any other banana company in the United States*"

Chairman: "*These different companies are not operating under any form of agreement with your company, are they?*" Preston: "*Absolutely not.*"

Chairman: "*With reference to regulating the quantity of fruit imported?*" Preston: "*No sir.*" Chairman: "*Or the price at which it is to be sold, or anything of that sort?*"

After a break for lunch, another congressman, Humphreys, took up the assault on Andrew Preston and the United Fruit Company. Whether it was the lunch or because he was tiring, Preston began to reveal the secrets of his company, essentially agreeing that it had operated as an illegal trust and had manipulated the price, production and delivery of bananas to the United States from Jamaica and Central America. Preston admitted his company had managed to get most of the banana growers in Jamaica and Central America under contract, thereby setting the price and locking its competition out.

Chairman Alexander said to Preston: "*State whether or not it is a fact that you are now in the position that you do control the production of banana except just a very small quantity?*" Preston admitted as much: "*I think in some countries we have the control; in others we do not.*" He hastily added. "*that control has not been obtained except in conducting our business legitimately...*"

Finished probing Andrew Preston, the House Committee on Marine and Fisheries called Joseph Di Giorgio, president of the Atlantic Fruit Company of 11 Broadway, New York, New York, to give evidence. Sworn in by the chairman of the committee, Joshua Alexander, Di Giorgio explained that his company had existed in many forms over many years. The original company, Di Giorgio explained, had been called the Atlantic Fruit and Steamship Company of Delaware and had been incorporated in 1905. This company, absorbed several companies — the Di Giorgio Importing and Steamship Company, the Italian American Fruit and Importing Co, the Cuneo Trading Co of New York, and the Fruit Importing Co of Philadelphia. His current company, simply titled the Atlantic Fruit Company, had been incorporated in 1913.

Di Giorgio admitted his company had been controlled by United Fruit from 1905 until 1910. The reason United agreed to sell its majority stake in his company back to him, Di Giorgio said, was because it feared an anti-trust investigation was imminent. The majority stake in Atlantic cost United a cash payment of $46,133.09 for 1,260 shares of the company's 2,500 shares at a cost of $31.75 dollars each. Five years after the purchase of Atlantic, Di Giorgio bought the shares back at $122.96 per share.

Chairman Alexander then asked Di Giorgio: *At the time the Atlantic Fruit Company was organized it took over practically all of the importers of fruit?* Di Giorgio: *It practically had to. We practically were in such a bad position that we had to.* Explaining how it was he came to sell controlling interest in his company to the United Fruit Company, Di Giorgio said he had been facing bankruptcy. Incredibly, the Atlantic Fruit boss claimed he had not realised the company that bought a majority stake in his firm was United Fruit. *"While I met with some officers of the United Fruit Company, the 51 per cent was not sold to United Fruit Co direct."* The sale, he said, was never transferred into their books or his. The identity of the purchaser of the 51 per cent stake in his firm was kept secret. *"Our books never did show they were stockholders,"* Di Giorgio told the committee. The Atlantic shares were sold, Di Giorgio said, to a wealthy French importer of bananas from Cuba, Marquis de Maury. Atlantic owed the French aristocrat a great deal of money, Di Giorgio explained, and selling him a large stake in the firm was the only way to settle his debts. *"We owed him a good deal of money on the fruit he used to ship to the U.S., and the transaction was made through him, to sell this 51 per cent, and we sold it."*

Chairman: *"You did not know that you were selling it to your competitors?"* Nervous that his answer would implicate him in anti-trust activity, Di Giorgio told the committee: *"I could not swear to it."* Explaining how the United Fruit Company got hold of the stock, Di Giorgio said the Marquis de Maury purchased his firm's stock and immediately transferred it, or sold it, to Bennett Walsh and Co, a New York City steamship brokerage with close ties to United Fruit.

While the committee digested this fantastic story, Di Giorgio was asked how United came to dispose of, or sell him back his shares. He asked first to be allowed to explain in detail how poor relations were during their partnership. United Fruit insisted, Di Giorgio said, on dictating the price Atlantic offered banana growers for their fruit and the ports at which Atlantic could sell fruit in the United States. The Atlantic chief said though he resented being told what to do by United's managers, they'd always run his company well, making enormous profits for Atlantic. Nonetheless, Di Giorgio told the committee, he wanted his freedom and independence returned.

When he tried to free himself from United's embrace, it because impossible for him to operate because all the banks and other financial institutions were controlled by United. Asked to be specific about financial institutions he believed were controlled by United, Di Giorgio dissembled. Committee chairman Alexander put it to Di Giorgio that United began disposing of his stock because it was nervous its illegal activities would be discovered. *"Do you know, as a matter of fact, about that time there was some hint that they might possibly get in trouble and be prosecuted under the Sherman anti-trust law?"* Di Giorgio: *"Yes."*

The hearings ran, on and off, from January 1913 to the middle of 1914. Despite the long and exhaustive investigation into the role United Fruit and Atlantic Fruit played in controlling the trade in banana, no prosecution was ever brought against the two firms nor was any personal penalty levied against either United president Andrew Preston nor Atlantic's president Joseph Di Giorgio.

Rumours of War

'And ye shall hear of wars and rumours of wars: see that ye be not troubled: ...the end is not yet'
Matthew 24:6

The year 1914 began peacefully enough in the United States. But by April there was talk of war. Three thousand American troops marched into the Mexican town of Vera Cruz on April 21. Mexico was in the midst of revolution and the United States claimed it sent troops only to protect American citizens living in Mexico and U.S. vital interests there.

In Jamaica, war was far from most people's thoughts. St Mary wasn't thinking about war. On New Year's Day 1914, the town of Port Maria held a market fair. There were refreshment stalls and fancy stalls and athletics races. The most popular race was the 'Bun' race. Those who could afford it paid for joy rides in automobiles. In the evening, around 7.30 pm, a concert starring the *Masked Minstrels*, was put on. It was an outlandish sort of entertainment for a mostly black audience: bug-eyed, black faced, red-lipped performers caricaturing black life. The minstrel show received favourable reviews, all the same.

"These merry lot of fellows kept the audience in a state of mirth and laughter from start to finish with their Negro sketches, comic songs, monologues and speeches," a reviewer said.

The market fair was brought to a close with a dazzling display of fireworks that lit up the St Mary sky. Despite the explosions, war was far from people's minds in January 1914.

By March things had changed. In Annotto Bay, east of Port Maria, a contingent of West India Regiment troops excited locals when they began military maneuvers there. So impressed were some of the onlookers, they demanded the officer in charge of the regiment sign them up on the spot. The country was hardly on a war footing, though. What fighting force existed on the island was in bad shape. The British government had withdrawn, then returned the British West India Regiment unit eight years before.

"The populations of the West Indies could not possibly be of any consequence in any imaginable war of the near future," Sydney Olivier, Jamaica's Colonial Secretary at the time said. After much protest, the British government returned the regiment to the island. The damage was done, though. Some Jamaicans complained Britain did not care about the island's security and had allowed the United States to become the dominant military and economic power in the region. In an effort at restoring its standing in what the United States had begun calling its 'backyard' Britain sent three battleships to Jamaica in December 1913. The war ships — the Suffolk, the Berwick and the Lancaster – put in for awhile at Port Royal. They were, though, really on their way to Mexico to safeguard British interests there as Mexico was in the midst of revolution.

In 1913, too, Lanasa and Goffe had a ship arrive at a Jamaican harbour. The firm's *S.S.Beacon*, which had been in the company's service for many years, recorded its 100th journey between Baltimore and Jamaica. This was quite an achievement considering the generally precarious state of the shipping business. Fruit steamers routinely caught fire and sank or were damaged in storms and had to be junked. The fruit steamer a shipper selected to carry its produce could mean boom or bankruptcy.

"The physical strains of tropical service are many times greater than in temperate zones," wrote Charles Morrow Wilson in his book *Empire In Green and Gold: The Story of the American Banana Trade*. Ships built for service in the Caribbean had to, Wilson said, be able to withstand the very high speeds they would be expected to travel in order to deliver delicate banana cargo quickly. They must be able, he said, to withstand reefs, bars, and shoals that are a constant menace in tropical waters. "They must be able to ride out the violent hurricanes never encountered on trans-atlantic runs. The complex refrigeration and temperature control mechanisms must be foolproof — because a single failure can be ruinously expensive."

In the five years the *Beacon* had been under charter to Lanasa and Goffe, it traveled more than 270,000 miles and brought more than 2.2 million bunches of bananas and hundreds of thousands of coconuts, oranges, grapefruit and limes from Jamaica to the United States. The captain of the *Beacon* all these years was J.E. Petterson. Petterson was an excellent skipper and had managed, somehow, to avoid serious accidents in the years he captained the vessel. In celebration of the ship's 100th journey, it was decorated with code flags and bunting, a lightweight, loosely woven fabric used chiefly for flags and festive decorations. The celebration was capped off with a big dinner onboard the *Beacon* at Port Maria. All the St Mary nabobs and bigwigs were invited. Most of St Mary's banana growers, though, weren't in a celebratory mood. Fruit prices were flat and the parish had been in the midst of a long and costly drought.

It was with this in mind that A.C. Goffe and his brother, Clarence, set off on a tour of banana areas in western Jamaica in March 1914. They were hoping to convince growers there to sign contracts to sell their bananas to Messrs Goffe Bros, the banana-purchasing wing of the Lanasa and Goffe Steamship and Importing Company.

On 1 March, 1914, A.C., and Clarence, along with S.C. Rust, a Messrs. Goffe Bros banana agent, set off in a motorcar on a tour of Westmoreland and St. James. The year before this Goffe's firm had opened an office and leased a wharf in eastern Jamaica at Morant Bay in St.Thomas. Expanding eastward had proved profitable. He hoped westward expansion would prove profitable, too. It wasn't a daring business strategy. The island's banana market was saturated and drought in St Mary mean't few bananas were available.

In Westmoreland and St James A.C., Clarence, and S.C. Rust planned to meet with banana growers who farmed medium-sized and small properties — anything from 50 to 5 acres or so. Though small growers produced much of Jamaica's bananas, they were often neglected or poorly treated by the fruit companies and banana's 'big men.' For the tour to be successful, Goffe had to convince the small growers that he had much in common with them. A.C. Goffe knew when to emphasise his race and colour, and when to neglect and ignore it. He was convinced he had the 'common touch.' He'd get a chance to find out if this was true at Bethel Town in Westmoreland. Bethel Town was known as a marketing centre where sugar cane, cacao, rice, coffee, spices, breadfruit and livestock were plentiful. Though not a big banana area, Goffe thought the district had great promise.

"On Wednesday evening at about 7 it was said that Messrs. Goffe Bros, would be in the district to see the banana growers (the small men, of course)," *The Gleaner* newspaper reported in March 1914. "This welcome news spread like forest flies." They arrived early on March 4 and convened a meeting the same morning at 8 o'clock in the town centre. Scores of Westmoreland banana growers came from the surrounding villages of Rat Trap, Lamb's River and Cornwall Mountain to hear what the St Mary banana men had to say about the banana trade. Goffe had a lot to say. He was not, he said, asking growers who'd signed contracts with other banana firms to break them. He did, though, he said, want to remind growers that his firm was composed of "sons of Jamaica — the only native firm carrying on the banana trade between the island and America."

Goffe told the crowd that big American companies — United Fruit and Atlantic Fruit — had struck secret deals with Jamaica's big planters. His firm had come, he said, to "take the rejected ones — the small men with their four and five acre plots." He had come to help them and they should help themselves by helping his company secure as much banana as it could." If the growers had been moved by his message Goffe said they should give him their support and he would give them his support in return. He would, he said, have a ship ready to collect fruit at Montego Bay on 1 April, 1914.

"If Goffe Bros were not in the field," Goffe told the growers, again appealing to common heritage, "the outlook would be black for the small man." He warned them they would receive enticing offers from other companies, foreign ones, but they should ignore them. "They should be loyal and never turn their backs on his company," Goffe said, bringing his speech to the growers to a close.

Next, the Westmoreland planter, H.A. Barrett, spoke. He echoed much of what was said before. "I am very proud to know that they are Jamaicans," Barrett said pointing to A.C. Goffe and his brother, Clarence, who were sitting on the stage beside him. "The people ought to support this company. The United Fruit Company has its great big fields, the Atlantic Fruit Company has its great big fields. Goffe Bros had no fields in these parts. You should support them. They are Jamaicans."

The next stop on his tour of western Jamaica banana areas took Goffe to the town of Cambridge in the parish of St. James. The town sat close to the border between St. James and Westmoreland and was only a few miles from the parish of St Elizabeth. The Cambridge area had several advantages: It was located in a fertile interior valley, produced very fine bananas, and was close to the railway. Keen to hear what the St Mary banana men had to say about the banana trade and St. James' part in it, the area's banana growers gathered in large numbers outside Dunn's shop in the town centre on the afternoon of 5 March 1914. As in Bethel Town the day before, A.C. Goffe again appealed to national identity to convince growers to support his company.

"My company is the only one run by Jamaicans and this is a strong argument in favour of us," the St Mary planter told the St James banana growers. "The other companies have taken the cream. We will take the leavings, and will try to make the single acre growers just as satisfied as the large contractors." Goffe told the growers to go off and collect as many bananas as they could. He would, he said, arrange for a fruit steamer to be in port on March 26. To show he meant business, Goffe said he would leave his brother, Clarence, behind in St James' capital, Montego Bay, to tend to the grower's needs. His firm had recently opened offices there and leased a wharf on which bananas could be deposited.

"Do not let us hang down our heads in disappointment if you promise to support us," Goffe said, chastising the growers. "If you give another company one hundred [bananas] then give us, Goffe, two hundred. By supporting Goffe you are helping yourself," he said.

The meeting in Cambridge over, A.C. and Clarence Goffe, and S.C. Rust, set off for Montego Bay, eight miles north. They drove through the villages of Seven Rivers and Bickersteth, and through the towns of Montepelier and Anchovy. In Montego Bay, the Goffes inspected their firm's new offices and Breaker's Pier, a wharf they'd leased there.

S.C. Rust, the Messrs. Goffe Bros agent, left the two brothers in Montego Bay while he motored off to the town of Somerton, about ten miles away. He'd arranged to meet with banana growers there. The meeting was convened by Charles Sequira, a St. James planter. S.C. Rust took the stage and said he wanted to express, first of all, his sorrows at how badly the area had been battered by the hurricane of 1912. He also, Rust said, wanted to say how impressed he was that the people of Somerton and the surrounding area had gotten their banana fields looking so prosperous again so quickly.

Asked what sort of price growers could expect from the Goffe firm, Rust promised St. James cultivators would not be short-changed. They would, he told them, receive the six pounds per bunch St Mary banana growers got, not the five pounds per bunch they were used to receiving from other firms.

The meeting over, Rust motored back to Montego Bay to collect A.C. Goffe for the drive home to St Mary. Soon Goffe and Rust were on the road from western to northeastern Jamaica. Goffe was in a hurry to return to Port Maria. He had important business to attend to there.

Using the coast road, the two made their way in their 20th century vehicle, the automobile, along Jamaica's rough, 19th century roads. Donkeys and drays blocked the country roads and horses and buggies blocked the city streets. Jamaica was a country, Goffe thought, not in a hurry to go anywhere. After a full day of driving, the two arrived finally in Port Maria.

The reason Goffe had been in such a hurry to return home was because he was scheduled to take part in the launch of an interesting new enterprise. 'COMPANY TO RUN A MOTOR CAR SERVICE IN PARISH OF ST. MARY,' a newspaper headline read. A.C. Goffe, several of his siblings and several of St Mary's best-known citizens had decided to start a motor car transportation company.

Though there were other motor transportation firms elsewhere on the island — Leslie Leonides Fraser, for example, operated Fraser and Co, a St Ann's Bay car company — the motorcar industry was still in 1914 very much in its infancy in Jamaica. It'd been only a few years since Ernest Nuttall had begun the Motor Union, an organisation to encourage the development of "mechanically propelled road vehicles."

Despite Nuttall's best efforts, the horse and buggy and the donkey and dray continued to be the way most Jamaicans got from one place to another. Goffe and his brothers were convinced this would change. In the United States there had been strong opposition to the motor car at first, but Henry Ford's Model T Ford had converted many and made him rich in the bargain. A.C. Goffe and his brothers were not planning to manufacture motor cars. They were going to provide transportation around the island by motor car. They convinced the Anglican priest J.H.H. Graham, Sam Walker, a member of St Mary's Parochial Board, J.A Benjamin, owner of the Coves banana estate, S. C. Barham, a businessman, and John Parodie, who had until very recently been employed by Lanasa and Goffe as a pilot on one of their ships, to join them in the enterprise.

Interestingly, though John Parodie had quit his job with Lanasa and Goffe to take up a better paid one with the United Fruit Company, relations between him and the Goffes remained warm. Parodie's father, Joseph, had been friends with their father, John. Both had been merchants in Port Maria in the 1850s and 1860s and both had owned property on the seafront in the town. Parodie's grandfather, Bartholomew Parodie, had, like A.C. Goffe's grandfather, Robert Clemetson, been among the first 'coloured' men to become ship's pilots in St Mary parish. A colour bar had kept black and coloured men from becoming pilots. But when these obstacles were removed in 1816, among the first to take advantage of the new opportunities were Parodie and Clemetson.

The Parodies were an interesting family. They had their hands in everything in Port Maria. One was involved in shipping and a motor car company, another was deputy Registrar of births, deaths and marriages, another operated a bar, and still another operated the town's mental asylum.

With lots of hoopla, the meeting to introduce the St Mary Motor Company on 9 March, 1914 to prospective investors and to those who might want to use its automobiles to ferry themselves from one place to the next, was called to order at Port Maria Town Hall.

"I expect it to develop into a great concern, as there is room for development," Alec Goffe, a director of the concern, told the gathering. A reliable motor car taxi service, he said, would transform the town. Though Port Maria was a centre of the island's banana trade, it did not have a railway station. Efforts to convince the island's government to build a rail extension there had failed. "Having a reliable motor service between Port Maria and Albany," Goffe insisted, would convince "a number of gentlemen who used their buggies to Albany to give up using same as the motor car service would be cheaper and more convenient."

Alec Goffe's words received hearty applause. Next, the important business of choosing directors and the executive of the new concern was conducted. Alec, A.C., and John Goffe, John Henry Heron Graham, Jose Antonio Benjamin, and Sigismund Cyril Barham were chosen as the six directors of the firm. John Parodie was chosen to be Secretary and Treasurer. Cecil Goffe was chosen Solicitor and T. A. Gentles Promoter.

'The objects for which this company is established,' the company prospectus read, *'are for the conveyance of passengers, mails, and freight on Motor cars, between the Town*

of Port Maria, and the Railway Station at Albany in the Parish of Saint Mary, and between other such places as the Company may from time to time determine.' The launching of the motor car company was well attended and over the next several weeks directors of the concern continued to try to convince locals to buy shares in the company. To draw attention to the firm, a demonstration of the service it was offering was arranged.

The St Mary Motor Company employed as a chauffeur a young man named Silvera. His skills behind the wheel were said to be extraordinary. It was Silvera's job to show locals exactly how fast and efficient the motor car company's 65-horse power automobile was. He did this by speeding a couple of passengers the eight miles to the railway station at Albany and the eight miles back to Port Maria. The journey took 50 minutes. Today it would have taken 15 or 20 minutes.

Two months after it was formed the Saint Mary Motor Company handed out shares to those who'd invested in it. A limited liability company, it began with a capital of £1,500 divided into 1,500 shares at one pound per share payable. Investors had to pay the first five shillings of their one-pound stake on application and the next five shillings on receiving their shares. The balance was to be paid each month after that. The St Mary Motor Company estimated it would cost them around £650 apiece for cars, including the cost of duty and freight to ship the automobile from the United States. This price seemed a little inflated as a Ford Touring Car cost only £133. A Chevrolet cost only £173, and a Maxwell Car cost only £200.

While the St Mary Motor Car Company was keen, of course, to attract passengers who wanted to get back and forth to the Albany railway station, what it was really after was the lucrative mail delivery contracts awarded by the island's government. Four years earlier, in 1910, the government decided the most sensible way to deliver the island's mail was by motor transport.

Mail delivery by motor vehicle in Jamaica began on 1 April, 1910, under a contract that the government agreed with the Post Office. Delivery vehicles were supplied by one of the very earliest of the private motor companies, the Jamaica Motor Company. The firm had offices in Kingston and in St. James. Unable to cover the entire island, the Post Office tendered out delivery contracts to private motor car concerns. The Parochial Board of Trelawny positioned itself to win one of these contracts. In March 1914, while A.C. Goffe was on his tour of banana districts in western Jamaica, Trelawny's Parochial Board decided it would support a proposition to ask the island's government to establish direct motor mail and passenger service in their parish from Kendall through the interior of Trelawny to Falmouth.

The St Mary Motor Company hoped a similar effort would be made in its home parish. But winning one of these contracts would not be easy. Neither would winning over people used to four-legged transport. The company's biggest obstacle, though, was it would be vying for passengers and mail contracts against a tough local competitor, The Port Maria Motor Company. Though this firm began operating in Port Maria several weeks before the St Mary Motor Company was launched, Goffe and his partners insisted they had the idea for a motor company first. They were upstaged, they said, by an upstart. *The Gleaner* took sides in the argument between the two car companies, coming down on the Saint Mary Motor Company's side. Sinister forces, the paper claimed, were conspiring to destroy the Goffe brothers' motor car firm.

"There is evidence of the presence of an 'undercurrent' — an element greatly to be feared by the promoters of the concern; and this is to be regarded as an attempt at forestalling the operations of these progressive movers," *The Gleaner* reported.

St Mary was familiar with banana wars, pitch battles that broke out from time to time between rival fruit firms. Now it had in its midst a new kind of commercial conflict- a motor car war. Soon, another motor car firm, The Clemetson Motor Car Company, run by A.C. Goffe's cousin, John Clemetson and by the Belnavis brothers, opened for business. It shut down awhile later when its driver, John Clemetson, was badly burned and the firm's Garford automobile wrecked in an accident on the Llanrumney Road on the way to Albany train station. The trade had its ups and its downs. Still, A.C. Goffe remained convinced his car company was far ahead of his rivals. The firm claimed it could get passengers to the railway in record time. The Port Maria Motor Company cut a couple pennies off its three shillings charge for the ride from Port Maria to Albany to undercut its rival.

"A spirit of rivalry prevails in the bus and motor passenger service between here and Albany," *The Gleaner* reported on 21 May 1914. "Just where it will end no one can tell. The St Mary Motor Company is in the mean time forging ahead."

Though the motor car had its supporters, it also had its detractors, it perhaps made more enemies in Jamaica. The automobile was, many of those who wrote letters to Jamaican newspapers in 1914 said, ruining the quality of life on the island.

"From recent occurrences it has appeared to the observant eye that it is time that the speed limits of motor cars through the town (Kingston) be regulated or if the law already exists that it be put in force," wrote an angry pedestrian to a newspaper in 1914. "On Saturday last, the driver of a car had but an hair breadth escape along Harbour Street. The car was passing a cart and ran down too near the water table of the street, brushing a lady's skirt. An hour later a Ford car on the same street knocked down a boy who fortunately received no injury to speak of."

Lawsuits abounded. It was the car versus horses, goats, cattle and pedestrians. In a typical case, a motor car driven by C. St. John Smythe struck and killed a mule belonging to David Morris on the main road leading from Annotto Bay to Kingston.

It was not just livestock that clashed with cars. Motor car owners clashed with one another, as well. In 1914, two of St Mary's best known citizens, Sir John Pringle and Henry George de Lisser, fought one another in court over who had the right of way and who was at fault when their automobiles struck each other on a St Mary road.

In 1918, A.C. Goffe, on a visit to St Ann's Bay, crashed into a car driven by the town's physician, Dr Hunter. Both cars were damaged. Goffe's car sustained the greater damage. Like it or not, the motor car would soon become a part of everyday life in Jamaica. Petrol stations started to appear, as did tyre repair businesses.

Though the motor car war between the St Mary Motor Car Company, the Port Maria Car Company and the Clemetson Motor Car Company had captured St Mary people's attention in the early part of 1914, by the middle of the year their attention was elsewhere. News that some of the most important men in the banana trade, among them two Jamaicans, were preparing to meet in New York City caused a stir.

On 7 May, 1914, the two Jamaicans with the largest stockholdings in the Atlantic Fruit Company, David Gideon, a member of the Legislative Council and chairman of Jamaica's Railway Advisory Board, and Sir John Pringle, owner of several large banana plantations, left for the big New York meeting.

The Atlantic Fruit Company's directors were an impressive lot. Among them was the American financier, I.H. Lehman of New York's Lehman Brothers Holdings and the British shipbuilder, Sir George Burton Hunter of the famous Swan and Hunter shipyard. Though Atlantic Fruit had made money for its shareholders — many of them old money Americans – they, nonetheless, regarded the firm's Sicily-born president, Di Giorgio, as an immigrant upstart out of his depth in the world of big business and high finance.

Di Giorgio knew his position at the head of Atlantic was in danger and so he decided the only way to win the confidence of the main shareholders was to call an emergency meeting. His strategy backfired. Di Giorgio didn't win the support of the majority. A month later, on 12 June 1914 he was forced to step down as president and general manager of the Atlantic Fruit Company, the firm he built into the second most powerful banana company in the world.

"He was induced to retire from the Presidency of the Atlantic Fruit Company of Delaware by the urgent pressure of Sir George Hunter, of Swan Hunter & Wigham Richardson, who was a large creditor and shareholder in the company," wrote Sydney Olivier, a former Governor of Jamaica in his book, *Jamaica — The Blessed Island.* "Sir George having been warned that the fighting policy of the United Fruit Company would never be relaxed so long as Di Giorgio remained with the Atlantic Company, and that no peace was possible felt that with Di Giorgio out of the business some toleration might be relied on, and he desired to save his investment." Di Giorgio was replaced by the amiable Englishman, Norman A. McLeod.

Stunned by his ouster, Di Giorgio, left for Europe to holiday in the fjords of Norway and to visit Austria. It was bad timing. War was coming.

The Not So Great War

'The lamps are going out all over Europe; we shall not see them lit again in our lifetime.'
Sir Edward Grey

When Archduke Franz Ferdinand, heir to the throne of the Austro-Hungarian Empire, was assassinated in Sarajevo on 28 June, 1914, by a Bosnian nationalist, few Americans believed the shooting would lead to World War a month later.

"To the world, or to a nation," argued North Dakota's *Daily Herald* newspaper, "an archduke more or less makes little difference." *The New York Times*, too, miscalculated. "A general European war is unthinkable," it said on July 28. "Europe can't afford such a war, and the world can't afford it, and happily the conviction is growing that such an appalling conflict is altogether beyond the realm of possibility."

In the West Indies, too, people were oblivious. With no clue what was going on, St Mary went ahead with a big agricultural show on July 3. The island's governor, Brigadier-General Sir William Henry Manning, had promised to attend. The day of the agricultural show – the first put on by St Mary's branch of the Jamaica Agricultural Society – was as hot as it could be. The event was held at Moore Hall Common. More than 3,000 people from all parts of the island came to see what St Mary had to offer. They came on horseback, in Parry carts, in single and double-seated buggies, in shiny new motor cars, and by railway. A special, chartered train brought people in from Kingston. Others came from St Ann, Portland, and from St Catherine.

A. C. Goffe and his brothers did well at the agricultural show. A horse and a native cow belonging to A.C. won awards. His brother, Cecil, won a prize for a native heifer and his brother, Clarence, won an award for a prize milch cow.

A few weeks after the St Mary Agricultural Show, on August 1, Germany, which was an ally of Austria-Hungary, declared war on Serbia's ally, Russia. Soon after, Germany declared war on France, an ally of Russia.

"Europe a Vast Armed Camp, stands on the Abyss of Universal War," is how a headline in The *Daily Gleaner* on August 1 described the goings-on in Europe. But, somehow, the declarations of war in Europe didn't cause much concern in Jamaica. In the same August 1 edition of *The Gleaner*, Ryan & Co., a Kingston clothing company known for its tweeds, muslins and embroidered flouncings, ran an advert which used the impending war to drum up sales for its products.

"WAR DECLARED in JAMAICA BY RYAN & CO Against The High Cost Of Living," the advert read. "This warfare in which we are engaged, does not bring unhappiness, but piece (sic) and joy; for by it you save, and to save is a joy indeed. We hereby issue a call to every one to enlist in this great engagement, and get their share of the spoils...COME ONE, COME ALL, and join us in the big fight against our common enemy, The High Cost of Living."

Adverts like this disappeared from Jamaican newspapers when Britain declared war on Germany on 4 August, 1914. Though far away from the action, Jamaica was ready and willing, the director of the Institute of Jamaica, Frank Cundall, wrote in his book, *'Jamaica's Part in The Great War.'*

"Owing to good cable communication, that colony, in common with other parts of the Empire," Cundall wrote, "knew almost as soon as England of the fateful assassination of the heir to the Austrian throne, and was not altogether taken by surprise when in the early hours of August 5, 1914, she learnt England had declared war against Germany the previous day." War declared in Britain, on August 5 Jamaica's governor, Manning, issued the government decree, 'Regulations Under Martial Law.' Newspapers were ordered not to publish anything that "might be of use to the enemy." A Board of Food Control was set up to ensure there were adequate food supplies and that retailers did not take advantage of war conditions to inflate prices. Government departments were ordered to suspend all but the most important activities, and a Jamaica Reserve Regiment was quickly formed, a contingent in every parish.

Though Jamaica was not in danger of being invaded, the island was put on a war footing. The population was told to be on the look out for spies and provocateurs in their midst. Inevitably, those with German sounding names attracted suspicion and hostility. With a large population of residents who were the descendants of German labourers who had come to Jamaica in the years after slavery, Seaford Town, in Westmoreland, fell under the watchful eye of government agents. Afraid its name would make it seem sympathetic to Germany, the venerable St Elizabeth boarding school, Potsdam, which had been named after a town in northeastern Germany, took on the more English sounding, 'Munro'. The Hamburg American Shipping Company, a large purchaser of Jamaican fruit, was blocked from conducting business in the island. Its ships were counted as enemy vessels. Only a few weeks before, many Jamaicans, A.C. Goffe among them, had been enjoying travel on the *S.S. Auguste Wilhelm* and on the *S.S. Prinz Joachim*, popular steamships of the Hamburg American Shipping line.

On 13 August, 1914, nine days after Britain declared war on Germany, Jamaica's governor issued a proclamation calling on Jamaicans to "…continue peacefully and tranquilly to pursue their usual avocations, carefully abstaining from all action likely to produce popular excitement, unrest or confusion…"

Though Governor Manning encouraged Jamaicans to go about their business as usual, for those in the fruit and shipping trade this was not possible. Britain had issued an order banning its colonies from selling produce to countries outside of its empire. Jamaica could not, for example, sell its oranges, cocoa, and banana to the United States as it had long been free to do. The island's governor issued a proclamation prohibiting the export of fruit to any port other than to Britain or to its colonies. This hit companies like Lanasa and Goffe hard. This prohibition all but put a stop to the firm's American business.

Another result of war and prohibition on exports was a collapse in fruit prices. Land prices collapsed, too. In St Mary parish, for example, land that'd been valued at as much as £44 per acre fell to as low as £10 per acre. Planters protested the British government measure. *The Gleaner* protested the measure, too. In editorial after editorial it demanded an end to the prohibition on the export of Jamaican bananas to the U.S.

The government didn't budge. In fact, it decided to drastically reduce the amount of fruit it allowed into the United Kingdom, as well. In a time of war, tropical fruit was something the British decided they didn't need and could not afford. Jamaican banana exports to the United Kingdom dropped from 217 tons in 1914 to barely half that figure in 1915. In 1917, a miserly 32 tons of Jamaican banana was exported to Britain. The British government's decision to reduce the amount of fruit it imported from Jamaica sent the island's planters into a panic.

"It could never be the government's policy to interfere hastily or wantonly with the export trade of this country," *The Gleaner* wrote. "For unless we ship fruit and other articles, we shall not be able to obtain flour and other articles in return." A few months later the British government did an about turn and withdrew the ban. Planters and exporters like Lanasa and Goffe were relieved. But by 1917 similarly tough prohibitions on the importation of foreign fruit were enacted in Britain again.

"Oranges, banana, grapes, almonds and nuts will be restricted to 25 per cent of the 1916 imports," British Prime Minister Lloyd George proclaimed. "People in England should depend upon their own produce." In 1915, the British government allowed eight and a half million bunches of bananas into Britain. In 1917, the government allowed only two million bunches to enter.

Restrictions on what could be exported to countries other than those that were part of the British Empire and reductions in the amount of fruit Britain purchased from its colony made life for planters and exporters of Jamaican fruit very difficult. But it was not these restrictions alone that forced many out of the fruit business during the war years. The availability of ships was another problem. Shortly after it declared war on Germany in 1914, Britain began requisitioning ships of all kinds for war service. The Quebec Steamship Company, the Royal Mail Steam Packet Co., Elders and Fyffes, and the Lanasa and Goffe company had steamships taken from them for war service.

In May 1917, the West India Committee, a planter's advocacy group in London that A.C. Goffe's brother, Rowland, was a member of issued a circular objecting to British policy. The West India Committee protested what it called the British government's sweeping powers in the requisitioning of merchant ships. While it was right, the circular said, that "every square inch of tonnage available, or that can be made available, must be devoted to bringing food supplies for our teeming population," it did not believe causing the suspension of the already meagre West Indian trade was a sensible measure. "In Jamaica special concern is felt and particularly by banana planters."

Despite protests, steamers were pressed into military service. This reduced severely the number of vessels available to ship produce. Insurance companies, too, made the leasing of ships difficult. Insurers took full advantage of war conditions to charge shippers as much as they could to insure their vessels. When asked why they charged so much, insurers pointed to the sinking of the *Lusitiania*. The *Lusitania*, a British cargo and passenger ship, was attacked and sunk by a German submarine on 1 May, 1915 while on its way from New York to Liverpool. Twelve hundred people died. One of the 764 survivors described the moment the first torpedo struck the ship as "like a million-ton hammer hitting a steel boiler a hundred feet high and a hundred feet long." The sinking raised tensions between the United States and Germany and contributed to the U.S. decision to declare war on Germany two years later. In 1917 alone, German submarines sank 3,000 cargo ships. One out of every four ships heading for the United Kingdom was sunk by German U-boats.

It wasn't just insurance companies that took advantage of war conditions. Ship owners also took advantage of war conditions. In May 1917, a consortium of Norwegian ship owners announced they were raising prices for chartering or leasing ships. Prices went up by more than fifty per cent.

Yet another problem for banana planters during the war years was praedial larceny. Praedial larceny, produce theft, usually increased during times of drought or after a hurricane, when fruits and vegetables were scarce. What food survived was often pegged for export, not for local consumption. Food that made it to markets in Linstead, Kingston or elsewhere was often very expensive. Hurricane, or what Jamaicans who lived in banana parishes called, 'banana blow,' made both food and work hard to find. Desperation led some to steal bananas, coconuts or whatever fruits or vegetables could be easily spirited away from a small settler's land or a big planter's estate.

The Great War, though far away in Europe, forced harsh conditions upon Jamaica thousands of miles away in the West Indies. Restrictions were placed on the sale of food and kerosene oil, and prices were set so as to discourage gouging. In Kingston and St. Andrew parish, salt beef could not be sold for more than eleven pence per pound, cornmeal, three pence per pound, fresh beef, six pence per pound, salt fish, seven pence per pound, and kerosene oil, five pence per quart.

Aside from restrictions placed on fruit export by the British government, yet another obstacle stood in the way of banana planters and fruit exporters during the war years. On its entry into the war in 1917, the United States passed the Trading With The Enemy Act and created a special War Trade Board under the auspices of the Department of State. The War Board was given the power to licence exports and imports, ration the amount of products that could be sold to neutral countries and initiated programmes designed at preserving commodities and shipping facilities for American and Allied use.

Though the War Trade Board was established to keep strategic goods out of enemy hands and prohibit the use of enemy credit and financial holdings in the United States, American fruit companies took advantage of its restrictions to keep rival banana producers like Lanasa and Goffe from getting easy access to the United States. The big US fruit companies also succeeded in placing executives from their companies on the War Trade Board's Caribbean Committee. Before a foreign fruit vessel could enter the United States it had to receive special approval and a special licence. At one point, seven out of eight members of the Caribbean Committee were executives of either the United Fruit Company or of the Atlantic Fruit Company. Jamaican fruit merchants had little chance against this rigged system.

"By pressure at Washington, a war measure was stretched to prevent us running a line of steamers to America and thus bringing about healthy competition," complained Charlie Johnston, one of the Jamaican fruit exporters hurt by the War Trade Board restrictions.

Few licences were granted by the Caribbean Committee: Thus was the United Fruit Company and the Atlantic Fruit Company, with U.S. government connivance, able to monopolise the banana trade during the Great War.

On top of these problems, Jamaica experienced the worst weather on record during the four years of the First World War. Bad weather destroyed banana harvests year after year. Jamaica was hit by two hurricanes in 1915, one in August and one in September. There were two more in 1916, one in August and one in October. There was another one in September 1917.

Battered by bad weather and by the war in Europe, banana planters called an emergency meeting in Port Maria in 1917. At the meeting, A.C. Goffe's brother, Alec, said St Mary planters were hurting and the only way to stop their pain was for the government to place a tax on bananas exported from the parish. The money from this tax, Goffe said, would be used to extend loans to desperate St Mary banana planters. "The idea is for the planters of St Mary and St Mary alone," insisted Alec Goffe.

Goodbye To All That

'Therefore, whoever wishes for peace, let him prepare for war.'

Anon

While the Great War was raging in Europe, another war of a kind was raging in Baltimore. As usual A.C. Goffe was in the middle of it. "Relieved Of Pier Lease," is how a headline in the *Baltimore Sun* on 15 December, 1914, described the latest controversy involving the Jamaican.

The trouble started in 1908. That year Goffe was arrested and implicated in an alleged plot to murder Joseph Di Giorgio. Freed from jail in late January 1908 – his business partner Antonio Lanasa remained in prison – Goffe set about restoring confidence in his firm and getting even with Di Giorgio, the architect of his troubles. Both Goffe and Di Giorgio had been desperate to secure a large chunk of Pier 2 at Baltimore harbour. The City of Baltimore's Board of Estimates granted Lanasa and Goffe the pier space the firm so desperately wanted. But Goffe's hatred for Di Giorgio clouded his judgment. Instead of agreeing to a year-to-year lease or a five or ten year lease, Goffe, greedily, signed a 50-year lease for Pier 2. This was a bad move which made no allowances for the boom and bust nature of the fruit exporting business. The lease of Pier 2 required Lanasa and Goffe to pay the then enormous sum of $9,336.24 each year to the City of Baltimore whether they used the pier or not or whether their business was good or not. The years between 1908 and 1911 were good ones for banana exporters. The years between 1912 and 1917 were not so good. Drought pockmarked Jamaica's agricultural belt and hurricanes blew down what fruit had not been dried to a crisp.

144

As for Lanasa and Goffe, their 50-year lease had become a heavy burden that was sucking cash out of their company.

"WANT TO GIVE UP PIER SPACE," read a headline in the *Baltimore Sun* newspaper. "Lanasa & Goffe Ask Release From Contract." The day before this report appeared, Lanasa and Goffe had a special meeting with members of Baltimore's Board of Estimates. They asked that their firm be relieved of its lease of a portion of Pier 2 in the new dock district. The company wanted, it told the Board, the right to use Pier 2 three days each week and wanted to be billed for its use at a per square foot rate. The rest of the pier space could be let, Lanasa and Goffe told the Board, to some other shipping company the rest of the time. Though it was outraged at first by the demands, the Board of Estimates gave them what they wanted. This was done, though the board chafed at it, to make sure the fruit and shipping company did not decamp from Baltimore to some rival city. Baltimore had been held to ransom, the city's newspapers said, by an Italian and a Jamaican.

'TO KEEP STEAMER CO. HERE,' read a headline in the *Baltimore Sun*. "Lanasa & Goffe Company Get Better Terms From City.' The new lease would, the Board of Estimates decided, be year-to-year as had been requested. The Mayor of Baltimore, James Preston, approved the measure. In order to give them what they wanted, Baltimore city laws had to be changed.

A bill to broaden the powers of the Board of Estimates in dealing with franchises had to be drafted and sent to the Legislature. Once this was done, on 14 December, 1914, both branches of the City Council passed a new ordinance allowing the Board of Estimates to grant what it wanted. It wasn't long before all kinds of businessmen began asking that laws of one sort or another be changed to accommodate their peculiar and special business needs. Banana companies were so important to Baltimore's economy, laws were re-written to accommodate them. But bending over backward to please Lanasa and Goffe wouldn't keep their steamship and importing business in Baltimore much longer.

The Lanasas and the Goffes had seemed, after almost a decade in the banana trade in Baltimore, like permanent fixtures. Three months after the company was incorporated, in April 1906, A.C. Goffe and Antonio Lanasa signed a contract which said the Lanasa and Goffe Steamship and Importing firm promised to provide ships to collect and distribute banana and other produce procured by the Messrs Goffe Bros. banana purchasing firm in

Jamaica. As the contract neared its expiration on 1 April, 1915 it became clear the Goffes and the Lanasas were not going to continue in business together. The *Daily Gleaner* had been watching developments closely.

"It is rumoured, what amount of accuracy your correspondent knows not, that the fruit and other produce interests of one of the largest planters in the parish will shortly be transferred to another, and we are awaiting developments." Those developments came days after the contract between the Lanasa and Goffe company and the Messrs. Goffe Bros. firm expired. Though Antonio Lanasa and A.C. Goffe had been partners since 1906, Lanasa moved quickly once the contract expired to form a new partnership with the Pringle Brothers, rivals of Goffe and his brothers in Jamaica. The Pringles took over the loading of Lanasa ships. "The move," *The Gleaner* said, "has caused quite a stir in banana circles."

On 16 April, 1915, fifteen days after the contract between Messrs. Goffe Bros and the Lanasa and Goffe Steamship and Importing Company expired, three of the Goffe brothers, A.C., Alec and Clarence, set sail from Jamaica for the United States.

"Going on business," is what A.C. and his brothers told the US immigration officer who interviewed them at New York City's Ellis Island. The immigration declaration forms the Jamaicans filled out makes for interesting reading. They are neither anarchists nor polygamists, they tell the official. They are, they say, of good mental and physical health and are not deformed or crippled. A.C. Goffe says he is five foot five inches, Alec, six foot one inch and Clarence, six foot exactly. The complexion of all three is listed as 'Colored.' Their hair is 'dark,' and their eyes also are 'dark.' Deciding on an alien's colour and racial type was an inexact science and varied from immigration officer to immigration officer. A.C. had been scrutinized many times before at Ellis Island. Sometimes they categorised him as a 'British African' and other times they categorised him as 'U.K. African Black.'

Interestingly, the ship A.C. Goffe and his brothers took from Port Antonio to New York was owned by the Atlantic Fruit Company. It was not by chance that they traveled to New York on the *Concettina Di Giorgio*, a steamer named after a family member of the founder and former president of the Atlantic Fruit Company, Joseph Di Giorgio. In New York, the Goffes met with the directors of Atlantic Fruit at the firm's Broadway offices. There they signed a deal to load the American company's ships in St Mary.

Done with their business in New York, A.C. and his brothers made their way to Baltimore. There wasn't much prospect a visit to Baltimore would heal the rift between the two families. It probably made things worse. The Goffes accused the Lanasas of reneging on a contract to supply them with ships to bring fruit from Jamaica. The Lanasas accused the Goffes of failing to procure sufficient high quality fruit to fill the holds of ships it sent to Jamaica. As a result, the Lanasas said, fruit steamers chartered by them were forced to return to Baltimore with too little fruit to justify the cost of chartering and coaling a large fruit steamer.

With Messrs Goffe Bros now contracted to the Atlantic Fruit Company and the Lanasa family arranging for their ships to be loaded by the Pringle organisation in Jamaica, there was little more for the Goffes and the Lanasas to discuss besides how their company would be wound up. Though people in Jamaica did not know what had come of the meeting in Baltimore, they could read the signs quite easily. While A.C. Goffe and his brothers were in the United States, the fruit steamer, *S.S. Kingston*, which was under charter to the Lanasa and Goffe company, arrived at Port Maria on 30 April, 1915. Instead of collecting fruit from Messrs Goffe Bros, the ship was loaded with fruit collected by the rival S.S. Smith company. The Pringle deal had, it appeared, fallen through. Filled to the brim, the ship left for Baltimore.

Seward Scott Smith, it became apparent, was Lanasa's new partner in Jamaica. The Smith firm was based in Port Antonio and had agents in all the key banana parishes. Samuel Magnus Walker, Alec Goffe's best friend and colleague on St Mary's Parochial Board, was an agent for the S.S. Smith Company in St Mary.

But the relationship between the Lanasas and the S.S. Smith Company did not get off to a very smooth start. The *S.S. Catherine Cuneo*, a ship chartered by Lanasa and Smith to bring their first load of fruit to the United States, met with an accident at sea on April 22. Unfortunately for the new partnership, Sam Walker, usually a shrewd banana man, had already purchased 3,000 bunches of bananas and had them delivered to a Port Maria wharf for collection. When the *Catherine Cuneo* did not arrive as expected, all 3,000 bunches were abandoned on the beach. It was an expensive mistake.

"This is a serious loss to the Smith Co," *The Gleaner* reported, "especially at such a time when profits are like angels visits – few and far between."

It was true. Profits were in those times a blessed thing for banana exporters and growers, alike. Further proof that the Lanasa and Goffe company had disbanded came in May 1915 when the onetime flagship of the firm, the *Antonio Lanasa* arrived in Port Maria harbour under a new name. Instead of the *S.S. Antonio Lanasa*, the ship was called the *S.S. Minnesota*. A few months later, after extensive repairs and the replacement of its boiler system, it was sold to a Norwegian firm and sent off to be used in the coasting trade of Norway.

While Antonio Lanasa and Seward Scott Smith's partnership didn't get off to a very good start, the partnership between the Goffes and the Atlantic Fruit Company got off to a much better start. On 3 May, 1915, Atlantic collected an enormous load from Messrs Goffe Bros wharf at Port Maria. It was the largest lot of banana handled by any St Mary firm in more than a year. The Atlantic Fruit ship, the *S.S. Van der Duyn* anchored at Port Maria at 7.30 am on 3 May, 1915 and left three hours later after taking on 8,600 bunches of banana.

Messrs Goffe Bros let growers know it was mounting a weekly service and, rather optimistically, that it expected to ship a minimum of 30,000 bunches of bananas to New York from St Mary each week. Many growers thought this arrangement between Atlantic and the Goffes a temporary one. They fully expected Lanasa and Goffe to make up and return to business together. It was clear this wasn't going to happen when this headline appeared on page seven of the *Baltimore Sun* on 8 October, 1915: "Lanasa and Goffe sued For $50,000." Messrs Goffe Bros. had sued the Lanasa and Goffe Steamship and Importing Company for alleged breach of an agreement to furnish it with steamships to bring bananas to the United States from Jamaica. The Lanasa and Goffe firm refused without cause, the lawsuit said, to supply Messrs Goffe Bros with steamships for the collection of fruit as it'd contracted to.

As for Joseph Di Giorgio, after being unseated as president of Atlantic Fruit he re-emerged in Chicago. There he erected a large fruit depot, built a fruit auction house, produce yards, a large cold storage plant for fruit and built an office building to accommodate fruit brokers and fruit dealers.

During this period, too, apparently untroubled by the restrictions and poor prices, several new companies entered in the banana trade. Among them was Soutar and Company, a firm begun by Simon Soutar, a Kingston shipping merchant and commission agent. Soutar, a former consul to Denmark, Sweden and Norway, was owner of plantations in the Stony Hill and Half

Way Tree areas of St. Andrew. In January 1915, the Phoenix Fruit Company, an American firm, began buying fruit in St Mary and St. James for export to New York. Like a phoenix it went up in flames. It did not, though, emerge from its ashes. In February 1915, the West India Importing Company of Philadelphia, launched with two chartered steamers. The new company took over the offices and warehouses of the old Cuneo company, one of the earliest of the independent banana traders.

Bad news in the banana industry was matched by bad weather. In August 1915, St Mary found itself directly in the path of a major hurricane. Damage to Port Maria was enormous. A hundred buildings were smashed. All of the wharves and landing points were washed out to sea. The United Fruit Company lost its wharf. So did Atlantic. So did C.E. Johnston. So did the S.S. Smith Company and so did Kerr and Co. Kerr's schooner, '95', was smashed in the harbour and tossed onto Port Maria's main street by the hurricane. Messrs Goffe Bros was luckier than most. The firm did lose its wharf, its wharf houses and fruit shed, but its building, made partly of wood and partly of stone survived.

The parish's banana walks were leveled. Fitz Herbert de Lisser, one of St Mary's largest planters, estimated the loss to growers at around four million dollars in bananas and around half a million dollars in coconuts. The hurricane, and the enormous losses it caused, forced S.S. Smith out of the export trade.

Another form of exporting looked as though it was coming to an end, too. The publication in April 1915 of a report commissioned by the Indian government detailing the abuses suffered by indentured Indian labourers in Fiji, Trinidad, Guyana and in Jamaica led the Indians to pass a resolution against the indentureship system. Thousands of Indians had been brought to Jamaica in the post-Emancipation period to replace African labour on sugar, and later, banana plantations. With St Mary the pre-eminent banana parish in Jamaica, inevitably hundreds of indentured Indians ended up there. With many Afro-Jamaicans abroad working on the Panama Canal, or in Costa Rica or Cuba working on banana plantations for higher wages than they could earn at home, low cost labour was at a premium.

"Owing to the scarcity of labour in India and the grave consequences resulting from the system of indentured labour, which reduces the labourers during the period of the indenture practically to the position of slaves," the Indian activist, F.G. Matesan, told the Indian Congress in 1915 that indentrueship should be terminated. Matesan said sending Indians to the West Indies to work for blacks was an intolerable blow to his people's national honour and pride. "This Congress strongly urges the total prohibition of recruitment of labour under indenture either for work in India or elsewhere."

As a result of Matesan's efforts and the report on the condition of indentured Indians abroad, no Indians were exported to Jamaica in 1916. Between 1845 and 1916, approximately 37,000 Indians had been brought to Jamaica. In time, though, indentures began to come again to Jamaica, partly due to pressure from Jamaica's planters.

As for the deal between Atlantic and A.C. Goffe, predictably, the partnership did not last long. Goffe chafed at the commission his company was paid by Atlantic Fruit. He wanted to tear up the deal they had, Goffe told Atlantic, and sign a new one. He wanted to start an independent export company and he wanted Atlantic to bankroll it. Atlantic Fruit would act, in essence, as managing partner, sharing in the profits as a major shareholder. Atlantic thought it a good plan, in prinicple. All that was left was for Goffe to charter two fruit steamers. Before the deal could be finalised, though, the Jamaican fell out badly with his American partners. The ships were withdrawn. To re-coup what had been invested in the venture, Messrs Goffe Bros filed a lawsuit against Atlantic Fruit. Before the case went to trial, the two sides reached a settlement.

Confined once again to acting merely as a provider of produce for American companies to ship and distribute, A.C. Goffe and his brothers looked for many and various ways of earning their pounds, shillings and pence between 1914 and 1918. In March 1914, with war in Europe only four months away, Goffe, his brothers, and several associates began the Saint Mary Motor Company. Later the same year he opened a hotel, the Kingsley, one of St Mary's first, three miles outside Port Maria in the lovely coastal village of Galina. Apart from H.P. 'Papa' Jones' small hotel in Port Maria, which was the place planters gathered for lunch and other entertainments, the Kingsley was for many years the only hotel in the whole of St Mary parish.

'An Ideal Health Resort, three miles from Port Maria, Every modern convenience. Motor Car Service direct from Albany Station. Sea Bathing A Specialty,' read an advert for the new hotel. The Kingsley was one of only a handful of hotels in the entire country in 1915. There were taverns which let rooms, and inns, but few hotels. Among the few which advertised each week in The Gleaner were Edwin Bell's Mandeville Hotel, James Browning Dick's Newleigh Hotel, also in Mandeville, Ben Oliphant's Moneague Hotel in St Ann, and the Sea View Hotel in Port Antonio.

Tourism had only very recently begun to be regarded as a serious industry, worthy of developing in Jamaica. When the Jamaica Hotels Law was passed in 1890 it enticed entrepreneurs to build and develop hotels. The island's government, desperate to encourage tourism in Jamaica, offered those willing to invest in large hotels large subsidies. But developing tourism in Jamaica, with its history of slavery, was not without its challenges. "This itself posed particular problems, as the Blacks and Coloureds in the hotel industry seemed acutely sensitive to racial slurs and infamy," writes Frank Fonda Taylor in his book, *To Hell With Paradise: A History of The Jamaican Tourist Industry.* "Even to come forward to greet the guest on arrival was frowned upon by the native staff, for such civility would smack of servility and remind the black or brown person who showed it that his or her colour was once the badge of slavery."

The Jamaica Hotels Law of 1890 boosted tourism in the island and advances in shipping also helped, making travel from North America and elsewhere both quick and relatively cheap.

With his hotel up and running, and proving profitable very quickly, A.C. and his brother Alec set off for the United States in April 1916. They were going to attend court in Baltimore in a breach of contract lawsuit against Antonio Lanasa. Messrs Goffe Bros demanded $50,000 in damages and $3,400 for the balance due on fruit it shipped to the United States which it said had not been paid. Before the court proceedings could begin, the two sides settled the lawsuit. On their return to Jamaica Alec and A.C. declared they were happy with the agreement they reached with Antonio Lanasa.

Much as they were interested in the goings on between Lanasa and Goffe, banana men in Jamaica had their own problems. On 9 August, 1916, a large deputation of St Mary banana planters set off for Kingston to meet with the governor, Sir William Henry Manning. The planters demanded the government help the banana industry. The leader of the deputation, Sir John Pringle, asked the governor to demand that Britain stop purchasing bananas grown outside its Empire.

Blunt as ever, Alec Goffe told the governor he was afraid of no man, nor any steamship company and that he expected the 'Mother Country' had a responsibility to buy fruit produced by its colonies before it bought fruit from other countries. Jamaica had pledged to contribute money and food to the British war effort, he told the Governor, but how could the island do this if its banana industry was destroyed because of government indifference. If the government did not come to the rescue soon of the Jamaican banana industry there would be widespread bankruptcies, Goffe said.

Anyway, as it became clear in 1918 the war was coming to an end, eager entrepreneurs, among them A.C. Goffe, began hatching plans to re-enter the export fruit and shipping field. Goffe would very likely have been among the first of Jamaica's banana men to re-enter the trade; that is had he not been in St Catherine District Prison in Spanish Town, awaiting trial for murder.

"TRIAL AT PORT MARIA OF ALFRED CONSTANTINE GOFFE ON A CHARGE OF MURDER," read the banner headline in The *Daily Gleaner* newspaper on 22 June, 1918. A.C. Goffe was in trouble again.

A. C. Goffe, 1908
(left)

A. C. Goffe, 1910, London
(right)

A. C. Goffe, 1884.
(left)

Cecil Goffe, 1912
(right)

Clifford Clemetson owner of
Frontier estate, St Mary, 1920.
(right)

Ernest Goffe, London, 1914
(left)

A. C. Goffe's father, John, 1870s
(right)

Rowland Parkinson Goffe,
London, 1910. (left)

Charles Edward Johnston, A. C.
Goffe's business rival, 1911
(left)

A. C. Goffe's mother, Margaret
1850s
(right)

A.C. Goffe (left), American
business associate(centre),
Clarence Goffe (right), 1920

Antonio Lanasa and wife,
Giuseppa, 1908, Baltimore.
(right)

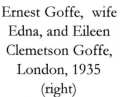

David Louis Clemetson
with Trinity College,
Cambridge rowing
team 1914.
(left)

Ernest Goffe, wife
Edna, and Eileen
Clemetson Goffe,
London, 1935
(right)

Alexander Davidson Goffe and Lesline Isaacs' wedding,
Oxford House, Port Maria, 1910.

Antonio Lanasa and family, 1930

THE ST. MARY MOTOR COMPANY, LIMITED.

Runs a Car daily between Port Maria and Albany to catch the
Kingston and Port Antonio trains—to avoid disappointment,
apply to T. A. Gentles for conveyance early.

PROSPECTUS.

(1) The name of the Company is "The Saint Mary Motor Coy., Ltd."

(2) The Registered Office of the Company is situate in the Town of
Port Maria, in the Parish of Saint Mary.

(3) The objects for which this Company is established are for the conveyance of passengers, mails and freight in Motor Cars between the Town
of Port Maria and the Railway Station at Albany in the Parish of Saint
Mary, and between such other places as the Company may from time to time
determine.

(4) The liability of the Company is limited.

(5) The Capital of the Company is One Thousand Five Hundred Pounds
divided into one thousand five hundred shares at One Pound per share payable at 5/ on application, 5/ on allotment, and 5/ each at the expiration
of two months from the last payment.

It is proposed to approach the Government for the Conveyance of the
Kingston and the Port Antonio mails between Albany and Port Maria which
will be a subsidy to the Company if obtained.

DIRECTORS:—A. D. Goffe, Rev. J. H. Graham, J. A. Benjamin, A. C. Goffe,
S. C. Barham, S. M. Walker and J. B. Goffe. Secretary and Treasurer:
John Parodie. Bankers: The Bank of Nova Scotia. Solicitor: C. H.
Clemetson Goffe.

ESTIMATED EXPENDITURE:—1. First cost of Car £650 including freight
and duty. 2. Running Expenses £50 10 per month.

ESTIMATED EARNINGS:—Passengers £90 per month. Freight, extra.
Contract for Mails, extra. Application for Shares to be made to
JOHN PARODIE, Esq., Secretary & Treasurer, Port Maria.

Jamaican newspaper cartoon, 1908.
(left)

THE BALTIMORE AND JAMAICA TRADING CO.

Regular Weekly Passenger Service

Between BALTIMORE, U.S.A., and JAMAICA.

The S. S. "PORT MORGAN" leaves for Baltimore, U.S.A., MARCH 29, to be followed by S. S. "PORT GALES".

For further particulars apply to

A. CONSTANTINE GOFFE,
Manager for Jamaica, Port Maria.

BLACK STAR LINE S.S. CO

The S.S. "Yarmouth" will sail on Wednesday, 24th inst., for Colon, taking freight and passengers.

W. E. WILSON, General Agent,
37 Orange St., Kingston, Ja.

Daily Gleaner, shipping adverts for A. C. Goffe's firm and
Marcus Garvey's Black Star Line Company, 1920.

TO THE

JAMAICA BANANA GROWER

Here is something that should be brought home to every Banana Producer in Jamaica, small and large, who has at heart the interests and the future welfare of Jamaica.

For comparison, we give you below the approximate weights of Jamaica Bananas landed and sold in America, as against Bananas from Bluefields, Bocas and Guatemala:

JAMAICA	BLUEFIELDS	BOCAS & GUATEMALA
9s - 43 lbs.	60 lbs.	66 lbs.
8s - 32 „	42 „	47 „
7s - 25 „	35 „	39 „
6s - 17 „	25 „	28 „

Jamaica Bananas are now sold in America at so much per 100 lbs.

Think it over and you will soon realize the seriousness of the situation. When you are asked to cut thin and immature fruit, think of the figures given above, and remember that unless we greatly increase the weights of our Bananas by allowing the fruit to fill out, the Banana Industry will receive a serious set-back. and our hopes of becoming once more the largest Banana-producing country in the world will not come to pass.

Be on Your Guard! Do Not Cut Thin and Immature Fruit.

Allow your fruit to fill out, and to avoid bruises. Wrap and Handle the fruit Carefully, and thus build up again the name of JAMAICA BANANAS. It lies within your power to do this, and you should not fail to act promptly.

FULL FRUIT IS WANTED.

JAMAICA FRUIT & SHIPPING COMPANY, LTD.

Jamaica Fruit and Shipping Company circular, 1919.

The Lanasa & Goffe Steamship & Importing Company
OF BALTIMORE CITY

STEAMSHIP "ANTONIO LANASA"
IMPORTERS OF FOREIGN FRUITS

ss *Antonio Lanasa*, 1907

Loading Bananas, Jamaica, 1905

DYNAMITE CASE

—:o:——

Alleged Attempt on Mr. Di Giorgio's Life.

——:o:——

THE GOFFES IN BALTIMORE

Baltimore newspaper headline
1908.

Black Hand Bombing Suspects
Baltimore 1908

Lanasa and Goffe in court Baltimore 1908

56 Hope Road, St. Andrew, 1970s.

A. C. Goffe's Windsor Hotel, 1950s.

Port Maria, St Mary, 1825

Banana Plantation, Jamaica, 1900s

Port Maria, circa 1890

Baltimore Harbour, 1930s

Blood on the Fields

'For everything there is a season..a time to live and a time to die'

Ecclesiastes 3:1-8

.C. Goffe had been the talk of the island ten years before, in 1908, when he was arrested in the United States and charged with conspiring with Antonio Lanasa and members of the Mafia-like Black Hand Society to murder Joseph Di Giorgio in Baltimore. The case against Goffe was eventually thrown out and he returned to Jamaica something of a hero. The St. Mary planter had been the victim, some said, of American manipulations and machinations. The Port Maria man had fallen foul, others said, of Americans determined and desperate to keep Jamaicans, especially black ones, out of the lucrative export fruit field. But that was ten years ago. Now, here he was again, on trial, this time in his homeland Jamaica, and this time in his hometown of Port Maria, St. Mary.

On 13 April, 1918, Goffe was busy in the fields of his banana and coconut estate, Kingsley. Near the lovely coastal village of Galina, three miles outside Port Maria, the property also housed a small hotel that was popular with visitors from abroad. The planter had little to do with the running of the hotel. He left what he called 'soft hand business' to others and attended to his bananas and coconuts.

Planters like Goffe had long complained that produce theft was ruining them. The police, planters complained, had done little or nothing to stop fruit bandits from pillaging their produce. *The Gleaner*, often called the 'planter's paper,' was outraged, too. Day after day during 1917 and 1918, the paper ran story after story on what it called, 'the great evil.' In one edition of the paper, a letter, really a parody, from a supposed 'praedial larcenist' was published.

'I am a praedial thief," the letter read, "and Solomon in all his glory never had much better time than I am having. I spend the days in drinking, smoking, and gambling and at night I go gather produce from the poor brutes who have been toiling and sweating in the sun for months to bring their cultivation to perfection." The fake letter, likely written by a member of *The Gleaner* staff, continued: "I am caught only one in ten, and nine times of ten I manage to coax, threaten or buy myself off so that my risk of conviction is about one per cent...I threaten the poor, timid cultivators, man, woman and children that I will knock the stuffing out of them or will put obeah on them, and they are frightened out of their wits." The letter was signed, 'AP THIEF, Kingston.'

The praedial larcenist was, next to the German during the war years, the most vilified figure in Jamaican newspapers. One paper warned the authorities they'd better act against praedial larceny or angry planters would begin arming themselves with guns and take the law into their own hands.

A.C. Goffe had been talking for some time now about taking the law into his own hands. Each day for the past several weeks, Walter Hyer, chief yard-man at Goffe's Kingsley banana and coconut estate brought reports of bunches of bananas severed from their limbs and coconuts gone missing. First twenty coconuts disappeared, then thirty, then fifty.

To try and put an end to pilfering of his produce, Goffe sought out a local man, Prince Henry, whom everyone said was good with a cutlass and with a gun. Henry was given the job of ranger on Kingsley after convincing the planter that as he was from the nearby village of Galina, he knew the terrain. He knew, he said, who were locals and who were outsiders come from other parishes to pilfer fruit.

A deal struck, Goffe gave Henry a gun, cartridges, a cutlass and permission to shoot first and ask questions later. But still chief yardman Walter Hyer came each day to report that coconuts were disappearing at an alarming rate.

Fed-up with his failure to ferret out the produce thieves, on April 11 Goffe fired Henry. Early the next day, he sent his chauffeur, Eustace Rutherford, to Prince Henry's home to collect the gun and cartridges he'd given him when he took the job as ranger. Henry handed them over with little protest.

The day after this, Rutherford took Goffe to town on business. They returned to Kingsley at around 3.30 pm. When the car pulled up, Walter Hyer was waiting with the usual bad news; this time, though, with a twist. Hyer had seen some fresh coconut husks piled high in a pasture. Hyer said he was convinced the coconuts had been stashed nearby. This meant the thief was sure to return.

"Rutherford, get the gun and let us go there," Goffe told his chauffeur. He was eager to send a message to any produce thief who thought his bananas and coconuts offered easy pickings. Rutherford grabbed the gun and cartridges he'd taken from Prince Henry. Goffe ushered his twelve-year old niece, Grace, and Walter Hyer into his automobile and drove in the direction of 'Parson Land,' where the yardman had found thirty-six coconuts covered with trash. "Let us watch for the thief," Goffe told the group. After a time, Grace walked the short distance home, the St Mary skies darkening overhead.

Left behind her, hiding in the bushes was Rutherford, Hyer and Goffe. They lay-wait the thief there from around 4pm until nightfall. At approximately 7 pm Grace, who must have considered it a great adventure, re-joined the three men in the pasture. Two more hours went by. Then around 8.30 pm a man appeared. Not aware there were people hunkering down in the bush near him, the man began loading the thirty-six coconuts into a box. "Stop, or I will fire," Goffe called out to the man. 'Stop, or I will fire.' But the man, Goffe told police later, got up from the box and began moving towards him. 'Bang.' Goffe discharged one cartridge from the double-barrelled shotgun, afraid for his life, and the lives of those with him, he would later say. Believing the man to have escaped without injury, Goffe told Hyer to collect the coconuts and the four left the estate for the night.

The next morning, April 14, before heading for church, Goffe sent Rutherford to search the pasture to see if anyone had fallen there. After a cursory investigation, Rutherford returned. He had found nothing. But, by now, the entire village of Galina had been roused. News that a thief had been shot on Goffe's place had spread quickly. At around 10 am, villager Ernest Wallace, arrived at Kingsley. He told Goffe he'd heard he'd shot at a thief on his estate in the 'Parson's Land' area. He asked for permission to go onto the property to see if he could find the thief. He believed the man might be Prince Henry, Goffe's former ranger, Wallace said.

Henry's common law wife, Maria Wilson, feared the worst when she heard a man had been shot. Henry hadn't come home and so she asked Ernest Wallace to go and find him. Wallace set off for Kingsley plantation. He found a dead body. It was 25-year old Prince Henry, as suspected. A 123-foot trail of blood led Wallace to the body, which was face-down, a single bullet wound in the chest.

Hearing this, and without checking for himself, Goffe, with Eustace Rutherford driving, went not to the body but directly to the home of St Mary's acting Chief of Police, Thomas James Hazlett. "Voluntarily Inspector, I come," Goffe told the policeman, "to tell you what happened last night.'"

A.C. Goffe had quite a story to tell. He did not deny he was responsible for Prince Henry's death. But it was done in self-defence and not premeditated murder, the planter insisted. Because of Goffe's wealth and influence in St Mary, and because his friends and relatives were in positions of power in the island, most people expected he would be let off easily. So, even when he was taken into custody on April 14 and charged with murder, it seemed merely a formality.

At a special sitting of the Resident Magistrate's Court in Port Maria held on 15 April, His Honour George Harvey Clarke, a close friend of Goffe's older brother, Cecil, an attorney, was preparing to grant bail when he was over-ruled by the Attorney General. Goffe spent the night in Port Maria jail. Still, it was not clear to the planter how serious his predicament was.

The next morning, April 16, after an uncomfortable night in jail, Goffe was brought before the Resident Magistrate again. This time bail was granted in the sum of £1,000. Two of his brothers stood surety at £500 each. He was ordered to return to the court a week later. Then a preliminary examination would be held to decide if there was reason to go to trial.

At the examination it was the job of the Crown to show cause why the accused should not be admitted to bail. Henry Milne Radcliffe, representing Goffe, said the case was one in which it was within the discretion of the court to grant bail. He cited the case of *Rex vs. Jones*. He also mentioned a case in which a woman awaiting trial for murder had been given bail. Mr. Justice Beard agreed the judge had the power to grant bail in this case, but said this should not be done if there was a violent presumption of guilt. But Henry Radcliffe told the judge he had represented a man in the parish of Clarendon not long ago who, in an attempt to chop a person with a cutlass, caused a shotgun to go off, killing the man. The accused was, Radcliffe said, granted bail so why should Goffe not be granted bail. If the court was concerned the banana planter would flee the island for America, Radcliffe said he would arrange for the planter to give up his passport and other travel documents.

The Attorney General agreed that under such circumstances it would be difficult to escape justice, but insisted there were countries other than the United States where the accused could flee and from where it would be impossible to have him extradited. Though Goffe's friends and family had tried to assure him that all would go well, things went very badly at the preliminary examination. To everyone's great surprise, A.C. Goffe was indicted on murder, refused bail, and sent to Jamaica's notorious St Catherine District Prison in Spanish Town. He remained there for two long months, till the day of his 20 June, 1918 trial at the St Mary Circuit Court in Port Maria.

Praedial Larceny

'Thief from thief, God laugh.'

Jamaican proverb

Eleven months before A.C. Goffe shot and killed the alleged coconut thief, Prince Henry, an emergency meeting was hastily convened in Port Maria to discuss the 'praedial larceny evil.' At the meeting, which was held at the Town Hall on 3 May, 1917, was a cross section of St. Mary society. There were small settlers, members of the clergy such as Presbyterian minister I.N.D. Gordon and Anglican archdeacon J.H.H. Graham. There, too, were several of St. Mary's big planters like H.J. Rudolf, owner of Hampstead estate, J.A. Benjamin, owner of Coves estate, Lewis Brodie Melville, and J. de Lisser, owner with his siblings of several large estates. Present, too, was A.C. Goffe and three of his brothers — John, Horace, and Alec. The planters were in bellicose mood. The government agricultural instructor, William Cradwick, said the authorities had employed several 'authorised persons' to make citizen's arrests. The pay was two shillings for an arrest and another two shillings for giving testimony in court. H.A.Webster of the Oracabessa Agricultural Branch Society said though he believed 'authorised persons' had done a good job, few praedial larceny prosecutions ever made it to court. The costs of bringing a prosecution for all but the parish's wealthiest citizens was, Webster said, prohibitive.

While a person caught trespassing on the property of another was usually fined around ten shillings for a first offence, the person who brought the suit had to pay the court eight shillings and sixpence just to mount the prosecution. Plaintiffs also had to pay the costs of those who testified on their behalf, making it even more expensive to mount a prosecution against a praedial larcenist. H.A. Webster said 'authorised persons' working in the Oracabessa area of St Mary had told him only six out of some 250 cases made it to court because of concerns over the cost of bringing a prosecution.

Outraged by the lack of prosecutions, banana planters at the meeting condemned the island's government. The clergy asked for patience. There had been, they said, a desperate shortage of food in the country since Britain declared war on Germany in 1914. Jamaica was a country at war and imported foodstuffs were hard to get and when they were available they were prohibitively expensive. Jamaica's governor, William Manning, was doing what he could to keep the cost of foodstuffs down, the clergymen explained. To stop profiteering, Manning put strict limits on what could be charged for everything from salt fish to salt beef, from cornmeal to baking flour.

But the planters would have none of it. No one, Messrs de Lisser, Rudolf, Benjamin, and Goffe complained had suffered quite as they had as a result of this confounded war. They'd lost markets for their bananas in the United States because Britain had placed severe restrictions on what could be exported to countries outside the British Empire. They were being driven out of the American banana trade by shortsighted politicians in London, the planters moaned, and were being driven to the edge of bankruptcy in Jamaica by praedial larcenists. The planters told the gathering it was time the island government or the Imperial government in London introduced measures tough enough to discourage produce thieves or they, the planters, would take action. Their blood up, some demanded the re-introduction of the dreaded 'Cat-O-Nine' tail for those caught stealing their produce.

The chief spokesman for the planters was Alec Goffe, chairman of St Mary's Parochial Board. His proposal for fixing the praedial larceny problem quieted the noisy Port Maria Town Hall meeting room. Modern times had no suitable punishment for thieves, Goffe said. The answer lay, he said, in a device from medieval, 'Dark Ages', England. Those found in possession of stolen fruit and vegetables should, he said, be placed in a specially designed stock, a medieval torture device for the public punishment of offenders. Bizarre as Goffe's proposal was, the detail with which he presented it showed he'd given careful thought to the idea. The stock would, he said, be erected in

Port Maria town centre between the clock tower and the Parish church. Anyone found guilty of stealing fruit or vegetables more than twice would, instead of being sent to the district prison to serve the standard sentence for praedial larceny, be locked in the wooden device, his hands and feet stuck through holes with bracket irons.

Once the convicted man was locked in the stock, citizens would be encouraged to begin the produce thief's punishment with a series of pokes and slaps. This was just the first course, though. The proceedings would quickly graduate to acts both terrifying and humiliating. A person placed in a stock knew that faeces, bodily waste, would be smeared into his mouth, into his ears and into his nose. Bucket loads of urine would be collected and pushed into his nose and the foulest collection of urine poured over his head. Next, the crowd would stone, burn or mutilate the person. If none of this broke the spirit of the offender, his feet would, be tickled till he could take no more.

Apart from the physical punishment a person locked in a stock endured, there was also the mental torture. Alec Goffe said because Jamaicans were a prideful and haughty people he was convinced fear of being publicly humiliated would frighten off those tempted to steal their neighbour's fruits and vegetables.

"As a rule you know that our people object to anything like ridicule," Goffe said, "and if they ridiculed a man they would drive him out of a district." Showing he was not a hard-hearted man, Goffe made clear that only adults would be punished in this way. Children caught stealing bananas and coconuts would, he said, be sent to a school of correction where they would be "flogged going in and flogged coming out."

What was wrong with a simple prison sentence, people asked Alec Goffe. A stock would, he said, yield much better results than simply confining a criminal to prison. An ex-convict had once told him, he said, Jamaica's prisons were not places of punishment but palaces of pleasure. The only thing prisoners really objected to, Goffe said the ex-convict told him, was being lined up with other prisoners and hosed down with freezing cold water three times a week.

The Port Maria meeting broke up without clear agreement as to exactly how St Mary should tackle its praedial larceny problem.

Though some thought Alec Goffe's plan for the punishment of praedial larcenists outrageous and sadistic, others thought his idea a promising one, full of good, solid, common sense. Praedial larceny was a concern for planters and it wasn't long before talk of Goffe's plan had spread from one end of the island to the other. A few days after the emergency meeting, *The Gleaner* entered the fray on Alec Goffe's side. Using a stock to punish thieves was a sound idea, the paper said. "We ourselves think that to expose a praedial thief to the stocks would do much good. We would therefore advocate the stocks," the paper said.

The newspaper did, however, take exception with Alec Goffe's depiction of Jamaica's prisons as being sumptuous and akin to palaces. "We don't agree that prison life here is so easy that the convicts regard a term in prison as a sort of holiday." Goffe was wrong. Those serving time in prison suffered terribly under the strictures of the so-called 'Silent System,' which was introduced into prisons in the 1860s. Convicts were kept not just apart from one another, but in total silence, their days filled with hard labour. The authorities were convinced this would eventually break the spirit of the most hardened convicts and make them easier to control.

It was the job of the prison, 'Silent System' advocates believed, to treat prisoners so harshly they would not want to commit another crime. Prison authorities believed the 'Silent System' would be particularly effective on the island because, it was argued, Jamaicans were not an introspective, inward looking people. Deprived of free and easy contact with one another, Jamaican prisoners would, the authorities argued, change their ways. Outlandish as this form of discipline sounded, it had many supporters in Jamaica. Indeed, *The Gleaner* newspaper argued in an editorial that tough justice transformed prisoners. Convicts, the paper said, banned from participating in what it called, "the much loved Jamaican habit of fiendish whistling" had, it said, become model inmates. Not being allowed to sing "songs in a minor key is a serious deprivation from the peasant's point of view," the paper said.

Tough sentences, though, did not stop praedial larceny. In 1917, incidents of produce theft rose. *The Gleaner* recommended planters be allowed to employ armed watchmen to patrol their fields in the nights. "We can see no reason," the paper said, "why the watchmen should not be armed: this will not mean they go about committing murder: it will simply be a precaution."

Praedial larceny had long been the planter's peculiar obsession. In 1915, Robert Percy Simmonds, St Mary's representative in the island's Legislative Council, asked the Jamaica Agricultural Society to find out from its counter-

part in Trinidad whether flogging had resulted in a reduction in praedial larceny there. Trinidad's Agricultural Society in its reply said its government did
not allow a produce thief to be flogged unless they'd committed at least two
offences. The island's administrators saw no reason, the society said, for
greater punishment. It wasn't the answer planters in Jamaica were looking for.

Though there had been relatively few cases of praedial larceny in Jamaica
in the 1890s, influential planters somehow convinced the island government to
pass a Produce Protection Law in 1896. Those found guilty of produce theft
were flogged. In one case a young boy was lashed twelve times for stealing a
single orange.

Opponents of the Produce Protection Law said it unfairly targeted the poor
and the black. The black activist, Dr Robert Love, a medical doctor and publisher
of the *Jamaica Advocate* newspaper, wrote an article in an 1896 edition of his
paper denouncing praedial laws.

"How many white men will be whipped for praedial larceny?" Robert
Love asked. "Not one…We hate this new law because while its penalty will
brutalise the offender, it will leave him no less an offender…By a strange
species of reasoning they propose to drive out of us by the lash, the evil
which they had driven into us, by the lash, for nearly 300 years."

Planters were not moved by these arguments. Black vagrants were responsible for the theft of produce and were aided in their crimes, they said, by
Chinese immigrants. Chinese immigrants, mostly from the poor southeast
region of China, had been arriving in Jamaica in ever increasing numbers
since the 1850s. The first 472 Chinese were sent as indentures in 1854. After
a period of indentureship on Jamaican plantations, many of the Chinese, who
spoke little English and had little education, turned to shop keeping to earn
their living. In St Mary, for example, John Chin Loy, William Lee Sang and
Edward Wan-Lan were all familiar names in the shop keeping trade. Their
shops, small wooden and zinc constructions, sold salt fish, bread, corned
beef, and a range of fruit and vegetable produce, as well.

"It was a fact that the Chinese did bring about praedial larceny," A.C.
Goffe's brother, Clarence, insisted at a meeting of St Mary's Parochial Board in
November 1917. A board member, Goffe did his best to work his colleagues
into a frenzy by telling them that bananas and coconuts from their fields were
being stolen on the orders of Chinese shopkeepers. The shopkeepers bought

the contraband cheaply, he explained, and sold it in their shops at a profit. This was how, Goffe insisted, Chinese shopkeepers had been able to sell produce at such low prices and thus squeeze native-born Jamaicans out of the shopkeeping trade.

St Mary ought to support St Ann's Parochial Board, Goffe told his colleagues, in its stand against the Chinese. St Ann's Parochial Board had recently passed a motion demanding the island's government reduce the number of licences issued to Chinese shopkeepers. If this was done, the argument went, native-born shopkeepers would once again be able to compete in the retail trade. Praedial larceny would decline, too, as with fewer Chinese in the trade, produce thieves would not have as many outlets for their bounty of stolen bananas and coconuts.

Trying to create a nationwide campaign against Chinese shopkeepers, St Ann's Board sent a letter to all thirteen of Jamaica's Parochial Boards asking for their to support. When the matter came up for discussion and vote in St Mary, Clarence Goffe was the only member of the board to vote in favour of the St Ann resolution. "No produce licence," Goffe insisted, "should be granted to them."

Despite campaigns against Chinese shopkeepers and the tightening of praedial larceny laws, produce theft did not decline much. Increasingly planters took the law into their own hands or hired thugs to intercept thieves for them. Few waited for the police to arrest suspects or for the courts to pass judgment. Planters became both judge and jury. Summary justice was harsh. In one case, a man caught stealing in a farmer's provision ground was killed by the landowner. Another landowner chopped to death a man he caught stealing bananas from his property.

Taking the law into his own hands didn't help A.C. Goffe. It got him put in Spanish Town prison.

St Mary, of course, had its own district prison. But St Catherine District Prison was the prison convicts, or those on remand, were taken to when their crimes were too big for a little parish prison. The crime Goffe was charged with was too big for St Mary's little district prison. Spanish Town prison, as people called it, had its own death row. Between eighteen and thirty-six people were executed there each year.

After being processed, Goffe would have been given prison clothing, a toothbrush, a mug, and a blanket. Next, he would have been assigned a single cell, as all prisoners were. He would have been placed in a section of the prison with men, who like him, had been charged with murder. Murderers were kept with murderers, rapists with rapists, robbers with robbers. Incarcerated in the prison, too, were likely more than one or two praedial larcenists.

With fifty-nine days to go before his trial, Goffe had time on his hands, time to ponder his fate. Doubtless Prince Henry, the man whose life he took for allegedly stealing coconuts from him, visited the planter in his dreams and gave him many restless nights.

Many men imprisoned in Spanish Town considered escape, but this was impossible. The prison's walls were 22 feet high and five feet six inches thick. It was no ordinary prison. Within its gates was a special debtor's prison, a county gaol, reformatory and a prison farm where a variety of new plants, among them banana plants, were experimented on. Prisoners were kept busy. They were put to work burning bricks, breaking stones or working at one trade or another. They had to do this work on a diet composed primarily of pap, a mushy grainy substance like porridge and a little bit of meat.

Prisoners were entitled to three ounces of meat and pap, sweetened with sugar, each day. Sometimes even this was not available. On occasion, prisoners had to take their pap brackish because prison warders had stolen the sugar allotted them. In one notorious instance, a warder was discovered leaving the General Penitentiary with four pounds of sugar up his sleeves and twelve pounds of meat hidden elsewhere on his person.

Though Goffe knew what the inside of a prison looked like – he'd been in one when he was charged with conspiracy to murder Joseph Di Giorgio in Baltimore ten years before – it was no preparation for this. The next two months would be a mental and physical torture for the planter.

In the cells around Goffe's were likely a former worker or two of his who, unable to make it on the meagre wages paid by him and other banana planters, turned to crime. Now, for a while at least, he would know life as most Jamaicans knew it. Not an especially religious man, what faith he had would be tested in the depths and darkness of St Catherine District Prison.

"For broad understanding and deep feeling," Fyodor Dostoevsky wrote in *Crime and Punishment*, "you need pain and suffering. I believe really great men must experience great sadness in the world."

It would have been impossible to have been an inmate at Spanish Town and not experienced great sadness. The prison, which was originally known as the Middlesex and Surrey County Jail when it was built in 1714, was a gruesome place even by the standards of Jamaica's other grim penal institutions. Inmates who could afford it, often paid prison warders to buy small privileges for them. Decent food and drink could be had for the right bribe.

Institutions like St Catherine District Prison took their lead on jailhouse discipline from Britain.

By the time A.C. Goffe arrived at St Catherine District Prison in 1918, the so-called 'Mark' system was being employed. Prisoners serving time for relatively minor crimes were not assigned fixed sentences. Instead, if they practiced good conduct they were rewarded with marks of accomplishment. If they collected enough marks and showed they were willing to accept society's rules, they were freed. Those convicted of murder could not benefit from this liberal regime. Female prisons in Jamaica employed a novel approach to reform convicts too. Prison officials decided the most effective way to encourage black women to give up criminal activity was to threaten to cut off their hair.

Often prisoners who could not read or write served more time than they ought to have. Not able to read prison notices, they did not know when their sentences were up and prison warders rarely bothered to tell them. In some instances a prisoner had to pay a jailer to alert them. Those without money often stayed in prison much longer than required to. There was little chance Goffe would forget what day he was to leave prison.

"Go now. Go this very moment, and stand at the crossroads;" Dostoevsky wrote. "Bow down, and first kiss the earth which you have defiled; then bow down to the whole world, to the four points on the compass, and say aloud, for all men to hear: 'I have killed!' Then God will send you life again."

A.C. Goffe's friends complained that his indictment and imprisonment was unjust and was being led by his rivals in the banana business. Enemies of the family, those who resented their domination of St Mary's political and economic life, were happy that its most outspoken member seemed about to get his come uppance. The Goffes, their assorted cousins and in-laws, some locals muttered, were a law unto themselves and had turned St Mary into their personal playground and kingdom.

A.C. Goffe's imprisonment and murder trial was the big news in Jamaican papers in April, May and June of 1918. Readers of *The Daily Gleaner, Daily*

Telegraph and *Jamaica Times* found great entertainment in the daily and weekly reports of the trials and tribulations of the St Mary planter. These were difficult times for Jamaicans and they were eager for anything that would take their minds off the Great War. Millions had died, including many of their own friends and family. They found some relief in the troubles of A.C. Goffe.

Craiglockhart

Dulce et decorum est pro patri mori.

" I feel that Jamaica will loyally and patriotically assume her part in maintaining the integrity of our Empire, and will comport herself gallantly to-day as she has done in the past," Sir William Henry Manning, Governor of Jamaica, said in an address before the island's Legislative Assembly a few days after Britain declared war on Germany in 1914.

Between 1914 and 1918, around 10,000 Jamaicans, all volunteers, joined the British West India Regiment, the so-called 'coloured' branch of the British Armed Services. Most of the Jamaicans who served were teenagers or in their early twenties. Some were already servicemen before war began. Others left their jobs or schooling in a fit of patriotism or derring-do and signed up. The sons of the wealthy became lieutenants and colonels and the sons of the poor became privates and corporals. Some went because of a desire to serve King and Country. Most, though, went for reasons unconnected with patriotism.

Unemployment had skyrocketed in Jamaica partly as a result of the war and wages were low. A salary for soldiering was better than no salary at all. Those who did not volunteer because of a desire to fight the enemy or because they needed a job, likely signed up for the sheer adventure of it; the chance to experience life outside of their small piece of the Empire.

Public calls to duty were printed in newspapers and recruitment meetings were held in towns and villages across the island. One such meeting was held in the courtroom of the Resident Magistrate in the St Mary town of Retreat on 24 November, 1915. St Mary had already sent 300 young men off to fight, but more were wanted. In attendance were local grandees, E.M. Mais, J.C. Sharpe, the Reverend W.T. Graham, and Sydney McCutchin, secretary of St Mary's recruiting committee. Also there were A.C. Goffe's cousin, Clifford Clemetson, who'd recently become a lieutenant in 'F' Company of the parish militia, and A.C.'s brother, Cecil.

"No country's subjects were better treated than those of the British Empire," Cecil Goffe told the audience. "The King had appealed, and so all able-bodied men should go forward and show their patriotism. Do not let your mothers, your sisters or sweethearts haul them back, but join at once and put shoulder to shoulder."

Also at the recruitment meeting was Alec Goffe. As if forgetting Jamaica's past, he told the assembly of mostly black men, "if it hadn't been for Britain's flag we might have been slaves today." If Jamaicans wanted to keep enjoying the privileges they did, Goffe said, "you better keep the British flag floating."

Rising to the task of stirring the blood of the country's young men, Alec Goffe told them this war was not just for honour, it was to protect their wives, their sisters, and their mothers. Cleverly, he recounted the story of Edith Cavell, a British nurse executed by the German military. Cavell was serving with the Red Cross in Belgium when the Germans invaded the country. Stuck behind enemy lines, she chose to remain to continue nursing the wounded. At some point, members of a resistance movement contacted Cavell. She agreed to help British soldiers trapped in Belgium escape.

When Cavell's activities were discovered, she was imprisoned and later shot by the Germans. Her execution became the stuff of legend. It was said she survived the bullets of two firing squads. But as she lay on the ground, a callous German officer walked over and shot the nurse in the head. Soon postcards depicting Nurse Cavell's execution were distributed among British troops. Whatever the truth of her death, it was exploited by the British to encourage young men in Britain, and in Jamaica, to join the military. The number of recruits doubled after the nurse's execution.

"Come I say, and revenge it, and you will feel you have done your duty," Alec Goffe told the young Jamaicans gathered at Retreat Town Hall in November 1915. Four months later, the recruitment bandwagon arrived in Highgate, St Mary. Alec Goffe was there, too. He did his best to get the blood up of all present. The recruiters had been to Highgate before but had little success there.

Of eighty volunteers, only twenty actually reported to camp when called by the military. Alec Goffe wanted to light a fire under the young men of the parish.

"Men of Highgate, you are called to fight for your God, your King and your country, and for your honour," he said. "The news from the 3,000 Jamaicans at the front is very cheering and encouraging," he said, misleading those who'd gathered at Highgate market to hear news of the war. "They speak of the kind treatment received from the English people." This wasn't true. Most reports suggested West Indian soldiers were having a miserable time of it. "The King's message is, more men; come forward then, and make up the 5,000 which Jamaica must send to the mother country."

Though recruiters did not always have the success they hoped for in the parish, St Mary was generally fertile ground for them. They were more successful there than in any other parish in Jamaica. Either the citizens were unusually patriotic or the recruiters unusually effective. The lead recruiter in St Mary, Sydney Cameron McCutchin, a director of the Gray's Inn charity, was very skilled at shaming battle-shy young men into joining up.

"The weight [to sign up for service] had been reduced to 116 pounds and the height to 5 foot 2 inches in order to meet the situation," explained McCutchin at a recruitment meeting in Port Maria. The implication was clear. Few young men had signed up so entry qualifications had to be lowered. It was an embarrassment for the British and for the recruiters. "It was a shame to be sending away small men," McCutchin said, "when there were men nearly six foot high hiding at home."

Not satisfied with the numbers, in 1917 the British government introduced the Military Service Law. This required all adult Jamaican men to register for service or face imprisonment. Following the introduction of the law, 122,218 young Jamaicans registered. But only 11,483 actually enlisted. Only men who were unmarried or did not have children could be called up. So reluctant were some Jamaican men to fight, they begun claiming children they'd fathered but had, until the threat of being called for military service, ignored. St Mary and St Catherine proved the most patriotic parishes. A total of 1,142 young men from St Catherine enlisted. St Mary was number one, enlisting 1,256 young men. The young men of Trelawny, Hanover and St. James were not so keen as other parishes to put their names among the 'glorious dead.' These three parishes sent the fewest number to the European conflagration.

Though A.C. Goffe's father, John, had served as an infantry officer in St Mary's branch of Jamaica's Home Guard in the 1860s, the men of the Goffe family were not exactly made of fighting stuff. They were a pragmatic breed, concerned first and last with their self-preservation. A.C. and his brothers were all in their forties and fifties so were too old to fight. But their many young nephews and cousins – some of them gifted horsemen and good shots – had no excuse. Those who did not heed the call to go abroad and fight for King and Country sometimes joined the Reserve Regiment at home in Jamaica, instead. A.C. Goffe's cousin, Clifford Clemetson, a 19 year old when war began, elected to stay home and become a lieutenant in St Mary parish's Reserve Regiment. In the end, only three members of the family were among the 1,256 men from St Mary who volunteered to fight. There was Kenneth Harold Goffe, who served in Egypt. There was 19-year old Egbert Victor Goffe. He was part of the first Jamaican War Contingent that sailed from Royal Mail wharf in Kingston for England on 9 November, 1915. It was a national event and an estimated 20,000 people came out to see the 550 soldiers off. One newspaper had this to say: "...young, virile, bubbling over with life, proud soldiers of that Empire on which the sun never sets; the great glorious British Empire...they were making history for Jamaica — writing possibly the most glorious page in the long, and chequered story of this isle of the Caribbean Sea...Jamaica, as Jamaica, was now in the war." Private Egbert Goffe's father, Albert, a much-loved shopkeeper from the Manning's Town district of Port Maria, was so proud his eldest child had gone off to fight for the Empire he encouraged other St Mary men to do the same at a recruitment meeting in Port Maria on 26 January, 1917: "So make up your minds, you all know him, and do likewise, and swell the British Army so that we may gain a successful victory, and thus better yourselves and your families, lifting up your heads to glory." The other member of the Goffe clan who enlisted was Clifford Clemetson's older brother, David, who signed up in October 1914.

David Louis Clemetson decided he'd fight though he had a lot more than most to lose. He was one of St Mary parish's largest landowners and had a very bright future ahead of him. But this sort of eagerness to come to the aid of the 'Mother Country' was misplaced. Privates, corporals and other enlisted men in the British West India Regiment spent most of their war digging trenches and toilets, burying the dead, and carrying foodstuffs and supplies for white soldiers.

West Indians who hoped to be admitted to an Officers' Training Corps, O.T.C., were usually disappointed. Take the case of the Jamaican, Roy Douglas

Manley. Manley was refused admission to an Officer's Training Corps in England though he'd served in the corps at his English boarding school and had been promised a place. Dutifully, he reported to camp for service, but when the army brass realised he was a man of colour his place in the corps was withdrawn and he was turned away. He served anyway as an enlisted man and died in action in 1917 in the third battle of Ypres in Flanders, Belgium.

Roy's older brother, Norman, who would later become a distinguished barrister and a Premier of Jamaica, had much the same experience as did his sibling. Blocked from becoming an officer, he enlisted as a gunner in the Royal Field Artillery. David Clemetson had better luck. Like Norman Manley he was a 21-year-old law student from Jamaica who found himself in England when Britain declared war on Germany on 4 August 1914. Manley was a Rhodes Scholar in his second year at Jesus College, Oxford and Clemetson was a second year law student at Trinity College, Cambridge.

Unlike Manley and his brother, Roy, Clemetson managed, somehow, to win a commission as an officer. Clemetson, five foot eleven and three quarter inches tall and weighing 165 pounds, served first in the Royal Fusiliers and then became a Second Lieutenant in the Pembroke Yeomanry, in command of a platoon of men. Usually only white men of pure European extraction who were born in Britain and whose parents had been born in Britain could win commissions as officers. Clemetson was not white nor close to it. As his war record shows, one of the questions he was asked at his enlistment interview at Cockspur Street in London on October 17, 1914 was: 'Are you of pure European extraction?' Clemetson answered truthfully, 'No.' For whatever reason, the War Office decided to overlook his colour and make him an officer. In the Jamaican's war record, his complexion is described, ambiguously, as 'dusky.'

Clemetson seemed to enjoy his war service, at first. He wrote often to his widowed mother, Mary. He told her he was enjoying life as a British 'Tommy,' and was eager to do his "little bit" for his King and Country. He told his mother he found soldiering "very attractive," and that he was gaining a lot of useful experience. Truth was, he did not see action until 1915, when he was sent to the 'Struma Front' or 'Southern Front' in Salonika, Greece, near the border with both Serbia and Bulgaria. In October 1915, Bulgaria declared war on the Allies and invaded Serbia. The Serbs called on the British for help. The French sent three divisions and the British sent four divisions. Clemetson's unit was among these. A solider who fought alongside David Clemetson in Salonika kept a diary of life on the Struma Front.

"Imagine, if you can, what it means to fight up a hillside under a deadly fire, wearing a hot mask over your face, dimly staring through a pair of clouded goggles, and sucking the end of a rubber nozzle in your mouth…In this plight you are called on to endure the blast of machine-gun fire, the pointed steel or bursting shell of the enemy…it is as much like hell as anything you can think of."

If a soldier was not killed by bullets or shells, then malaria likely got him. British forces suffered more than 160,000 cases of the disease on the Struma Front. Second Lieutenant David Clemetson was one of these. During his eight months fighting in Salonika, he contracted a particularly virulent strain of the disease. This was followed by a mental breakdown. He was diagnosed with neurasthenia, or shell shock, a condition which left many soldiers suffering from hysteria, delusions, limb paralysis and loss of speech.

The War Office used the term 'shell shock' to describe soldiers so traumatised they were unable to carry out their duties on the battlefield. Earlier in the war, shell-shocked soldiers were often accused of being cowards and shot. Those spared execution were often imprisoned, placed in solitary confinement and given electric shock treatment. The War Office called this 'physical re-education.' Before the war was over more than 80,000 British soldiers were treated for shell shock. German military figures show over 600,000 of their troops were treated for cases of nervous disorders during the war.

By 1917, the British military had grudgingly accepted shell shock was a legitimate disease. A special hospital, the Craiglockhart War Hospital, was opened in Edinburgh, in Scotland to treat British officers suffering from shell shock. When it was clear David Clemetson would not recover from his condition without treatment, he was sent to Craiglockhart. On the way there on 26 May, 1917, the hospital ship he was travelling in, *Dover Castle*, was torpedoed and sunk in the Mediterranean Sea off Algeria by a German submarine. The hospital ship, filled with wounded men, was on its way to Malta from Gibraltar when it was attacked. Six men were killed. Luckily, another British hospital ship, *Kaspara*, was in the area and rescued the 270 survivors, among them Clemetson.

Clemetson was taken to Malta and later in June, to Craiglockhart. Craiglockhart's doctors believed their patients could get well by talking about their troubles. They encouraged the officers to face 'the phantoms of the mind.' It was also believed social activity would help officers like Clemetson heal. Patients were encouraged to participate in gardening, carpentry, and in swimming. There was a natural history society, a yacht model making club and a photography club. Officers put on plays, concerts, and began their own magazine, *The Hydra*.

Interestingly, Clemetson was a patient at Craiglockhart at the same time as Wilfred Owen and Siegfried Sassoon, two poets whose work showed the misery and devastation of war. Owen was suffering from shell shock and Sassoon was sent to the hospital after a tract he wrote, *Declaration against the War*, was read out by a supporter in the British parliament.

"I can no longer be a party to prolong these sufferings for ends which I believe to be evil and unjust," Sassoon's declaration read. "I am not protesting against the conduct of the war, but against the political errors and insincerities for which the fighting men are being sacrificed. On behalf of those who are suffering now I make this protest against the deception which is being practised on them; also I believe that I may help to destroy the callous complacency with which the majority of those at home regard the contrivance of agonies which they do not, and which they have not sufficient imagination to realise."

Records show 1,736 men were admitted to Craiglockhart. The number of admissions varied from 50 to 100 admissions per month. The average treatment period was two to four months. Soldiers were discharged as medically unfit (DMU) or given Home Service (HS), which was usually a desk job, or transferred to other hospitals, or sent back to active service.

As for David Clemetson, he was likely the only black soldier resident at Craiglockhart. His medical records says "he sleeps badly" and that he suffered memory loss and had delirium and malaria. The job of Craiglockhart's doctors, sympathetic as they appeared, was to get the soldiers fighting fit and return them to the Front. Clemetson was initially assigned to Home Service and given 'light duty.' He was, though, eventually sent back to the fighting. The Jamaican was sent to the Western Front in October 1917. He survived a year there before being killed on 21 September, 1918, aged 24, in a major battle near the town of Peronne in northeastern France.

The Great War ended just seven weeks later. Clemetson was buried in the Unicorn Cemetery in Vendhuile and a year after war's end, his mother, Mary, was sent the balance of his army pay, which amounted to 142 pounds and 12 shillings. Also included in the package was the two pounds and seventeen shillings her son had on him when his body was recovered. A portrait of

David Louis Clemetson was displayed for a time in a special war collection at the Institute of Jamaica in Kingston. This poem, dedicated to him by a friend, was published in *The Gleaner* in 1918:

IN MEMORIAM

Somewhere in France you are sleeping
The warriors last sleep
Far from the land that gave you birth
And the eyes that for you weep.

Where the cannon's roar and shrapnel burst
Echoes around your head
While circling airplanes above
Look down on our honoured dead.

Where the thunder of a thousand guns
Resounds throughout the day
And myriads starry shells at night
Light up the "milky way"

Oh lads, you've given yourselves your All.
But you have not died in vain –
For the chariot wheels of Victory press
And peace is in your train.

So a last salute we'll offer you,
And a last farewell we'll wave;
God rest our gallant countrymen
Till we meet beyond the grave.

FROM A FRIEND

By the time the Great War ended in November 1918, eight and a half million people had been killed. Of the 11,000 or so Jamaicans who went to war, 1,000 of them did not return home.

Trials and Tribulations

'Every man is guilty for all the good he didn't do.'
Voltaire

The pretty port town of Port Maria had been a sleepy, off-the-beaten-path sort of a place before the banana boom that A.C. Goffe and his brothers helped spark turned it into one of the most prosperous and busiest towns in Jamaica. In June 1918, Port Maria was abuzz with news that one of its best-known citizens was about to go on trial for murder.

"Not for a long time in the history of the town of Port Maria had there been a case of such island-wide interest as was tried here today when Alfred Constantine Goffe, the well known St Mary planter, was arraigned on a charge of murdering Prince Henry a young man who had been a ranger on his property Kingsley," *The Gleaner* newspaper reported. Recognising the case had caught the attention of people up and down the island, the newspaper filled its pages with coverage of it.

Jamaican newspapers had filled their pages with little except coverage of the war these past few years: 'The Hun Has His Back Against The Wall' and 'Certain Victory At Verdun' were typical headlines. *The Gleaner* was thrilled to have a story in its pages which titillated its readers. There was, the paper suggested, a moral to be found in A.C. Goffe's troubles. 'Thou shalt not kill,' the fifth commandment says. 'Thou shalt not steal,' the seventh commandment says. 'Thou shalt not covet thy neighbour's house…nor anything that is thy neighbour's.' The trial served, some said, as a morality tale of rich versus poor.

187

Nonsense, others said, it was simply a case of right against wrong, gentleman against vagrant. For those not concerned with guilt or innocence, the trial offered cheap – newspapers cost just a penny in 1918 – entertainment at someone else's expense.

On the day of *Rex v Goffe*, A.C. Goffe's trial at Port Maria, *The Gleaner*'s Port Maria correspondent was at the courthouse bright and early. He captured vividly the excitement generated by the case.

"It was nearly an hour before the time fixed for the opening of the Court that the first few spectators were observed wending their way into the Court House to secure their seats in the building. Thereafter the spacious courtroom filled rapidly. Extra chairs were brought in and every inch of space was utilized. Outside was a scene of unusual bustle and excitement; motor cars were rushing swiftly in all directions; buggies drove up to the front of the building and deposited their occupants; horsemen came cantering in from all sides."

The crowd was a thoroughly mixed one. There were simple labourers, people who likely toiled on one of Goffe or his brothers' plantations. Small settlers who struggled to farm five or ten acre plots in the shadow of the big estates with their thousands of acres were in attendance, as well. Also there were the moderately large planters and the big property owners, those who were most likely to sympathise with Goffe for taking the law into his own hands to protect his property and produce.

"The place was so packed as to become intensely uncomfortable, but so profoundly interested were the spectators, that so long as their physical powers could possibly withstand the close, reeking, atmosphere, so long were they prepared to endure discomfort," *The Gleaner* correspondent reported. "Many persons from other parishes of the island were observed among the spectators. The brothers of the defendant – all well known in the planting line – were also present." Prosecuting on behalf of the Crown was Jamaica's Attorney General, Sir Charles St John Branch. Defending Goffe was Henry Milne Radcliffe. His solicitors were Harold ('Hardy') Wilmot Whitehorne Dayes and A.C.'s brother, Cecil, a Port Maria attorney.

On 20 June, 1918, Goffe was taken from the cell where he'd been held at St Catherine District Prison to St Mary Circuit Court in Port Maria. Before leaving, he cleaned himself up. His brother, Cecil, had brought a gray tweed suit, tie, white shirt, hat, and white rose to decorate his buttonhole.

Both Goffe's friends and his foes knew it was going to be difficult for a jury composed of St Mary people to find the banana man guilty of murder. Though A.C. Goffe was a widely disliked figure, he was too important to the prosperity of the parish and the well-being of its citizens, hundreds of whom worked in one or other of his family's businesses, to sentence him to death. The planter had already confessed to shooting Prince Henry. The question was whether a jury of his peers would decide he killed in self-defence or not.

'All Rise for Chief Justice, His Honour Sir Anthony Michael Coll,' the bailiff bellowed. Justice Coll took his seat. Soon the preliminaries were done with and the prisoner was brought into the courtroom.

"He was neatly attired in a well-fitting suit of gray tweed and wore a white rose in his buttonhole," *The Gleaner* reported. "The long incarceration at Spanish Town and much mental worry had a visible effect on him." His step, the newspaper said, was a trifle unsteady. "As he entered the dock he brushed with his handkerchief the tears of remorse – for the defendant never denied having killed the man – that welled up in his eyes."

A.C. Goffe, *The Gleaner* said, wore an air of contrition throughout the trial and at certain moments showed signs of breaking down.

The testimony of three of the people who had lurked with Goffe in the dark grounds of Kingsley plantation – his chauffeur Eustace Rutherford, his yardman Walter Hyer, and his niece Grace – was as expected, favourable.

The testimony of two others there on the night Prince Henry was shot and killed was not so helpful. Sylvester Easy, a coachman, and Alexander Mendez, a schoolboy, had been riding past the Kingsley estate in a buggy at around 8 pm when they heard a shot, both said. Sylvester Easy earned his living in the coach and carriage trade. The advent of the motor car and of companies like the St Mary Motor Company, a transportation firm begun by Goffe and his brothers, had begun driving away what few passengers the coachman had left. The coachman told the court that upon hearing the gunshot he made his way to the pasture with the young Mendez. There he found Goffe, Goffe's yardman, Goffe's chauffeur and his niece. Believing someone might have been shot and injured, Easy tried without success, he testified, to convince the group to search for what he believed was a wounded man. Alexander Mendez's testimony was equally damaging.

"Sylvester said, 'Let us go and search for the man'," Mendez told the court. The schoolboy's words made the planter seem every bit as callous as many in the parish believed him to be. "Mr. Goffe said," Mendez told the court, "'I can't bother with that.'" It was damning stuff. But the schoolboy's testimony was thrown into question when he revealed that the dead man, Prince Henry, had been kin to him. "Prince Henry was my cousin and the next morning I saw his dead body," Mendez said.

Mendez was led from the stand. Replacing him there was Port Maria's acting inspector of police, Thomas Hazlett, and a detective constable, Charles Nembhard. Nembhard said they did not find a weapon of any kind on Prince Henry's person. Both agreed this was unusual. It was unusual not because the deceased was supposed to have been a thief, but because a Jamaican was rarely far from his trusty cutlass, especially in agricultural areas. Praedial thieves, the policemen said, usually brought a bag or a box to collect stolen produce and a knife or a cutlass to cut and chop the banana or coconut away from its stem and, if necessary, to fend off those seeking to capture them. Henry, the policemen said, did not have a weapon of any sort.

Taking the stand next was Dr George Lescesne, a St Mary District Medical Officer. A senior physician in the parish, Lescesne's testimony, too, caused problems for Goffe. An outspoken, independent-minded man, Lescesne had become a D.M.O. shortly after completing his medical studies at Edinburgh University. Lescesne raised uncomfortable questions as to exactly what took place on the night of the shooting. Though Eustace Rutherford insisted Prince Henry rushed straight toward Goffe, Lecesne said the angle the bullet entered Henry's body did not indicate this.

Lescesne also pointed out that while the deceased had died from a single gunshot which struck him near his heart, there was, strangely, no damage to his left arm, at all. This indicated, Lescene said, that far from attacking Goffe and his group, Henry was probably taking defensive action to protect himself. Goffe also said, Lescesne pointed out, that he had shot the deceased at close range. But the District Medical Officer said the burning that occurred when a person was shot at close quarters was not in evidence on Prince Henry's corpse. It wasn't looking good for A.C. Goffe.

It was time for Goffe's barrister, H.M. Radcliffe, to try and sway the jury in his client's favour. His client had not, Radcliffe argued, intended to kill anyone. Goffe had gone to his banana and coconut estate armed with a double-barreled shotgun merely to protect himself should he be met by gun or knife-toting thieves, the barrister argued. Goffe had suffered badly at the hands of praedial thieves, Radcliffe told the jury. One of the planter's employees had been badly injured by a produce thief not that long ago, the barrister explained. Radcliffe asked the jury members if they did not see the tremendous irony that existed in this case. Goffe had employed Henry to track down praedial larcenists looting his estate. As it turned out, Henry, the man he employed as a ranger and entrusted with a gun, was, in fact, the thief himself. Henry was a produce thief, Radcliffe said, and by some strange, maybe just logic, he'd been killed with the very gun and bullets he'd returned to Goffe after being sacked for failing to stop the thefts. Was it not the right of a man, Radcliffe asked the jury, to feel safe, to not feel threatened on his own property?

Finally, it was the accused's turn to speak. A.C. Goffe entered the witness box and faced his barrister.

"From what direction did the deceased come?" Radcliffe asked.

"From the surveyor's track," Goffe answered.

"Wouldn't the surveyor's track be on the left hand side of where you were sitting?" Radcliffe asked.

"Yes," answered Goffe, brief and to the point as he'd been instructed to do.

"Weren't you sitting in a mass of honeycomb rock?" Radcllife asked.

"Yes," Goffe answered.

"And wasn't there a lot of bush there?" the barrister pressed.

"Yes," the planter answered.

"It was a very rough place indeed?"

"Yes"

"And it would be a very difficult place to get away from if someone was coming at you?"

"Very difficult indeed," answered Goffe.

"Did you hear Miss Grace Fraser call out," Radcliffe asked, *"'Oh Lord, Uncle Fred, he is coming?'"*

"Yes"

"The man never stopped after the young lady called out?"

"No"

"Weren't you very much afraid that night when the man was coming towards you?"

"Very much afraid," Goffe said.

"After you heard the gun could you see the man turn?"
"I saw him make a short wheel and he went towards the surveyor's track."
"Had the man wanted to run away couldn't he have gone in another direction?"
"Yes."

H.M. Radcliffe was finished with his witness. The prosecuting attorney, Charles St John Branch, Jamaica's Attorney General, was not so gentle with the banana planter.

"If you fired at the man, didn't you think he'd been shot?" Branch demanded.
"I thought if I'd caught him at all it would have been on his leg," Goffe replied sheepishly.
"Was it your intention to shoot anyone who came there?" Branch asked.
"No" Goffe said.
"What was your intention?" Branch demanded as the rapid-fire cross-examination went on.
"To protect myself," Goffe answered, becoming bolder.
"I put it to you that you shot the man when he was over the box," said Branch.
"No sir, not at all." Goffe responded.

After a forty-five minute grilling by the Attorney General, Goffe got some respite when Chief Justice Coll called for the proceedings to be adjourned for lunch. Lunch over, the prosecution and defence gave their closing statements. This was followed by the Chief Justice's instructions and summing up of the facts of the case for the jury. In his instructions, Coll said Prince Henry had been a praedial thief and praedial thieves were a curse on the island. He said certain plantations used armed guards. But the fact that praedial thieves were usually armed did not justify a man taking another man's life.

"It would be a terrible thing in this island if it got out that the life of a fellow creature had been taken away in any circumstances except those which the law recognized," Coll said coming dangerously close to telling the jury to convict Goffe. Coll had been accused in the past of trying to sway juries. One aggrieved attorney, who'd lost one too many cases before him, remembered Coll as a judge who possessed, "a keen intellect," but suffered "from unjudicial temperament." Coll, the attorney Ansell Hart said, usually made up his mind about the right and wrong of a case before he'd heard the evidence. "Usually everybody was wrong," Hart said, "and, joyous joy! Coll was there to set them right." Coll, Hart said, "heckled and grilled plaintiffs and their counsel." Hart conceded, though, that the Chief Justice was "incisive" and "usually right." All the same, Coll "played the very devil," Hart said, "with judicature in Jamaica."

Coll continued his instruction to the jury in *Rex vs. Goffe*. "If a person did not bring himself within the principle which the law required then he must be prepared to take the consequence. Persons could not be allowed to take life as they thought fit."

Whether A.C. Goffe took the life of Prince Henry in pre-meditated fashion or in self defence would be for the jury to decide. The jury was composed of a fairly representative group of St Mary citizens: There was the butcher, William Ellis, the coachbuilder, Henry Stultz, two shopkeepers, Mortimer Henriques and Wilfred Lucus Lindo, two overseers, Francis Langbridge and Arthur Roper, three clerks, Peter Slader Wilson, Ernest Prendergast and Ernest Bartlett, and three planters, William Evelyn, John George McGregor and Cecil George Silvera. Silvera was almost disqualified from serving on the jury when Goffe's legal team discovered that Silvera's brother, Leopold, had been defeated recently in a bitter land dispute case tried by Goffe's brother, Cecil, a St Mary attorney. But rather than have Silvera disqualified, Goffe's attorneys decided to keep him. They calculated that as Silvera was a part of the parish's landed gentry he would see Goffe, a planter like himself, as the injured party in this case.

The 12-man jury retired to consider its verdict at 3:15 pm. The defendant waited in the hot, crowded courtroom, his expensive attorneys on one side of him and his brother, Cecil, on the other side. The accused didn't have to wait long. It took the jury barely 15 minutes to ponder and render its verdict.

"As the jurors filed back into Court, it is safe to say the intensity of feeling took hold of every person present," reported *The Gleaner* breathlessly. "Anxiously they listened to the momentous query of the Clerk of the Courts as to how the jurymen found and every eye was riveted on the Foreman and the sense of hearing strained to the utmost as he replied in a firm, distinct voice, "Not Guilty." The jury had found, against all the evidence, that A.C. Goffe shot Prince Henry in self-defence. Goffe family members, friends and supporters were delirious.

"Despite the vigorous cries of 'Order, Order! by the police, the spectators in the courtroom broke forth with loud and continuous clapping," *The Gleaner* wrote. In an instant Goffe had become the people's champion for killing one of the people. "As Mr. Goffe left the dock," the paper reported gleefully, "he was borne in triumph on the shoulders of three or four young men of the working class. Men, women and children tossing up their hats, executing wild gestures of delight, shouting at the top of their voices, joined in one great demonstration of rejoicing. Not within living memory had such a scene been witnessed in the quiet seaside town."

But not everyone in Jamaica thought the verdict something to celebrate. The verdict, some said, was a shame and a disgrace and showed how unjust a country Jamaica was. *The Gleaner*, 'the planter's paper,' had supported Goffe throughout the trial and had been generous to him in its coverage. "All Jamaica would have been unspeakably shocked had the case against Mr. Alfred Constantine Goffe ended in a verdict against him," the paper wrote. "It will not be disputed that Mr. Goffe was being shamefully robbed…Besides, it is unfortunately a not uncommon occurrence for men to be attacked when merely protecting what is their own, and in no country in the world (save possibly Russia at the present time) will public opinion admit that a man has not the right to defend himself or his property against aggression."

But another newspaper, the *Jamaica Times*, a weekly published by W.R. Durie and edited by Tom MacDermot, better known as poet Tom Redcam, did not see things this way, at all. The paper condemned the decision, saying Goffe had been found innocent because Jamaicans valued the life of a rich man above the life of a poor one.

"The praedial thief deserves punishment and should get it swiftly and severely, but that punishment is certainly not to lose his life," wrote MacDermot. "Such a condition would be worse than the old time system of hanging a man who stole a sheep or a woman for stealing a loaf of bread." This view was echoed in several letters to the *Times*, including one from a Charles Kent. "The recent acquittal of Mr. A.C. Goffe of the capital charge of murder, or its alternative manslaughter, has raised much in some people whose minds are obsessed by the idea of ownership; that they fail to discriminate between the value of life and the value of property. To what are we drifting?" Kent asked plaintively. "The recent issue was between the rich and the poor, between a large property owner and a man who may not have even owned 6 foot by 6 inches, between society and a wastrel." Kent went on to say that the trial would have dire consequences, showing as it did to all and sundry that there was one law for the rich and one for the poor. "Nothing in the nature of property stolen can ever justify the taking of a man's life," he wrote angrily. "I am fully convinced if the accused was of Henry's class he certainly would have been brought in for murder, if not for manslaughter."

One reader suggested A.C. Goffe make recompense for the killing of Prince Henry by offering financial support to the dead man's family. "My suggestion is, that some provision be made for the dependents of the deceased, (for a period) in keeping with the amount of the financial loss sustained by them, as a result of his death," wrote Egerton M. MacMillan of 27 Duke Street, Kingston in a letter to the *Jamaica Times*. "I venture to think that this thoughtful, kind, humane act would not only lessen the weight of the blow, but will convince the man's people of Mr. Goffe's heartfelt sorrow, regret and sympathy with them in this their hour of great sorrow and trial, but he will be commended by all right thinking persons, and this act will further endear him to his people." Whether Goffe took this advice to heart is not known.

Emboldened by the result of the Goffe murder case, the planter class in St Mary went on the offensive against praedial larceny in the parish. They had a champion in the person of A.C. Goffe. So, days after his acquittal, a group of St Mary planters and public officials set up the Cane-Heap Committee of Protection Against Praedial Larceny.

The committee held its first meeting in the parish on June 24, 1918. Sir John Pringle, the parish's largest landowner, was the keynote speaker. His speech was a thinly veiled call to arms. God would only help those among them who helped themselves in the matter of praedial larceny, Pringle said inciting the banana men to take the law into their own hands as A.C. Goffe had done.

"The government in Jamaica had done all that the government in London would allow them to," Pringle said, referring to the Protection of Produce Act of 1896. "The people were therefore to…rid the districts of praedial thieves." Flogging was no cure, Pringle said. It was hardly a deterrent, at all. He told the Cane-Heap Committee of Protection Against Praedial Larceny they were to watch out for men who "only worked part of the week, the gamblers, the loafers and idlers and such like." They were the people, he said, who were "prowling in their neighbours fields at night." They were to watch every "suspicious person" who came into their village.

Pringle said horse theft had been rampant in St Mary in the past, but had been driven away by vigilantes. Pringle said better enforcement by the authorities of the Vagrancy, Gambler's and Trespass laws was one certain way to defeat produce thieves. Pringle asked those in attendance to put their hands over their hearts and swear a special oath:

"I hereby promise never to steal my neighbors goods and pledge myself to discourage the habit of praedial larceny," the citizens repeated, "and will report immediately and bring to light every thief or suspected person in the village in which I live."

A few weeks later another Goffe, Alec, found himself in court in Port Maria. Two young men, Felix Morgan and Clifford Lynch, were found guilty of stealing 15 bunches of marketable bananas from land owned by Alec Goffe. Goffe stood up and had his say in court.

"These boys, sir, steal all the time bananas and coconuts from my property," he complained. "They won't work, only gamble all day and they always have money. I have set out a watch for them long time and have just succeeded in catching them…I would like you to give them," Goffe asked the magistrate, "exemplary sentences." He got his wish. Felix Morgan, who had a long criminal record, was sentenced to six months imprisonment at hard labour in the General Penitentiary and given 12 strokes of the tamarind switch. Clifford Lynch, whose first offence it was, was given five months hard labour.

As for A.C. Goffe, if he was tortured at having taken a fellow Jamaican's life for stealing thirty-six coconuts from him, he didn't show it. Within weeks of his murder trial, he was off to the United States to put the final touches on a plan to re-enter the banana export business as soon as the Great War was over with.

Like other Jamaicans, Goffe was forced out of the export trade during the Great War by restrictions placed upon the importation of foreign produce by the American government. Foreign importers were not allowed to bring their produce to the United States without special licences granted by a special Caribbean Committee. As the members of this committee were mostly the executives of American banana firms few foreign exporters like Goffe received licences. With restrictions on the export of fruit to the United States, Canada and England, as well, there was little for a banana man to do during the war years but sit the conflict out and wait patiently for its end to begin business again. The Lanasa and Goffe Steamship and Importing Company had been the only Jamaican firm in the banana export trade immediately before the war begun in 1914. A.C. Goffe wanted a company owned and operated by him and his brothers to be the first into the market at the end of the war.

The End Of The Affair

Jamaica For Jamaicans

'Nationalism is power hunger tempered by self-deception.'

George Orwell

With the war finally over in November 1918, banana prices quickly recovered to their pre-war levels. Jamaican banana people were keen to get back to business. But by the time A.C. Goffe was ready to launch his new company in 1919, an upstart, the Jamaica Fruit and Shipping Company, had already gotten there before him. The managing partners of the new company were Sibrandt Duhn List, a Danish born American citizen who'd been a United Fruit Company manager, and Charles Edward Johnston, a Jamaican banana merchant who began his life in the banana trade at the tender age of twelve. Johnston's father, Patrick, a merchant from the town of Lucea, in Hanover in western Jamaica, had begun shipping a few loads of bananas in the 1880s to cities in the southern United States.

Charles Johnston, or Mass Charlie as everyone called him, quickly established an impressive record of achievement in the banana trade. He was part of the team that set up a banana company in Portland, Jamaica in 1893. He was part of the team that set up the Fruit Importing Company in the United States in 1904. He was also part of the team that established the Atlantic Fruit Company in 1905 in Baltimore. It was because he had such an impressive resume that Johnston was able to convince a Who's Who of Jamaica's biggest landowners and banana planters to join his new firm, the Jamaica Fruit and Shipping Company Ltd, in 1919.

Among those Johnston convinced to join him, surprisingly, was A.C. Goffe's brother, Alec. Joseph Di Giorgio, a longtime enemy of A.C. Goffe, also became a partner in the enterprise. That Alec Goffe should choose to join forces with Di Giorgio and Johnston smacked of betrayal to his brothers. Wasn't Di Giorgio the same man who had almost led to A.C. being sent to prison in 1908? A.C. Goffe viewed the Jamaica Fruit and Shipping Company as an unholy alliance which threatened his interests in the banana trade.

Yet the truth was Goffe and his brothers had happily done business in the past with those they considered enemies. In 1899, for example, Messrs Goffe Bros, the banana purchasing company set up by A.C. and his brothers, leased a large banana plantation in Annotto Bay, St Mary with David Gideon and Charlie Johnston. In 1910, Alec Goffe, in a private venture apart from Messrs Goffe Bros business, joined Herbert Robinson, a Kingston solicitor, in the purchase of the 1,240 acre St Catherine sugar estate, Cherry Garden. This venture proved so successful the two purchased the 50-acre St. Andrew property, Liguanea Villas together a few years later.

It wasn't Alec alone that did business with people outside the family. In 1915, his brother, Clarence, bought the 1,650-acre St Catherine sugar estate, Treadways, with Sam Walker. By 1921 the two were ready to sell the property, though they had signed a 10 year contract promising Percy and Rupert Lindo of the Keeling Lindo Company they would provide them with the entire output of canes from Treadways for the Lindo's Bernard Lodge factory.

Treadways was fertile. It had 117 acres in cane, 23 acres in cocoa, 150 acres in guinea grass, 800 acres in commons, 15 acres in bananas, and an endless supply of logwood. In 1917, 2,500 coconuts were planted. The property had a large population of renters, another source of income.

Like other family businesses, Messrs Goffe Bros was fraught with sibling rivalry. Yet, despite differing personalities and outlooks, family had always come first. This time, though, blood had been, A.C. and his brothers believed, betrayed by ambition. It probably didn't escape their attention that a popular film in Jamaican cinemas at the time was the American feature, *Freddie's Family Feud*. Alec Goffe had found himself a new set of brothers. Their names were: Charlie Johnston, Joseph Di Giorgio, and Sam Walker.

Sam Walker, like Alec Goffe, was a big landowner in St Mary parish. Unlike him, though, he was a mostly well-liked figure. When Walker's daughter, Alma, whom a society columnist called 'one of St Mary's beauties,' married Alec's nephew, John, gossips in Port Maria joked that it was less a marriage than a business alliance.

Sam Walker liked to call himself a 'self-made' man. Determined to accentuate his humble beginnings, Walker was fond of telling people he'd been so poor when he got his first job in the banana industry as a cashier for the West India Trading Company, he slept at nights in the firm's offices wrapped in banana trash with the company's money tied to his body.

But Walker's friends said this was a tall tale. His father, Hugh Walker, had been a small landowner and Sam had not grown up in poverty, as he suggested. Samuel Magnus Walker's family had some connection to the wealthy Jewish Jamaican family, the Magnuses. Though the exact nature of the connection was not clear, Walker called his only son after them: Magnus McDonald Walker.

Though he was a wealthy and widely respected man by the time his son was accepted at Cambridge University in 1917, Sam Walker was much more excited at this achievement than any of his own. He hadn't had the chance to attend fancy Jamaican prep schools like Mary Villa and York Castle that Alec Goffe had. He felt unschooled and unsophisticated. After beginning his working life with the West India Trading Company, Walker became the St Mary representative of the S.S. Smith banana company, a post he continued to hold even after he became a director of the Jamaica Fruit and Shipping Company in 1919.

His wealth increased and he invested wisely. In quick succession he bought the large properties, Albion, Cromwell, and a piece of the huge Tremolesworth estate. He grew bananas, coconuts and raised cattle on his properties and became an executive of St Mary's Cattle Association and won a seat on St Mary's Parochial Board in 1910.

Though Walker was Alec Goffe's best friend, he never sought to become a member of the St Mary Country Club nor the Port Maria Tennis Club. With Goffe president of both the clubs, had Walker wanted to join the so-called 'soft-hand set' he could have. Walker preferred shooting, fishing and billiards to hob-knobbing with snobs. Walker did, though, like Goffe, become a Worshipful Brother of the District Lodge of Jamaica. But that was probably more to do with business than pleasure.

Alec Goffe was a bon vivant. He loved the social whirl, the networking, and the pressing of the flesh. Comparing Alec Goffe to Sam Walker, Daniel Hill Jackson, clerk of St Mary's Parochial Board and son of the legislator Richard Hill Jackson, said "taking the temperament of the two gentlemen into consideration I would sooner, to use a broad word, take a liberty with Mr. Goffe than Mr. Walker, as his rebuke in his calm way and look, would be far more stinging than Mr. Goffe speaking at the top of his voice."

Others, though, remembered Walker quite differently. "Unfortunately he never countenanced opposition," said St Mary resident and author Robert Meikle. Walker pursued those who opposed him with, Meikle said, "ruthless efficiency."

Sure, Sam Walker wasn't the orator Alec Goffe was, but Goffe wasn't the politician, Walker was, either. The two's strengths and weaknesses were in full view on the speaking tour they arranged in 1919 to introduce the Jamaica Fruit and Shipping Company to banana growers in St Mary. They motored to the usual St Mary spots – Guy's Hill, Belfield, Windsor Castle, Gayle – their cohorts in tow, exhorting to all and sundry that they ought to sign with the new company. Many big planters and small growers did come out to hear what Walker and Goffe had to say.

Growers knew Alec Goffe had a long and successful track record in the banana business. Just a year before, Goffe had won the respect of large and small planters when he stepped forward with a proposal to revitalize St Mary's banana industry, which had flagged badly during the war. Things had become so bad that even some established banana growers had been talking about giving up banana for sugar cane. At an emergency meeting at Port Maria Town Hall, Alec Goffe, offered a plan he said would save the parish's banana industry. Essentially, the proposal was for the island's government to help with a special reserve fund for St Mary growers, partly funded by applying a small tax on bananas exported from St Mary ports. Goffe figured around £100,000 could be set aside to help the parish's planters.

"The idea is," Goffe said at the meeting, "for the planters of St Mary, and St Mary alone." The government did not back the proposal and planters had to make do with whatever St. Mary loan banks extended them. Goffe had been instrumental in getting the island's government to help with the setting up of loan, or co-operative banks, in the parish. Hundreds of St Mary banana growers, with government support, established the Port Maria People's Bank Ltd.

The Governor saw to it that a loan was granted to the bank and an average of £20 each was extended to members of the institution. From humble beginnings the bank grew to around 500 members.

The bank's founders – mostly small banana growers – made Alec Goffe, chairman of the concern. Though Alec had done a good job, some said choosing a Goffe to manage the affairs of a small banana grower's co-operative bank was like choosing a fox to guard a chicken coop.

Because Alec Goffe played an important role in helping set up a co-operative bank in St Mary he was guaranteed an audience when he tried to interest settlers in his newest enterprise — the Jamaica Fruit and Shipping Company. At the meeting to introduce the firm to banana growers, Goffe began with a question. Had they, he asked the planters, the big men in the parish, not realised what had been occurring in the fruit trade these past several years? The United Fruit Company had been paying a pittance, Goffe said. It was common knowledge the American firm bought a bunch in Jamaica for only two shillings or so and sold that same bunch in the United States for three times as much. Only Joseph Di Giorgio had helped keep prices high, Goffe said praising his new Jamaica Fruit associate. He ignored, though, the part played by A.C. Goffe and his brothers in the banana trade, and made no mention of them. Without greater competition, Goffe said, alarming the growers, the price for a count bunch would drop as low as just one shilling and three pence.

If they did not want this to happen they should support the Jamaica Fruit and Shipping Company, he told the growers. If they wanted to know what his company had done for Jamaica in its short time in the trade, he would tell them, he said. Just a year before, growers received only seven pounds and ten shillings per 100 bunches from the United Fruit Company. Now, Goffe said, the price per 100 bunches of bananas had more than doubled to 15 pounds. "Jamaica like most other parts of the world has been suffering from profiteering," he said. "The worse sinners, however, seem to be the shipping profiteers," Alec Goffe said waxing lyrical from the stump. "Profiteers are the cannibals of commerce. They gorge themselves with the substance of their victims until their eyes bulge out with fatness, leaving the poor like Patience on a monument, smiling at grief."

Alec Goffe had his say, and then it was Sam Walker's turn. Goffe had been, at turns, poetic, fiery and condemnatory. He celebrated Charlie Johnston,

Joseph Di Giorgio and condemned the United Fruit Company and condemned Jamaican banana men whom he said were apathetic and complacent. Sam Walker was not tough on his countrymen. The Jamaican banana grower's woes could all, he said, be laid at the door of a single foreigner – Andrew Preston, boss of the United Fruit Company. Walker reached for a newspaper cutting buried in his pocket. Preston, Walker said, had boasted to a newspaper that United Fruit once had many competitors, but those rivals had all fallen by the wayside. United Fruit's competition in the banana business was, Walker said quoting Preston, "now in the graveyard." But Jamaica Fruit was very much alive, Walker said.

A 'Jamaican Company for Jamaicans' is how the Jamaica Fruit and Shipping Company described itself in a circular distributed in Jamaica in 1919. This wasn't exactly correct. Sibrandt Duhn List, one of the firm's managing directors, was a Danish- American who'd been rewarded for his achievements as a sea captain and executive of the United Fruit Company with a knighthood from the King of Denmark. Another director of the company, Italian-American, Joseph Di Giorgio, had presided over the Atlantic Fruit Company when it had conspired with United Fruit in 1910 to fix banana prices. Despite this, though, Jamaica Fruit continued to emphasise how Jamaican it was. 'Every Penny We Make Remains In Jamaica' and 'You Have Nothing To Lose But Your Chains,' were just two of the slogans employed by the firm in its advertising in 1919.

The company calculated that appealing to black pride and to a lingering distrust of Americans would win Jamaican banana growers loyalty. Other businesses, too, used similar methods to sell their products. The Lascelles de Mercado Company, for example, began selling a brand of matches called, Jamaica Born. "All Born Jamaicans should use the "JAMAICA BORN" Match," a 1914 advert reads. "Employ your own countrymen before you employ Swedes and others...They are fully as good as any other...JAMAICA BORN are just the same price as other good brands on the market...You give employment to your fellow country men when you buy JAMAICA BORN. This is the point which should plump down the scale in favour of the locally produced match."

Charlie Johnston and the other Jamaica Fruit executives recognised that black Jamaicans, many of whom had fought in the First World War, were not as docile as they had been before the war. They were more self-confident, self-possessed and determined to assert their identity and their independence.

"Be as proud of your race today," said Marcus Garvey, the Jamaican Black Nationalist, "as our fathers were in days of yore." Garvey had launched his Universal Negro Improvement Association in 1914 in Jamaica. Its goals, were he said, "to promote the spirit of race pride and love...To reclaim the fallen of the race...To conduct a worldwide commercial and industrial intercourse." In 1916, Garvey moved to the United States, and before long the UNIA had a membership of more than a million in America.

"If we are...to become a great national force, we must start business enterprises of our own; we must build ships and start trading with ourselves between America, the West Indies, and Africa."

But despite, or perhaps because of Garvey's success, some critics, like *Daily Gleaner* editor H.G. de Lisser, sniped at him and his movement.

"You will remember that Marcus, after having decided that Africa was to become a republic, at once proceeded to create some dukes, knights and other noble personages," de Lisser said sarcastically in one of many such articles he wrote about the Garvey movement in *The Gleaner*. "I think I met one or two some time ago: the Earl of Stewed Orange, and the Baron of de Banana...Garveyism is not democratic. It is autocratic. It is arrogant. It is amusing..."

Still, despite detractors, Garvey's movement continued to grow in the United States, and in Jamaica. "We have a beautiful history," Garvey said, "and we shall create another in the future that will astonish the world." The world was astonished when on 15 September 1919, the first of Garvey's *Black Star Line* of steamships prepared to launch in New York City. "Yesterday was a red letter day in the history of Negroes of the U.S.," a report in an American newspaper said. "The first ship of the Black Star Line Steamship Company of which Marcus Garvey is president was inspected by thousands of Negroes in New York." Garvey even won over some in the African-American community who'd opposed him, like William Pickens, a director of the National Association for the Advancement of Colored People. "The creation of a shipping line even in embryo," Pickens said, "is one of the greatest achievements of the twentieth century Negro."

In Jamaica, Garvey's talk of black self-determination and black pride was having an effect, too. But his call for repatriation to Africa was rejected by most Jamaicans. 'Jamaica for Jamaicans' proved a far more compelling slogan for Jamaicans than Garvey's 'Africa for the Africans.' Henry Ward, a Presbyterian minister, member of the Parochial Board in St Mary and a leader in the movement that sprang up after the war to create a banana co-operative, recognised this.

"Today the new slogan is "Jamaica for Jamaicans," Ward wrote in the *Jamaica Critic* journal in 1926. "It is not the word of a narrow insularism; it is a claim of a fundamental right, an expression of the law of self-preservation. This is the land of our fathers, for which they toiled and suffered and died; it is the only land we dare call home."

Secrets and Lies

'Ambition breaks the ties of blood'

Sallust

A.C. Goffe was short – five foot six inches or so tall – and dark-skinned. He was a little man with a big voice. By all accounts, he was not well-liked nor did he want to be. By contrast, Alec Goffe, who was tall, 6 foot one inch and light-skinned, was a popular man about town in Port Maria. He had been a president of the St. Mary Country Club, a president of the Port Maria Tennis Club, and a Worshipful Brother of the Port Maria chapter of the District Grand Lodge of Jamaica Under The Grand Lodge Antient of Free and Accepted Masons of Scotland, a Masonic brotherhood. He sat, too, on the board of Gray's Charity, a poor house for the exclusive benefit of the 'respectable poor of St. Mary.'

He was a highly clubbable fellow to whom few doors were closed. Alec Goffe was, said George Harvey Clarke, a longtime Resident Magistrate in St. Mary, known for lavish hospitality and a fund of inexhaustible, highly amusing stories. One of the stories Alec was most fond of telling concerned St Mary's Parochial Board. Board members, upset at what they believed was an over-use of foreign words by some board members, passed a resolution banning the use of other than English words in the discussion of parish business. But Alec Goffe, who was fond of showing off his boarding school education – he had won a prize for excellence in Greek at York Castle – forgot the ban, and ended a speech with a Latin phrase. "Our motto, gentlemen," Goffe implored, "must be 'nil desperandum.'" The Parochial Board member who had pushed for the introduction of the ban on foreign words jumped to his feet in disgust, and pointed at Goffe and said angrily: "Yu see dat now? I gawn...Him talking French."

Alec Goffe was a sophisticate, well schooled and urbane, and he didn't care who it upset. It won him enemies and it won him friends.

"Some few persons of colour had what might be called a flair for society, and might be admitted," wrote author and attorney Ansell Hart of Jamaica's racial caste system. Alec Goffe was one of those few men of colour admitted. "By and large persons of marked colour were not on visiting terms with the whites or near whites," Hart explained, "nor were they readily accepted in the more exclusive clubs in Kingston." As well as being a member of all of the clubs in St Mary that mattered, Goffe was a member of Kingston and St. Andrew's most exclusive clubs and associations, too. He was a member of the Jamaica Imperial Association, the Liguanea Club, the Jamaica Jockey Club, the Kingston Cricket Club, and the St. Andrew Club. Here he would have rubbed shoulders with the Governor, members of the Legislative Council, itinerant English aristocrats, and large planters of sugar and, like him, large planters of bananas and coconuts. Members of these clubs liked to tell themselves that here at the Liguanea and at the St. Andrew Club was where Jamaica was really being governed.

The rivalry that existed between Alec and A.C. Goffe was not just of their own making; others actively encouraged it, as well. When it became clear in 1919 that Robert Percy Simmonds, St Mary's longtime representative in the island's Legislative Council, was ready to step down, competing sides rushed to nominate candidates. Unhappily for the brothers, the names of both Alec and A.C. were put forward for the seat. A Mr. H. St. J. Jones of 93 Orange Street, Kingston took it upon himself to submit a slate of names of Jamaicans he felt ought to be nominated to stand for Legislative Council seats. He selected A.C. as the man he believed ought to represent St Mary. This was a surprise, as A.C. had not participated at all in the political life of his parish. Three days after H. St. J Jones' list appeared in *The Gleaner*, a fan of Alec's, Leo Rankin, a former member of St Mary's Parochial Board, wrote an angry letter to the paper saying that H. St. J. Jones was talking nonsense and knew nothing of St Mary parish's politics. It was Alec, not A.C., who should be put forward to fill the empty seat in the Legislative Council.

"Someone suggested Mr. A.C. Goffe, in your Monday's issue as a suitable representative for St Mary," wrote Leo Rankin. "As one who has been identified for a number of years with elections in the parish and having a knowledge of the possible candidates for election," Rankin explained, "I do not hesitate to say that I do not consider A.C. Goffe a fit successor to Mr. Simmonds." Rankin's language was unusually harsh. "Mr. Goffe has been too busy for years in the fruit business, and in the rush of his business, he has not been able to find the time to devote to even the administration of parochial affairs. He is an excellent and conscientious man but does not carry that sound acquaintance and experience that form a sine qua non in the qualifications for election to Council."

Leo Rankin pointed to the only man he thought fit to represent St Mary. "Mr. A. Davidson Goffe is the proper person – the man of the hour – and it would be a pity if he failed to come forward! Electors should induce him to run. From 1905 the name of Mr. Davidson Goffe has been associated with the Legislative Council." If he had any thought of stepping forward, A.C. did not after Leo Rankin said he would make a poor candidate. Alec was, as expected, selected to run for the Legislative Council seat.

A few years later, in 1924, the simmering feud between the two brothers boiled over. A.C. accused Alec of mismanaging and misappropriating monies from Oxford, a large banana plantation owned by the two and by their brothers Ernest, Clarence and Rowland and their sister, Laura. A.C. demanded the property be split up.

Oxford had been a profitable property for its owners over the years. It produced large amounts of bananas, coconuts and oranges. Chunks of it – five and ten acres here and there – were leased to small cultivators who could not afford to buy their own plot. It, and Lee Wharf and the Kirk Corner Buildings, seem well managed, but A.C. was bitter his siblings had elected Alec, who was two years his junior, manager of Oxford, and not him.

The two disagreed about everything. They argued over how Messrs Goffe Bros ought to be run, how the Lanasa and Goffe Steamship and Importing Company ought to be managed. None of this mattered much until Alec decided to join Charlie Johnston and Joe Di Giorgio as a partner in the Jamaica Fruit and Shipping Company in 1919 instead of joining A.C., as his brothers John, Horace, Cecil, and Clarence had in a new banana export firm, the Baltimore and Jamaica Trading Company.

When Charlie Johnston later leveled a bitter series of attacks against A.C. Goffe in *The Gleaner*, suggesting he was a traitor to Jamaica and was conspiring with American big business to undermine the Jamaican banana industry, and Alec, a frequent writer of letters to the island's newspapers, did not send a letter condemning Johnston's attack, it was clear the sibling's relationship had come to an end. It was time for a legal separation. That came in 1925 with a lawsuit filed by A.C. demanding partition of property owned by him and his siblings.

'And whereas some time in the year One thousand nine hundred and twenty four disputes arose between the said Alfred Constantine Goffe and the said Alexander Davidson Goffe as to such management and the said Alfred Constantine Goffe threatened to issue a Partition Suit claiming a partition of Oxford Plantation and the premises aforesaid."

A.C.'s share of the estate and other holdings were bought out by Alec and his other siblings. A.C. went his way, eventually, to neighbouring St. Ann parish, and Alec, who eventually became sole proprietor of Oxford, went his way, never to meet, at least on friendly terms, again in life.

Alexander Davidson Goffe existed in a strange and rarified world which seemed, at first glance, to pay no heed to colour. His friends included the eccentric English aristocrat, Sir George Vernon, who stayed with him at his St Mary plantation whenever he was in Jamaica. Vernon left his family estate Hanbury Hall in Worcestershire and his family fortune on his death to his farm foreman's 16-year old daughter in an act of spite. Vernon was a strange friend for Alec Goffe to have. He was a member of the British Union of Fascists and a close friend of its leader Sir Oswald Mosely, whose Berlin wedding Adolf Hitler and Josef Goebbels attended.

With World War imminent after Hitler's re-arming of Germany in 1936, Nazi sympathisers like George Vernon would have been closely monitored by the authorities and it's anyone's guess what British Intelligence made of the knight of the realm with a fondness for fascism and a strange relationship with a black Jamaican.

Alec Goffe's marriage to Lesline Isaacs, the daughter of a Jewish merchant from Brown's Town, St Ann was, in its way, just as strange a relationship. At the turn of the 20th century, when Alec and Lesline married, mixed marriages were very rare. A white man could take a black or coloured woman as a mistress, as a concubine, but if he married her he would have been ostracised by other whites.

"Roughly speaking, Black and Coloured Persons 'knew their place,'" wrote author Ansell Hart, "an awkward situation arose when he aspired to marriage."

For a man of colour like Alec Goffe to seek to marry a white woman in early 1900s Jamaica, the Edwardian era, would have been condemned by many black and coloured people as brash and presumptuous. Whites would have thought such a pairing unacceptable or even unnatural.

"Would any white man…fail to shudder at the idea of consigning his daughter into the arms of a Negro husband?" asks a character in the Jamaican novel, *Marly, A Planter's Life in Jamaica*. "Black men may become rich. White parents may then be so unfeeling as to consign to the arms of the old and frail though wealthy Negroes their lovely daughter. This must happen in the course of time."

It did happen in the course of time. But Goffe, almost 30 years older than the 18-year old white girl he took for a wife, wasn't the first in his family to take a nubile, well-born white woman as a bride. Alec's older brother, Cecil, a Port Maria attorney, described by one admirer as 'pure, golden of heart and with the North shore's most powerful voice when cross examining,' married Mildred Bryson, daughter of George Samuel Bryson, owner of the St Mary property, Konigsberg, on Thursday 19, April, 1906, at St Cyprian's Church at Highgate, St Mary, the very day the new church was dedicated and opened.

"Open me the gates of Righteousness that I may go into them," the Archbishop of Jamaica demanded at the dedication of the church. The doors were opened, and the church blessed. The dedication ceremony over, it was time for the first event held in the new church: The marriage of 25-year old Mildred Maitland Bryson to 46-year old Cecil Herbert Clemetson Goffe. The bride's wedding dress was made of ivory duchess satin. Her two sisters, who acted as bridesmaids, wore green crepe merle, trimmed with white chiffon and hats of green and white with pink banskia roses and "sheperd's crooks" with pink boquets. The bride's mother wore a dress of grey volle with a hat to match, trimmed with pink chrysanthemums. It was, eyewitnesses said, a splendid affair.

Cecil and Mildred do not appear to have suffered much discrimination. Their child, Eileen Clemetson-Goffe, though, lived a tortured existence, happy she was the daughter of a white woman, distressed she was the daughter of a black man. Born in 1909, three years after her parents married, Eileen was raised in comfort and splendour on her father's St Mary estate, Roslyn. Ironically, whatever privileges she enjoyed came not as a result of her mother's white family, but as a result of the wealth and influence of her father and his black family. Cecil had been educated at boarding schools in England and qualified as an attorney there before returning home to Jamaica.

Eileen's mother's family – the Brysons – was not a prominent family in St Mary. From English expatriate stock, they were not a part of the local society world. The Brysons lived in a state of genteel poverty. Like other English Creole families, their forbears came out to the West Indies in the years before Emancipation expecting to make a fortune. This didn't happen.

The Goffes, the Clemetsons, the Marshes, the Silveras, the Prendergasts, the de Lissers got rich off the banana; the Brysons didn't. By the time of her marriage to Cecil in April 1906, Mildred's father was dead. Her mother, two sisters and five brothers didn't stand in the way of the union. They'd fallen on hard times and had taken, humiliatingly, to working as overseers on the plantations of others to make their meagre living.

For the Brysons, Jamaica had exhausted its potential and its possibilities. In time they all left. Two of the brothers – J. Maitland Bryson and George Naughton Bryson – fed up with their black luck in the West Indies set off to begin a new life in the frozen wilds of Canada, far from their sister Mildred, their black brother-in-law, Cecil, and their coloured niece, Eileen.

Like her uncles, Eileen was determined to get out of Jamaica. Privileged or not, it was still for her a prison, a racial one. After school at St Hilda's in St Ann parish, she went off to continue her studies in England. She returned home for a time, doing nothing more useful than arranging tennis and golf tournaments and organizing outings at the local movie house. For a sophisticate it was a miserable existence. She returned to England during the Second World War and somehow managed to hide her race and join the Women's Auxiliary Territorial Service.

The British Armed Services had erected a 'colour bar' to keep blacks and other non-whites out of, at least, the important positions in its military. Crafty and cunning, Eileen skirted their racial barrier and became a staff sergeant in the Women's Auxiliary Territorial Service anyway. Though most of the women who joined the Territorial Service did nothing more exciting than work as secretaries, telephone operators and postal workers, others got much more challenging assignments. Some were sent to Occupied France on spying missions that required them to hide themselves among locals without their true identities being discovered.

She wasn't on a mission, but Eileen went deep into Nazi dominated Europe in 1936. On a sightseeing tour, and seemingly oblivious or indifferent to the Jews and other ethnic minorities fleeing the Continent, she visited Hitler's homeland, Austria, which had adopted pro-German policies and just signed a co-operation treaty with the Nazis meant to bring the two German speaking countries closer together. In 1936, Austria wasn't a friendly place for Auslanders, outsiders. It was a hostile time and place for Europeans who were not Aryan, much less a black woman from Jamaica.

Whatever Eileen Clemetson-Goffe's job was in the Territorial Service, she was so successful at it she was later assigned to the British Army staff in Washington D.C. It's clear the British top brass had no inkling that a black woman was hiding among the staff they sent to work at their diplomatic headquarters in Washington. It would have caused an international incident. The United States was still a deeply segregated country in the 1940s and had the Americans discovered Eileen they would have demanded she be replaced. She remained undetected, however, and was able after the war to become a permanent resident in the United States.

She steered clear of neighbourhoods where others of her race might expose her ruse. She moved instead to the waspy, white town of Darien in Connecticut. Eileen's training in the Women's Auxiliary Territorial Service stood her in good stead there. She lived undercover in this Anglo-American bastion for forty years until her death, her black and Jamaican roots hidden from friend and foe, alike. Her cover was never broken. When a Jamaican cousin asked Eileen to play host to her on a visit she was planning to the United States, she was rebuffed. 'You'll mess things up here for me,' the cousin was told. The cousin shot back, 'Remember your father will always be a coloured man.'

Unlike their daughter Eileen, Cecil and Mildred Goffe confined their lives mostly to Jamaica. The two did, though, travel together to Baltimore in July, 1907. Daring, or maybe just foolish, the black Jamaican man and white Jamaican woman did somehow manage to escape harm in a city where black men were lynched for far less than consorting with a white woman. A black man accused of glancing in the general direction of a white woman in the American South in the 1900s could expect to be hunted down by a mob of whites and hung from a tree, his sexual organs cut off. While Cecil and Mildred were visiting Baltimore in July 1907, in the town of Crisfield, nearby, a black man, James Reed, was lynched, his body dismembered by a mob of whites.

As for blond, blue-eyed Lesline Goffe, Alec's wife, she, too, went to Baltimore with her black husband. Married in 1910, she moved into 'Oxford House', his 500-acre St Mary estate. The house, four miles from Port Maria, had five bedrooms, a dining room, a drawing room, hot and cold water plumbing, a swimming pool, and a verandah with a splendid view of the Caribbean Sea.

It wasn't until almost a year after the two married that they went on a honeymoon. They went to Baltimore on 15 July, 1911 aboard the Lanasa and Goffe steamer, the *Katie*. In the manifest of alien passengers, Lesline's complexion is described by the immigration officer as *white*, her hair as *light*, and her eyes as *blue*. The 18-year old, 5 foot 3 inch Lesline and the 45 year old, 6 foot one inch Alec must have made quite a sight on the streets of Baltimore in 1911. Sixty black men were lynched in the United States that year, two of them in Maryland in July 1911 while Alec and Lesline were visiting the city. Lesline's first visit to Baltimore couldn't have been that traumatic as she returned for another visit two years later in 1913. Interestingly, though she'd been classified by immigration officers as *white* on her first visit, this time, in the company of not just her husband, Alec, but his brothers, A.C. and Clarence as well, her race was classified, as was that of the Goffe brothers, as *African British*.

But Lesline didn't have to go abroad to feel the sting of exclusion. Her embrace of a man of colour was a journey of no return away from her white family in Jamaica. They told her never to darken their door again.

"Her parents told her to take whatever furniture she wanted," confided Dickie Jobson. Jobson, director of the Jamaican film, *Countryman*, first met Lesline in the 1960s when he used to visit friends who lived at her home on Hope Road in St. Andrew's parish. "I don't think she ever went back to her parent's house and her parents never spoke to her again. That's what she told me. It wasn't accepted no, not at all."

Accepted or not, Alexander Davidson Goffe married Lesline Gertrude Isaacs on 15 June 1910 at St. Andrew Parish Church. She was 27 years his junior. He was 45 years old and she was only 18. "On or about December 1910 human nature changed," wrote English author Virginia Woolf. "All human relations shifted." They didn't shift in Jamaica. Had Alec and Lesline not been black and white, they would likely have received hundreds of words of fawning coverage and a large picture in *The Gleaner* newspaper, as was usually the case when the well-to-do and the well-placed married one another. The nuptials received only a standard notice in a column bought for a few shillings: *GOFFE-ISAACS- At Half-way Tree church on Wednesday, 15th June, by the Rev. E. J. Wortley, Lesline Gertrude, youngest daughter of the late A. A. Isaacs Esq., of St Ann's, to Alexander Davidson Goffe, J.P. of Oxford, St Mary.*

The surviving photograph of Alec and Lesline's 1910 wedding shows a happy, multi-racial gathering, everyone elegant in the Edwardian fashions of the time. Though the bride's family boycotted the affair, and the groom's large family is not much in evidence either, the couple's friends came out in support.

"I was amazed to see a picture of a mixed marriage in those days," said Island Records founder Chris Blackwell, who grew up in Jamaica in the 1950s. He, like Dickie Jobson, first met Lesline when visiting friends who'd rented rooms from her at her home on Hope Road. "A black and white relationship must have been quite something in those days," said Blackwell, a white Jamaican whose late wife was African-American. "It was quite something when I was growing up in Jamaica, so it must have been something back then in the early 1900s. But what I like about the wedding photo is that everything seems very relaxed, natural as can be."

Pictures, though, tell only part of the story. Alec and Lesline made a tough accommodation to sooth racial prejudices. The couple's 35-year long marriage remained childless not because Lesline couldn't have children, but because they were afraid they would have a child with too strong a touch of the tar brush.

"Lesline had to promise not to have a child by Uncle Alec," explained 92-year old Mary Jane Todd, Lesline's niece and the couple's godchild. Born in 1911, a year after the two married, Todd spent a good part of her youth in the 1920s and 1930s with the couple at their estate in St Mary. In town,

Kingston and St. Andrew, the couple enjoyed a rich, varied social life filled with friends and large expensive parties that became legend. None of this made up, though, for the Faustian contract they signed with the Devil.

"She told me that and I heard that many times that because of the way things were," explained Todd, "she promised her family that she would not have a child by him because he was a coloured man and it would not be a good thing. It was a promise to the family because colour played a very big part in those days."

Colour certainly did play a big part in life in Jamaica in those days. As for Eileen Clemetson-Goffe, who was born in 1909, a year before Alec and Lesline Goffe married, though she was a favourite of the couple, if she was an example of how a child born of a black man and a white woman would come out, then, it was decided, it would be best not to tempt Fate.

Eileen Clemetson-Goffe's struggle was in vain, too. Sure she was pale of skin, but her features and the texture of her hair betrayed her roots. Likely she made use of the revolutionary new hair products which had been developed in the United States for Negro women and could be found in Jamaican shops. 'Wonderful Hair Grower,' read an advert for the Madame C.J. Walker company, a leading manufacturer of beauty products for black women in the early 20th century. 'Nourishes and stimulates the growth of stubborn, lifeless hair.'

The Madame C.J. Walker line included Complexion Soap, Vanishing Cream and a revolutionary wide toothed Straightening comb and chemical hair softener and straightener which claimed it could de-kink or straighten Negro hair.

Black women had used various potions to straighten their hair before. Madame Walker's products were the first not to endanger the user's well-being or life. In times past, black women placed their hair on tables or other flat surfaces and pressed it with a fiery hot flat iron. One of the first places in Jamaica to sell Madame C.J. Walker's revolutionary new products was the Kingston general store owned by Alfred Noel Crosswell, a close friend of Eileen's father, Cecil. Jamaica made it hard to forget race, colour and caste matters. Sometimes even a simple film like, 'The Masked Woman' and 'UnMask', two films shown at Port Maria's cinemas in the 1920s, seemed, somehow, to refer to the island's racial anxieties. "A mask," an advert for "The Masked Woman" read, "might save your face but not your reputation."

It would take more than fancy hair straighteners and expensive foundation creams to make a black woman into a white woman, though. For anyone considering passing for white the Rhinelander case, which was splashed across American newspapers for much of 1924, offered a cautionary tale. The 'Roaring Twenties' was a time of unprecedented economic prosperity in the United States. Barriers of all sorts came down. It was in this climate that Kip Rhinelander, the son of a white New York tycoon, fell in love with Alice Jones, a woman of mixed race ancestry who'd worked as a domestic in the homes of some of America's wealthiest families. After a three-year long romance, in which almost a thousand love letters were exchanged, Kip Rhinelander married Alice Jones.

Within months, a court battle began. Rhinelander's father had employed detectives to investigate his daughter-in-law's pedigree. The detectives told Rhinelander Snr that his daughter-in-law was a black woman passing for white. Kip Rhinelander was pressed by his father into seeking an annulment of the marriage on the grounds his wife, Alice, had deceived him into believing she was white. Mrs. Rhinelander was neither wholly black nor white. She was, like Eileen Clemetson-Goffe, a quadroon, that is, a person with one white parent and one parent of mixed black and white blood.

Mrs. Rhinelander told the court her husband had spent many long hours with her father and brother and could not have failed to notice their dark skin. She also told the court that before their marriage, her husband told a friend that he didn't care what race she belonged to. Kip Rhinelander's physician testified at the trial that it was likely the love and affection Mrs. Rhinelander showed her husband that helped heal his bad stammer and other nervous afflictions.

It was clear that the driving force behind the case was Kip Rhinelander's father, a bigoted real-estate magnate worth millions of dollars. He was pressing his son to seek an annulment so the Germanic family name and bloodlines would stay "pure." It was a desperate spectacle, one in which the judge approved a motion by attorneys to have Mrs. Rhinelander strip naked to reveal her true colour to jury members. The trial went on for several months and stayed on the front page of American and other newspapers for more than a year. Finally, Kip Rhinelander was given his annulment much to the relief of white America.

Other marriages between blacks and whites also attracted the attention of the media. "Hoax Wedding By Coloured Paris Dancer" the British *Daily Express* newspaper reported on 20 June 1927. "Josephine Baker, the Coloured dancer and star of the Folies Bergere in Paris, is now Countess di Abantino of Palermo." Unlike in the Rhinelander affair, the parent's of the Italian aristocrat gave their full support to the marriage. "His mother came up from Palermo," Josephine Baker told the *Express* newspaper, "to look me over, and she being satisfied we had the knot tied."

Tragic is how many people described the Rhinelander case and tragic is how Sally Henzell, wife of Perry Henzell, the director of the Jamaican film, *The Harder They Come*, an indictment of corruption, prejudice and hypocrisy in Jamaica, described the relationship between Alec and Lesline Goffe and the accommodation to racism they made by agreeing not to have children.

"She wasn't a crusader, at all," said Sally Henzell of Lesline, whom she met when she rented rooms at her Hope Road home in the 1960's. "She just happened to fall in love with the Brown Man, Goffie, as she called him."

'The Brown Man', Alec Goffe, paid a very high price for white acceptance. But not having a child – who was likely to be black like him – probably seemed a small price to pay for access to a world of white privilege in Jamaica. An invitation that arrived at their home in St Mary in January 1931 probably made it all seem worthwhile. Alec and Lesline were among a select group of Jamaicans invited to a reception with members of the British Royal family. Desperate for proof that they, too, were top drawer, the island's high and mighty waited anxiously for their invitations. Hundreds attended the event on 4 February, 1931 at the governor's residence at King's House in St. Andrew. Afterward an informal dance, which began at midnight and ended at 5am, was arranged at the Constant Spring Hotel for the Prince of Wales, Prince George and some of their staff and a few locals, among them Alec and Lesline. Later still, the Prince of Wales, who a few years later gave up his Crown for the love of an American divorcee, held an even smaller gathering – a breakfast party for eighteen. Alec was not invited to this, but Lesline and her cousin, Hope, were. *The Gleaner* pointed out the next day, as if it mattered, that the Prince of Wales spent most of the night dancing with Jamaican beauty, Hope Cahusac.

Strange Fruit

'They gorge themselves with the substance of their victims until their eyes bulge out'

Alexander Davidson Goffe

The year 1919 looked as though it would be a good one for A.C. Goffe. A favourite pig of his, 5 foot 6 inch in length and 3 foot wide, was judged one of the finest hogs ever produced in St. Mary.

The year 1919 looked even better for his brother, Alec. It looked certain he would be selected to contest the St. Mary seat in elections for the island's parliament in 1920. Alec had also become a partner in a new banana export firm, the Jamaica Fruit and Shipping Company. He'd set out on a tour of St Mary banana areas to introduce the company to growers. But while Alec and the other directors of Jamaica Fruit had been busy motoring across Jamaica from one banana district to another telling growers what their new firm had to offer them, A.C. Goffe had also been busy starting a new banana company. Acquitted of murder in June 1918, Goffe left Jamaica in September for the United States to see if he could find American moneymen willing to bankroll a banana company he wanted to start.

He met with investors in Pennsylvania, New York and Delaware. But nothing came of those talks. Not surprisingly, he found what he was looking for in the American city he knew best, Baltimore. Though it seemed at one point Goffe would resume his partnership with Antonio Lanasa, this didn't happen. What was past was past. Goffe had new partners now, and a new banana company called the Baltimore and Jamaica Trading Company.

Goffe's partners were: Ernest L. Dinning of the McCall-Dinning shipping agency; James Morfit Mullen; Charles Vincenti, and Andrew Ciotti. Two were Irish-Americans and two were Italian-Americans. The officers of the company were Charles J. Ciotti, Hector J. Ciotti, and Charles N. Doughty. The stockholders were described in a company circular as "capitalists of Baltimore, Pittsburgh, West Virginia, Virginia and Canada." On 23 October, 1919, A.C. Goffe and his partners incorporated the Baltimore and Jamaica Trading Company.

'Know all men by these presents that we the undersigned, do certify and state as follows, that the purpose or purposes for which the said corporation is formed…are the following…to plant grow cultivate and market all kinds of fruit vegetables nuts and produce and to buy store and sell all kinds of fruit vegetables nuts and produce. To engage in the importation of all kinds of fruit vegetable nuts and other produce and products raw and manufactured from West Indian and other ports places to trade generally in all manner of foreign or domestic products raw and manufactured to export to foreign ports and place American and other products raw and manufactured. To own control and acquire by lease purchase construction or otherwise steamships barges and vessels of all kinds of interest therein and to operate the same anywhere on the navigable seas and waters…and generally to engage in the business of shipbuilding and owning and operating steamships and other vessels and in the transporting of freight and passengers within and without the United States of America and elsewhere.'

His team in place in the United States, Goffe returned home to assemble the Jamaican team. James Hodge Byles, an experienced banana man, was made the Baltimore and Jamaica Trading Company's agent at Richmond in St Mary. Clarence Goffe was made the agent at Highgate, St Mary and W.E. Schliefer, was made the agent in Port Maria. The *Fort Morgan* and the *Fort Gaines* – the two steamships the firm chartered and had specially adapted for transporting tropical fruit – could each carry approximately 30,000 bunches and travel at a speed of 12 knots. The sailings were fortnightly at first. Accommodation for passengers was available, but was extremely limited.

The United States in which A.C. Goffe had set up the Lanasa and Goffe Steamship and Importing Company in 1906, was very different from the United States he returned to in 1919 to set up the Baltimore and Jamaica Trading Company. More than a decade had passed and a World War had come and gone. The United States emerged from the Great War an economic powerhouse, its economy in fine fettle. The 1920s was the 'Jazz Age', a time in America when many social, class and colour barriers appeared to be coming down.

This was the time of Al Capone and of the emergence of the Mafia. The Black Hand that caused Goffe so much trouble in 1908 had come and gone, replaced by bigger and badder gangsters.

This was also the time of the so-called, "Red Scare." both the US government and big business were terrified a worker's revolution would occur in the United States. In 1919, the Worker's Party, later the Communist Party of the United States, was formed. Mass arrests of political and labour leaders soon followed. In January 1919, the Dry Law, or Prohibition, came into effect, making the selling of liquor and beer illegal.

At the same time, in Paris, the League of Nations held its first meeting. In February 1919, a fledgling German political party, the Nazis, held its first important rally in Munich. The keynote speaker was Adolph Hitler. With all the turmoil, it is a good time for women in the United States. In 1920, women are granted the right to vote. It is also a time of great technological advances, as well. The first radio broadcast in the United States – featuring election returns from the Harding-Cox presidential election – is made by the Westinghouse Corporation of Pittsburgh.

This was, then, what America was like in the 'Roaring Twenties.' There were advances all around. There had been advances, too, in Jamaica. By the time Goffe launched his new fruit firm in Baltimore and returned to Jamaica in January 1920, the fruit firm his brother, Alec, was aligned with, Jamaica Fruit, was up and running and having some success convincing growers on the island that it was, indeed, a Jamaican company for Jamaicans. Its directors had set out on speaking tours and in a very short time made themselves well known to banana growers from one end of the island to the next. So success-ful was Jamaica Fruit it soon came to be called simply, 'the new company.'

Apart from banana, in 1920 Jamaica was busy, too, with Legislative Council elections. In Clarendon, the race involving James Alexander George (JAG) Smith, the popular black barrister and landowner, was attracting a lot of attention. People wondered whether Smith, whom his supporters styled 'the friend of the common man,' would be re-elected after his astounding victory in Clarendon in 1917.

In St Mary, the battle was for the seat vacated by Robert Percy Simmonds. Alec Goffe fancied his chances. Selected as a candidate to contest the St Mary seat in November 1919, Alec's opponent was the Anglican minister, William Thomas Graham, rector of St Cyprian's Church in Highgate. Graham was brother to the archdeacon of St Mary's Parish Church at Port Maria, John Henry Heron Graham. Graham was a late entry into the field. Clergy were difficult candidates to run against. They had the aura of the Church about them and a pulpit available to them. Alec Goffe calculated that St Mary, though it had its share of churches, was less concerned with clerical matters than it was with ones of commerce. He was devilish to his opponent, taunting the Reverend and asking audiences what a man whose job was to concern himself with their immortal souls could do for them here on Earth.

"I can do more for you in the Council than Mr. Graham who has care of his flock and the spiritual welfare of their souls to look after," Goffe told a crowd gathered in Port Maria. "He is a minister of the Gospel and his work is to save souls."

Alec Goffe's rhetoric sometimes got him in trouble. In 1913, seven years before his bid for a seat in the island's Legislative Council, he was severely critcised by *Gleaner* editor H.G. de Lisser in an editorial entitled, 'Workers Not Orators Are Needed At Parochial Boards.' Goffe had become chairman of the St Mary Parochial Board after Sir John Pringle, a Scotsman, stepped down as chairman to return to Britain to attend to personal business. Though duly elected as chairman, Goffe vacated the seat when Pringle returned to Jamaica in January 1913. Unkindly, H.G. de Lisser took Pringle's return as an opportunity to direct a slap at Goffe and the other black Parochial Board members whom he considered upstarts.

"Sir John Pringle is once more installed as Chairman of the St Mary Parochial Board – and obviously not a day too soon," de Lisser wrote stingingly. "In saying this, we must not be understood as casting any reflection on Mr. A. Davidson Goffe who patriotically vacated the chair…All we mean is that the members of the St Mary's Board – or at least some of them – require a strong man to handle them properly…one who on account of his age, experience, wisdom, dignity, and social standing, is admittedly their superior," de Lisser wrote. It wasn't really true that Pringle was Goffe's superior. After all, Pringle, a humble government medical officer when he arrived in Jamaica from Britain in the 1870s, only won his high social standing in Jamaica by marrying Amy Zillah Levy, daughter of wealthy Jamaican Jewish businessman, Isaac Levy. "There are a good many stump orators occupying seats at the Board: Gentlemen who like to hear themselves talking," de Lisser wrote, "who take a positive delight in playing to the gallery, and who never miss an opportunity of airing their views at unconscionable length on even the most trivial of matters."

Though he stepped aside for John Pringle, Alec Goffe didn't heed H.G. de Lisser's warning. He continued to use the parish's Parochial Board chambers to sharpen his rhetorical skills for the day when he, too, like his grandfather, Robert Clemetson, would become a member of the Legislative Council.

His opportunity came in 1920. He decided it would be best to run, essentially, as the candidate of the banana industry. A former assistant Superintendent of Roads in the island's Public Works Department, in a speech in Port Maria he said he would make it his business to convince government to construct better roads so the transporting of bananas would be quicker and easier. The Public Works Department had, Goffe said, made a hash of the country's roads and should be called the 'Public Waste Department.' Port Maria, he said, ought to be the very next place on the island to have a railway extension, crucial as the town was to the island's banana industry.

Popular as this talk was in Port Maria, it didn't win Alec Goffe any votes in other parts of St Mary. Other parts of the parish had long envied Port Maria. It got too much attention, they complained, and too much of the parish's resources. To lobby for their own interests, residents in Gayle set up the Western St Mary Citizens' Association. People in other parts of the parish followed suit. In the Oracabessa area, Wilford Ellis White, the owner of a well-known bakery, H.A. Webster, I.S. Magnus, R.A. and V.E Silvera help set up the Northern St Mary's Citizens' Association. All that was needed was for eastern and southern St Mary to set up their own associations, as well. St Mary was not a united place.

Something all parts of the parish agreed St Mary needed was better health care facilities. People agreed with Alec Goffe when he said District Medical Officers were not doing a good job. They should be paid, he said, a fixed salary and prevented from having a private practice.

As for education, poor children were, Goffe said, being turned out of school at far too early an age. Teachers were not to blame, he said. They were doing a fine job and ought to be better paid. He also called for an industrial college for St Mary and for a raft of scholarships to be set up for the parish's children.

"It is hard," Goffe said, "to find out how the labourer who is paid 1/3 pence a day can buy these dear things and cater for the needs of a family. My idea is to see if we cant get off some of the taxes from necessities of life and see that our poor people are better paid so as to be able to meet their humble demands."

Though Alec Goffe and the other hopefuls for a seat in the Legislative Council promised to improve this and promised to improve that, Jamaicans, at least according to the annual report by the Income Tax Commissioner, had never had it so good. The year 1920 was one of the most prosperous in Jamaican history.

"A good number of people had grown rich all of a sudden and decidedly a number of people were better off than they had ever been before," the Income Tax Commissioner's report for 1920 said. But this prosperity, figures show, was limited to only a very few. Only 9,000 out of around a million people had incomes high enough to pay taxes, at all. Many of Jamaica's less fortunate, unable to earn a decent income in the country, had left the country over the past several years to help build the Panama Canal. After the canal was completed many Jamaicans stayed on to work in the Canal Zone or labour on the banana plantations there. On the campaign trail in his bid for the St Mary seat in the Legislative Council, Alec Goffe returned time and again to the subject of expatriates and what their absence meant for Jamaica. Too many young Jamaicans, he said, had left the country to work in Cuba and Panama.

"Jamaica will be denuded; the island will be impoverished," Goffe said, "instead of being benefited we have to do something or other here to keep the strong young men in the island, and to attract those who are away to return." With wages in Jamaica two to three times lower than wages in the Canal Zone, a quick return was unlikely. What Goffe didn't say was it was plantation owners like him who'd helped drive wages down in Jamaica by encouraging the island government to bring indentured Indian labour, willing to work for a fraction of what Jamaican labourers demanded, into the country. "We allow our men to go away to enrich Cuba," Alec Goffe complained, "while Jamaica is famishing for their services."

He said the country had to try to create a fair wage system, "and keep our

sons here." I am, Goffe said, "a patriotic son of the soil. I am one of you."
He convinced no-one. His speech done, Goffe asked if there were questions.
Reverend E.J. Touzalin had one; a tricky one he knew would trip up this member of the plantocracy. Touzalin asked Goffe if he would see to it that large
properties were broken up so the small man could get a chance to be
landowners. "This," Goffe answered gruffly, "is being done."

The talking over, it was time for the voters to vote. They did this on 5
February 1920. The polls, two of them at the Court House in the centre of
Port Maria, were opened at 8am. Within a couple of hours some 70 odd
votes had been cast. This was a lot considering how small a number of people met the qualification to vote. Alec Goffe's supporters were dressed in their
candidate's gold and black colours. Supporters of his opponent were dressed
in their candidate's red and black colours.

"From the start motor cars and motor vans were busily engaged in conveying
voters from the country parts into the town," *The Gleaner* reported. As Goffe
and Graham partisans went back and forth into Port Maria Town Hall, each
tried desperately to convince the other to switch loyalties. "A staunch
Grahamite was ascending the steps when a supporter of Mr. Goffe greeted
him with these words," *The Gleaner* reported, "are you going to give your vote
to Mr. Goffe?' 'No!' loudly replied the voter, and enquired, 'do I look like a
fool?' Another man similarly accosted said, "Go away from me. I am no slave!"

It took five hours and twenty minutes to count the votes. The final tally
showed Alec Goffe was well beaten by the man of the cloth, Reverend W.T.
Graham. Goffe polled only 147 votes against Graham's 429 votes. The breakdown of the vote was revealing. While Port Maria and the surrounding area,
where Goffe and his family wielded the most influence, voted overwhelmingly
for the banana planter, outside of the capital town he hardly got a vote. In the
town of Richmond, for example, he got only four votes. In Windsor Castle,
he got just three votes. In Retreat, he got a measly four votes. In Belfield, he
got a paltry five votes, and in the town of Gayle in western St Mary, which
had long complained about Port Maria's so-called 'Banana Mafia', Goffe did
not receive one single vote. The *Jamaica Times*, a liberal weekly edited by Tom
MacDermot, exulted at the Goffe defeat. MacDermot had tangled with the
family 18 months before when he complained in the *Times* that because A.C.
Goffe was rich he'd gotten away with murder when he was acquitted of killing

an alleged coconut thief. "We said that Mr. Graham could beat anyone in St Mary," MacDermot wrote, "and he has done so handsomely. We welcome him heartily to the Council." Rebuffed, Alec Goffe turned his attentions from political battles to the war that was coming in the island's banana trade.

While Alec Goffe had been busy on the campaign trail, A.C. had been busy telling Jamaica about his new banana company. Any banana man who wanted to get the attention of banana growers knew a required stop was the town of Guy's Hill in the St Mary highlands. Perched on the border between St Mary, St Catherine and St. Ann, a gathering in Guy's Hill was sure to attract people from all three parishes.

A.C. and his cronies, L.A. Stephens, Hubert James Crooks, a onetime member of St Mary's Parochial Board, Boss Morris, and J.A. Benjamin, arrived by motor car in Guy's Hill on Saturday 13 March 1920. It was market day and the town was busy. A good number of people had come to town to hear the latest goings on in the banana trade. The past few years had been deadly quiet, but things had begun to look up. In the past few weeks alone, two new companies, Jamaican companies, had come seeking fruit from growers in Guy's Hill. The meeting to introduce the Baltimore and Jamaica Trading Company took place outside A.A. Pitkin's general store. L.A. Stephens introduced A. C. Goffe. "Mr. Goffe is known to everybody in Jamaica and so he needed no introduction," Stephens exulted. To his mind, Stephens said, Goffe was second to none in uprightness and honesty in business and for this reason he was convinced the settlers would give him their full support after hearing his plan. To loud applause, Goffe stepped forward to explain his plan.

"Fellow parishioners, fellowmen and fellow-women," he said, "having been unsatisfied with the condition prevailing in the banana fruit trade last year, I was determined to bring about a better state of affairs and I came to the conclusion that the only way to accomplish this was to establish a link between the producer here on the one hand and the consumer over there on the other hand." He was a fine speaker, prone sometimes to long windedness, but an effective communicator, all the same. The Baltimore and Jamaica Trading Company was, Goffe explained to the large crowd gathered outside Pitkin's shop, the small man's alternative to the big man's company – United Fruit, Atlantic Fruit, and Jamaica Fruit. Goffe, in his typically self-aggrandizing way, told the audience he'd had some amazing adventures in America that he'd like to share with them. He set sail, he said, in September 1919 for New York determined not to return to Jamaica until he formed a new banana export company.

"Here I am today to tell you that my efforts have been crowned with unbounded success," Goffe told the gathering immodestly. "I worked with might and main to bring about the desired effect. If you support this new Company I will see to it that you are properly remunerated, so that you may be able to improve your holdings and so make your district a better one. I would endeavour to give you your just dues."

His new company, the banana exporter said, would bring unmatched prosperity to Jamaica. He expected, he said, that American merchants and businessmen, principally from Baltimore, would begin coming to Jamaica in search of business opportunities of all kinds. That was all fine and dandy one person said, but he wanted to know, frankly, whether Mr. Goffe's company was independent or, as had been rumoured, simply an offshoot of one of the big American companies – a kind of wolf in sheep's clothing. The planter's ire had been raised. This was no more than evil gossip, spread, Goffe said angrily, by his rivals. There was, he said, no connection between his company and any other firm, foreign or domestic.

"Be careful," Goffe told the gathering, "not to be fooled by the big companies." He had his say. He sat on one of the chairs laid out for the visiting banana men. It was time for Hubert James Crooks, a well-known banana man from the Windsor Castle district near Guy's Hill, to have his say. "In times past when the banana price had dropped," Crooks said, "Mr. Goffe came to the rescue and assisted the growers to obtain good prices. Therefore," Crooks pleaded with the assembled banana growers, "support Mr. Goffe's last and present venture by giving all the available fruit."

The next speaker up was J.A. Benjamin, another of St Mary's big planters. Jose Benjamin was brother to Percival Austin Benjamin, founder of P.A. Benjamin's, the well-known medicinal and toiletries company which made the very popular *Khus Khus Bouquet* and *Bay Rum*.

Benjamin's speech was deliberately provocative. His words were calculated to cause a storm, and they did. By the time Benjamin finished flattering Goffe, the directors of Jamaica Fruit and supporters of Marcus Garvey, an unlikely tandem of mostly wealthy white planters on the one side and black nationalists on the other, were furious with the St Mary planter.

"There are two prominent men in the shipping world today," Jose Benjamin said, "who Jamaica and Jamaicans are bound to respect, in that they by their ability, resourcefulness and dogged tenacity...were successful in organizing two such companies as the Baltimore and Jamaica Trading Co., and the Black Star Line: A.C. Goffe and Marcus Garvey." Jose Benjamin believed if anyone was qualified to speak about Goffe, one of his best friends, and Garvey, who had once worked in the printing department of his brother Percival's company, it was he. Benjamin's comparison angered many of Goffe's rivals in the banana trade and angered fans of Garvey, as well. Neither side was happy about it and both would in time let A.C. Goffe know how they felt.

A.C. Goffe was becoming a popular figure in Jamaican banana parishes, a banana Messiah come to bring small growers a fair deal. Praise, too, came from outside Jamaica. Hearing that Goffe had set up the Baltimore and Jamaica Trading Company, a Jamaican expatriate in New York City wrote to the *Gleaner* to praise his countryman.

"Permit me to mention the doings of a great Jamaican," wrote T.N. Francis, who described himself in his letter as a resident of the United States for 12 years. "Being in contact with live wire businessmen, it gives me great pleasure in seeing one of our native sons displaying in great measure the same zeal and enthusiasm so admirably displayed by the people of America. Many men laughed at him when they heard what his intention was. Little did they dream that men of Mr. A. Constantine Goffe's type do not easily succumb to apparent difficulties."

Excited by the support he was receiving, Goffe placed an advert for the Baltimore and Jamaica Trading Company in the March 23, 1920, edition of *The Gleaner*. "*THE BALTIMORE AND JAMAICA TRADING CO. Regular Weekly Passenger Service Between BALTIMORE, USA, and JAMAICA,*" the advert in the newspaper's shipping section read. "*The S.S "FORT MORGAN" leaves for Baltimore, USA. MARCH 29, to be followed by S.S. "PORT GAINES." For further particulars apply to A. Constantine Goffe, Manager for Jamaica, Port Maria.*"

Not by accident, the Baltimore and Jamaica Trading Company advert was placed beside an advert for Marcus Garvey's Black Star Line Company. It was a smart move. Goffe's rivals at Jamaica Fruit had already fashioned a slogan for their firm, 'Jamaican company for Jamaican people'. This, of course, was meant to echo Marcus Garvey's famous cry of 'Africa for the Africans at home and abroad.'

The banana business, it was clear from the slogans Jamaican companies were adopting, was not just about fruit. 'You have nothing to lose but your chains,' and 'Every penny we make remains in Jamaica,' were other slogans adopted by Jamaica Fruit.

Jamaican commerce had taken on a decidedly radical tone in the years since the end of the First World War. A.C. Goffe, too, calculated that by placing an advert for his company next to one belonging to Garvey's company would, somehow, encourage readers to see the two as one. Perhaps Goffe was not so different from Garvey, after all, he hoped readers would think. Garvey had once worked in the banana business. He worked for the United Fruit Company in Kingston and later, when he migrated to Costa Rica, Garvey took employment there as a timekeeper on a United Fruit Company plantation. A.C. Goffe hoped Jamaica's black banana growers and banana workers would come to see him as not so unlike their hero. Goffe was already enjoying some celebrity among growers thrilled at what competition in banana trade had done for banana prices.

But Goffe was hardly a man of the people. Only two years before this, in 1918, he had been on trial for murdering a man alleged to have stolen coconuts from him. But if playing the race card would encourage Jamaica's black majority to support his company, that was fine with Goffe. As for Garvey, he had an undisguised contempt for so-called 'coloured' people like A.C. Goffe. They were, Garvey said, self-hating and 'stiff-necked.'

"I was openly hated and persecuted by some of these colored men of the island who did not want to be classified as Negroes, but as white," Garvey wrote in an essay he penned in 1923, The Negro's Greatest Enemy. "They hated me worse than poison. They opposed me at every step... a few of the stiff-necked colored people began to see the reasonableness of my programme, but they were firm in refusing to be known as Negroes."

A.C. Goffe would certainly not have been happy to have been called a Negro or anything like it. All his life his dark skin had been a source of discomfort for him, surrounded as he was by family members who were often a shade or two lighter than he was. It was his money that opened doors for him in Jamaica and abroad, not his colour. "He was a dark man," 82- year old Linton Hedge who grew up near a plantation owned by Goffe in St Mary remembered. "He was a black man." In Jamaica his colour was open to negotiation. In America, where he'd witnessed racism at its harshest, it was not. He was a black man, and that was that. If banana growers wanted to see in him a champion who would challenge the 'lily white' and 'nearly white' in Jamaica, that was fine with Goffe as long as it was good for him and good for business.

As A.C. Goffe had predicted, the Baltimore and Jamaica Trading Company was profitable in a very short time. Its fruit steamers, the *Fort Gaines* and the *Fort Morgan*, arrived in Port Maria for the first time in March 1920. They were back and forth, week in and week out, laden down with bananas, coconuts and oranges destined for marketplaces in Baltimore and elsewhere in America. On June 17, the *Fort Gaines* left with an enormous load of exactly 31,620 bunches of banana in its refrigerated holds.

Business couldn't have been better and Goffe went out among the growers of St Catherine to tell them so. "My dear people," he told an enthusiastic crowd of growers at a rally in June, "don't allow your intelligence to be trampled upon by any class or colour," the banana man said playing the 'man of the people.' He was a hero in the banana walks, and in the pages of the planter's favourite newspaper, *The Gleaner*. The paper sent a correspondent to follow him to the various banana parishes.

"Taking into consideration the popularity of Mr. Goffe amongst the masses," the reporter said, "and his untiring interest and grit, the local enterprise is sure to have a successful career." Not if his rivals at Jamaica Fruit had their way, it wouldn't. The company had said it often: the Baltimore and Jamaica Trading Company, and A.C. Goffe in particular, was a menace and had to be stopped.

Maas Mike vs. Maas Charlie

'Friends come and go, but enemies accumulate.'

Anon

St. Mary people believed, as did people in the island's other banana parishes, that they had the best banana lands, the best banana men, and of course the best tasting banana, as well. Jamaican banana people agreed on little and fought over much. They fought, for example, over who could rightly be called the island's 'Banana King.' Just who was the 'Big Banana' was the subject of many long and bitter arguments. It made sense that banana talk roused passions. With so many Jamaicans earning their living from the industry, how could talk of banana be cool and dispassionate?

Jamaicans knew that Americans had taken to calling Captain Lorenzo Dow Baker, the Massachusetts ship captain who'd helped begin the international trade in banana in the 1870s, the 'Banana King.' He had, after all, founded the first important banana export firm, the Boston Fruit Company, which an American banana man said was "one of God's agents to right some of the ills" of Jamaica. Baker also helped found the mammoth United Fruit Company. But Baker was an American, not a Jamaican and Jamaicans believed the American had been given far too much credit, anyway.

"Who said Captain Baker was the founder of the banana trade?" a writer asked in the journal, *Jamaica Critic*, in 1926. Others shared this view. Sir John Pringle, one of the island's leading banana planters, made his views known at a special 65th birthday celebration put on for Captain Baker at the Myrtle

Bank Hotel in Kingston in 1903. Baker was presented with a large silver encrusted cup upon which was inscribed, 'Godfather of the Jamaican Banana Trade and Foremost Friend of Jamaica.' In speech after speech, praise was heaped on the American. The only one not to lavish Baker with praise was Pringle. He took great exception to Baker being crowned the 'Banana King' and described as the pioneer of the Jamaican banana industry.

"Captain Baker had been, I would not say the pioneer," Pringle said in his speech, "but one of the great pioneers of the banana trade." The good captain took immediate umbrage at this, and shot back with a verbal volley of his own. "I was not and do not claim to be the first shipper of banana from Jamaica," Baker said, obviously embarrassed. "I do not claim anything, save a wish to do something to benefit those around me."

Well, if Captain Baker wasn't the 'Banana King', who was? Portlanders said their representative to the Legislative Council, David Gideon, who started one of the island's first fruit companies, was the island's true 'Banana King.' After all, hadn't he been a director of the Atlantic Fruit Company and wasn't Gideon chairman of the government's Railway Advisory Board? In fact, when it was revealed in 1914 that Gideon was chairman of the Railway Advisory Board – his appointment had been kept quiet – many Jamaicans protested. Wasn't it, they wanted to know, a conflict of interest that the man responsible for management of the island's railway was also a director of a big banana company? St Mary banana people saw conspiracy. They believed Gideon, a Portlander, used his influence in both the Legislative Council and on the Railway Board to stop Port Maria getting a railway extension.

St Mary people, naturally enough, claimed that a native son of their own, A.C. Goffe, was the 'Big Banana,' the 'Banana King.'

"The St Mary banana man, large or small," a writer said of Goffe and other banana men from the parish, "was never quite the same as the banana grower of other parishes...the leading planter families of the parish had a marked individuality. Their self confidence...their love of putting their opinions over, made them a power that had to be reckoned with by the United Fruit Co., the Government and democratic politicians..."

Residents of Hanover, the western Jamaican parish, didn't agree. They insisted their native son, Charles Edward Johnston, was the real 'Banana King.' Johnston had been in the banana trade since he was a young boy and had like Gideon been associated with the Atlantic Fruit Company. He was now a managing director of the Jamaica Fruit and Shipping Company. Johnston was born on 20 December 1871 in Lucea in Hanover, a small, neglected part of Jamaica. It wasn't a banana parish. Banana, of course, grew there. Green Island, Lucea and Mosquito Cove provided a fair amount. But Hanover was not a banana parish like St Mary, Portland, St Catherine, and St. Thomas. In Hanover, only Charles Edward Scudamore on his property, Greenwich, A. Watson Taylor on his property, Haughton Court, and Henry James Rudolf on his property, Spring Valley, committed more than 150 acres to the growing of bananas. Besides, H.J. Rudolf was a St Mary man. Father-in-law of A.C. Goffe's cousin, Clifford Clemetson, most of Henry Rudolf's landholdings were in his home parish.

The big landowners in Hanover grew lime, yams, rice and breadfruit. A good chunk of their properties were given over to raising cattle. The Charleys, the Sanftlebens, and the Kerrs were the big landowners there. These were the people who towered over the parish when Charlie Johnston was a boy. Johnston's father, Patrick, was at different times a schoolteacher in the parish and the owner of a small general provisions and liquor store in the capital, Lucea.

Though the elder Johnston was making a living in the grocery business, it was not sufficient to take care of a growing family. As a result, Charlie left elementary school aged just twelve to earn his living as a junior clerk for a banana company. Still little more than a boy, Charlie left his home in Lucea, going 28 miles east to the large port town of Montego Bay in St James parish to work for J.E. Kerr & Co. Kerr was the first Jamaican company to successfully export bananas to Europe with relatively little spoilage.

After a few years with Kerr, Johnston, now a teenager, resigned and moved on to the parish of Portland on the other side of Jamaica. His father, Patrick, had moved there and begun buying and shipping fruit from Portland to several American cities. In time, Charlie Johnston entered the shopkeeping trade, opening a chain of stores in Portland and in St Mary. He also became a tavern keeper, opening a beer hall and eatery in Port Antonio. His main business, though, was bananas.

Charlie Johnston's life changed when he met Joseph Di Giorgio in the late 1890s. He'd been a success in Jamaica, but a partnership with Di Giorgio meant success abroad in America, a vast, lucrative marketplace. The two began a long and profitable business arrangement. Di Giorgio was looking for a business partner in Jamaica who could provide him with bananas. This Johnston did, loading the ships of the Di Giorgio Fruit and Steamship Company.

Apart from their banana agreement, Di Giorgio also brought in products for Johnston's general stores at significantly reduced shipping rates. Johnston provided Di Giorgio with good quality fruit at reasonable prices. It was a good arrangement and made them both prosperous.

When Di Giorgio begun Atlantic Fruit in 1905, Johnston became an investor and associate in the company. By the time the First World War was over in 1918, Joseph Di Giorgio had been forced out of Atlantic and eventually sold his large stockholding in the company. Though he kept his shares in Atlantic, Charlie Johnston launched out on his own, beginning Jamaica Fruit in June 1919. Johnston believed there was room in the banana trade for what he called, 'a Jamaican company for Jamaicans.'

The Jamaica Fruit and Shipping Company wasn't the first Jamaican company to enter the banana export trade after the First World War. Already in the market was the St. Ann's Bay firm, Fraser & Co., which was owned by fruit merchant, Leslie Leonidas Fraser. Charlie Johnston didn't view Fraser & Co. as a rival because the St Ann firm only intended exporting a few hundred bunches of bananas, none of it from territory where Jamaica Fruit intended making large purchases of fruit. The launch of A.C. Goffe's new firm in October 1919 was another matter, altogether. Various bits of advertising began appearing in Jamaican newspapers in February 1920 announcing the arrival of Goffe's new firm.

"THE OFFICIALS OF THE BALTIMORE AND JAMAICA TRADING COMPANY WILL SOON COMMENCE OPERATIONS IN THIS ISLAND…"

It wasn't that Charlie Johnston hadn't filled the papers with news of Jamaica Fruit, too. 'TO THE JAMAICA BANANA GROWER…Be On Your Guard! Do Not Cut Thin and Immature Fruit. FULL FRUIT IS WANTED. JAMAICA FRUIT & SHIPPING COMPANY LTD,' read one advert from November 1919.

Two weeks later another Jamaica Fruit advert appeared. 'TO THE JAMAICA BANANA GROWER: While prices of foodstuffs the world over continue high DOWN GOES THE PRICE of Banana suddenly in America!..Jamaica Fruit & Shipping Ltd.'

Then, on March 25, 1920 the Cold War ended and the Hot War began. The first volley in a long running private war between Charlie Johnston and A.C. Goffe went public.

"I address to you by this method in what I consider the greatest crisis which has ever arisen in the Banana Industry of Jamaica," read an open letter published on almost an entire page in *The Gleaner* on 25 March 1920. Charlie Johnston, managing partner and founder of Jamaica Fruit, wrote the letter. Far from being independent, Johnston insisted, Goffe's Baltimore and Jamaica Trading Company was merely a front bankrolled by United Fruit and created as part of a conspiracy by that monopoly to spark a price war which would push banana prices far beyond what his company could afford to pay. With his firm forced out of the trade, United Fruit and other big American companies could pay Jamaican growers whatever they pleased.

Fear of United and what it could do was well founded. It had been only a few years since federal investigators in the United States discovered that 700 businesses thought to be independent, were actually owned or controlled by United Fruit. In Johnston's open letter – a long, sometimes rambling treatise – he outlined his grievances against A.C. Goffe and the Baltimore and Jamaica Trading Company.

"Let us recall to mind," he wrote, "several events in which Mr. Goffe had a prominent part." Johnston draws a harsh portrait of a conniving, double-dealing businessman. At one point Goffe had, Johnston said, been interested in starting up a "so-called independent line of steamers; the vessels were however at once recognized as those of a company then and now operating here." The company Johnston is referring to, but doesn't mention for fear of a law-suit, is Atlantic Fruit. "Not many weeks passed before disputes occurred between Mr. Goffe and that Company, the ships being withdrawn, a lawsuit threatened by Mr. Goffe and a compromise finally effected."

Johnston's attack on Goffe was relentless. Jamaica Fruit's founder said short-ly after Goffe fell out with Atlantic, not minding whom he did business with as long as he made a profit, Goffe quickly began a relationship with the hated United Fruit. Goffe, Johnston suggests, agreed to become the American firm's coconut buying agent in Jamaica. But that agreement, too, quickly went sour.

"Before long he came to the writer here in Kingston and related his tale of woe," Johnston says in his open letter, making public private business dealings he had with Goffe. Johnston says United Fruit betrayed Goffe and had he, Johnston, not intervened the St Mary planter would have been ruined because the American firm demanded immediate repayment of a large loan it had extended to the Jamaican. Goffe could not come up with the money, Johnston said, and was faced with bankruptcy.

"Resenting as I did what I considered to be a rank injustice to a fellow Jamaican," Johnston said, "I forthwith drew my cheque for the amount and gave it to Mr. Goffe." Johnston said he was surprised when not long after he helped Goffe escape financial ruin at the hands of double-dealing Americans, the St Mary planter told him he held no hard feelings toward United Fruit and that perhaps too much had been made of the incident.

"He met me again and to my great surprise spoke in most flattering terms of the Company that he claimed had so mistreated him in his coconut deal," Johnston wrote. "To my expressions of surprise he replied that it had all been a mistake, they were all kindness itself, that accommodation had been arranged for him on their steamer and as well an interview fixed with the President of one of their Companies; that he intended forming a Banana Company to whom anybody could subscribe, and he added with a chuckle," Johnson points out, "that of course he could not examine to find out where the money came from but he had to make a living."

To those who counted themselves friends of Goffe, this was a false portrait of the man. To those who were his business rivals or enemies, this was an accurate portrait of a man they believed would betray anyone to advance his own interests.

Continuing his attack on Goffe in his open letter in *The Gleaner*, Johnston suggested it became clear to him Goffe was being bankrolled by United Fruit when the St Mary planter stopped at Johnston's Kingston office after returning to Jamaica from the United States in January 1920. Goffe, Johnston said, boasted to him that a group of bankers associated with United had asked him if they should purchase several Jamaican plantations that had recently come on the market. Were these banana properties fruitful, the bankers wanted to know, and were they worth what United Fruit had agreed to pay for them? In his letter, Johnston asks, pointedly, if there wasn't a business connection between Goffe and the Americans, why did United Fruit involve him in its private business affairs?

"It would be interesting to hear Mr. Goffe's explanation of the reasons why he was in such close contact with the Bankers of the Fruit Company on the eve of his formation of an Opposition Company," Johnston wrote. These were valid questions and ones A.C. Goffe might have had some difficulty answering.

Further developing his conspiracy theory, Johnston asked how was it that with so few fruit steamers available for lease, Goffe was able to charter two ships specially adapted for the banana trade, the *Fort Morgan* and the *Fort Gaines*. His own firm, Johnston said, had to make do with inferior steamers because United Fruit told Norwegian shipping companies it would cease doing business with them if they leased their ships to Jamaica Fruit.

The most interesting part of this unusually public battle between two of Jamaica's leading banana men came later in Charlie Johnston's open letter. Johnston cites an article written by a *Gleaner* correspondent in March 1920. In the article the St Mary planter, J.A. Benjamin, had flattered A.C. Goffe by saying: "There are two prominent Men in the shipping world today who Jamaica and Jamaicans are bound to respect...A.C. Goffe and Marcus Garvey." Charlie Johnston, a man who would have been considered 'white' in Jamaica though he was of 'mixed' ancestry, felt Benjamin's comparison was really a slap at him and an appeal to black racial solidarity. In other words, Garvey was a black man and was for the black man. Goffe, too, was a black man and was for the black man. Where, then, did that leave Johnston? Though Goffe hadn't mentioned race in advertising his company, Johnston was convinced Goffe was trying to use race and colour to appeal to Jamaica's black majority and to undermine him.

"This is a direct attack on the Jamaica Fruit and Shipping Company and myself individually," Johnston protested. Though Johnston was considered a white man in Jamaica, in the United States, where he traveled often on banana business, Americans couldn't quite figure out what to make of him. US immigration officials at New York's Ellis Island described him on one occasion as being 'fair of skin' and on another as being 'dark of skin'. Just what colour Johnston's eyes were was also a matter for debate. One immigration officer described the Jamaican as having 'gray' eyes and another said the banana man's eyes were 'brown.'

Worried Jamaicans would view him and his company as somehow not as Jamaican as Goffe's firm, Johnston went on the attack. His firm he said was, "the only company which is Jamaican with its formation, ownership and headquarters here; the others, including Mr. Goffe's company, being American. The introduction of Mr. Garvey's name in association with Mr. Goffe's was merely to secure for the latter some of the popularity enjoyed by the former, for the reason that Mr. Garvey has no connection with the fruit business but runs a Passenger and Freight service."

Garvey would have been amused to see these two members of Jamaica's plantocracy involved in a bizarre public feud in which they questioned each others' patriotism and each others' commitment and connection with Jamaica's black masses, people whom coloured and white Jamaicans had conspired together to ruthlessly exploit and keep as far a distance from as possible.

It wasn't just Goffe whom Charlie Johnston took to task in his open letter in *The Gleaner.* Johnston also took on J.A. Benjamin, the black planter who compared A.C. Goffe with Marcus Garvey. Johnston viewed Benjamin as a friend – a friend he wanted Jamaica to know he'd lent a considerable amount of money to in the past. Johnston felt Benjamin had sided with Goffe simply because he and the St Mary planter shared the same skin colour.

"Perhaps it would not be amiss to ask Mr. Benjamin if he thinks so highly of Mr. Goffe as a 'Jamaican for Jamaicans' why it is that now he advises other Jamaicans to turn to Mr. Goffe as a 'Jamaican for Jamaicans' for help," Johnston wrote, "when at another and more serious time for him, it was not to Mr. Goffe but to another he turned for help?" It was there for everyone to see, he a white man had befriended and extended money to two black Jamaicans and they'd both betrayed him, hiding behind the bonds of racial solidarity.

Not only had Charlie Johnston come to the rescue of Benjamin and Goffe, he wrote, he had come to the rescue of Jamaica, itself. "I may be pardoned, I hope, if I recall that since the early '90's when I with my own funds undertook, in order to keep alive for Jamaicans, an active competition in the Banana Industry, the establishment of a line of vessels in New Orleans…My effort to-day is to the same end."

By contrast with his own obvious patriotism, Johnston as good as accused Goffe of betraying Jamaica. Johnston said during the war "the two large

Companies (United Fruit and Atlantic Fruit) had it all their own way, with Mr. Goffe loading some of their steamers and paying his fellow Jamaicans the pittance he did?" Johnston went further, suggesting A.C. Goffe had cheated St Mary banana growers. "Was Mr. Goffe the Organiser of the St Mary Fruit Growers Association, and if so, what became of that Organisation? How much was subscribed to it by the small cultivators of St Mary; how much money did they lose by it, and how much of their money did they get back?"

These were serious charges. A banana war that had been confined to Jamaica's wharves was now being fought out in the island's newspapers.

"I ask that you consider these facts and, therefore, that we banana growers (of whom I too am one) should do everything to encourage the great movement of which you men of Jamaica," Johnston said stirringly, "have begun to bring industrial independence into your midst."

Charlie Johnston's attack on A.C. Goffe did not go unanswered. It seemed at first there would be no reply. But, nine days after Johnston's open letter appeared in *The Gleaner*, an open letter from A.C. Goffe to the Banana Growers of Jamaica appeared.

"The advent of the Baltimore and Jamaica Trading Company into the field for securing to you a fair and legitimate price for GOOD, FULL, CLEAN, FRUIT, has aroused the ire of Mr. C.E. Johnston," wrote Goffe. "He is endeavouring by distributing his letter in pamphlet form far and wide to hoodwink the growers by all kinds of insinuations into believing that The Baltimore and Jamaica Trading Company is an offshoot of a Trust; a suggestion which is absolutely false, and he knows he cannot prove." Next, Goffe, obviously embarrassed and angry, took Johnston to task for mentioning in a public forum that he had extended large loans to him and to J.A. Benjamin in the past.

"With reference to the fact that this gentlemen has loaned money to Mr. Benjamin and myself, may I ask of what interest is that to the Banana Growers of Jamaica and does it not show that Mr. Johnston has forgotten the first instincts of a gentleman, when he publicly refers to private transactions on account of competition in business?" Goffe does concede, though, that he had in the past loaded ships for the Atlantic Fruit Company, a fact, he said, was well known and not something he felt he needed to hide.

"Is it not surprising for Mr. Johnston to trot this out," Goffe said, "when he was at one time the Manager in Jamaica for that same company…and held as he possibly now does a large amount of stock therein?" Annoyed that Johnston had depicted himself as an altruist whose only concern was the well-being of the Jamaican banana industry, Goffe said Johnston was a businessman like any other businessman.

"Do not entertain the idea that Mr. Johnston is a philanthropist, and his interest in your welfare is disinterested and unselfish. Nothing of the kind, 'Mr. Fruit Grower.' On the contrary, he is fearing his material interest…will be affected, hence his WAIL. It is well Mr. Johnston should know that nothing he can do or write, will prevent The Growers of Fruit from supporting The Baltimore and Jamaica Trading Company. I am convinced that you fruit growers will not be camouflaged by any clap-trap advertisement."

Just as Charlie Johnston called into question Goffe's business ethics and patriotism, so Goffe called into question Johnston's ethics. "Mr. Johnston's several past acts in dabbling in the fruit business," Goffe said, "were primarily to obtain preferential freight rates for his merchandise business, especially during the time The United Fruit Co. embarked extensively in merchandise in Jamaica, instead of its being what he now attempts to put forward. viz: His unselfish interest in the Banana Growers."

As to why it was Goffe had private meetings with bankers handling the purchase of large plantations in Jamaica for the rival United Fruit Company, Goffe explained, less than plausibly: "I went to America to form a Company, and it is only natural I should come in contact with Bankers, and if my opinion is asked in reference to anything in Jamaica, where does the harm come in? I am sure no one but Mr. Johnston will see any underlying motive in my reply."

As for the fruit steamers Johnston said Goffe's company had been able to charter because of its connections with United Fruit, Goffe denied this, saying, in essence, Johnston was frustrated because he wasn't as able a businessman as he was.

"I think Mr. Johnston pays me a compliment when he states that I have been able to secure two fruit steamers, when he has not been able to secure any," Goffe said. "His suggestion that they are controlled by a large Banana Corporation savours of pique. If that were so would it be necessary for the Baltimore and Jamaica Trading Co. to deposit three months charter money, cash in advance, to secure the ships?"

To the charge that Goffe cheated St Mary banana growers who belonged to the St Mary Fruit Growers Association, the St Mary planter said, "will Mr. Johnston attempt to say that this is the only fruit concern that has gone out of existence? It does seem that his chief desire is to be abusive by insinuation which is the most contemptible method of abuse."

In a coded reference to his brother, Alec, who left the family business to join Charlie Johnston's Jamaica Fruit and Shipping Company, Goffe said if Johnston wanted information about the St Mary Fruit Grower's Association, "he could easily have the same from one of his agents at Port Maria, who was not only a large stockholder, but also a Director."

In closing, A.C. Goffe said he had considered ignoring Johnston's attack on him, but decided to give him a war if he wanted a war. "I first thought of treating Mr. Johnston's letter that everyone describes as a lamentable display of bad taste, with the contempt it deserved but as some of my supporters may misconstrue my silence, I now make my position clear."

There was good reason for the bad feeling; there was a lot at stake. The American companies, United Fruit and Atlantic Fruit, shipped approximately three million bunches of bananas each from Jamaica to the United States in 1919. The Jamaica Fruit and Shipping Company shipped exactly 529,666 bunches. Johnston was rightly concerned that Goffe's return to the banana export trade would cut into the small market he'd managed to secure for himself.

Banana War

'God don't make no one ugly. They do that to themselves.'
Zora Neale Hurston

So, a banana war had been declared. Like a civil war, brother lined up against brother. Alec Goffe lined up with the Jamaica Fruit and Shipping Company. His brothers, John, Cecil, Horace, and Clarence lined up with A.C. and the Baltimore and Jamaica Trading Company.

"A big banana war is now on in Jamaica," *The Gleaner* announced on 17 June 1920, "and the battle for the fruit is raging with more or less severity throughout the length and breadth of the island. For some time there have been grave mutterings about the coming struggle and the fight started in grim earnest on Monday morning." Because of the banana bidding war that had broken out, growers, big and small, were being paid getting more for their fruit than they'd ever done before.

"Throughout the history of St Mary the parish had never seen or heard of the prices paid this week for the fruit," a newspaper said. In Kingston, for example, the lofty price of eleven shillings was happily paid for a bunch by the agents of the four companies in the market, United Fruit, Atlantic Fruit, Jamaica Fruit, and the Baltimore and Jamaica Trading Company, or the Goffe Company as it came to be called.

These prices, almost twice as much as was being offered elsewhere in the island, were unprecedented in the history of the banana business in Jamaica. Just a year before, in 1919, before the Baltimore and Jamaica Company's entry into the market, the price for a bunch of bananas was closer to three to four shillings in Kingston. Now on 17 June, 1920, at Port Maria a bunch was selling for the very high price of around 8 shillings and six pence. Goffe's Baltimore and Jamaica Trading Company did well on this June day. One of its ships, the *Fort Gaines*, in dock at Port Maria, took on stevedores, went down the coast to St. Thomas parish to collect bananas there before returning to St Mary to collect more fruit. Eventually the ship set sail for Port Antonio where it was cleared to leave Jamaican waters with, all told, 31,620 bunches of bananas on board.

Banana prices were highest in Kingston and in St Mary. Elsewhere on the island growers were enjoying the best prices they'd ever known, as well. In Christiana, in the parish of Manchester a bunch went for around six shillings and six pence. In St. Thomas, a bunch fetched around six shillings. At Montego Bay in St. James and elsewhere in the western section of the country, the price of a bunch was between six shillings and five shillings. In Port Antonio, £55 was paid per hundred payables. Some of the companies, desperate to convince growers to sell their fruit to them, went as far as giving growers wagons and other equipment to haul their produce from the interior to the railway station and shipping ports. This was not typical behaviour. But it was a seller's market not a buyer's, and growers could do business with any one of the array of banana exporters jockeying for their produce.

Both A.C. Goffe and Charlie Johnston had complained publicly about the state of the market. Prices needed to come down, both said, and the quality of the island's bananas needed to be improved. Growers, eager to cash in on high prices, had been selling fruit that had not matured properly and exporters had been happy to buy it. Under-grown, immature produce Americans called 'rat-tails' had begun to flood the market. By 1921, a new law, the Fruit Inspection Law, had come into effect. Under it, fruit intended for export from Jamaica had to be closely inspected to ensure immature, unfit fruit was not sent abroad. Government fruit inspectors were given far-reaching powers which allowed them to 'enter any land, building, place, vessel, boat or vehicle at any time of the day or night and examine and search and inspect any fruit.' Those found guilty of breaking the law could be imprisoned for up to six months at hard labour.

The 'banana war', one company outbidding the other, continued unabated through much of 1920 and into 1921. The United and Atlantic Fruit companies shipped 2 million bunches of bananas each in 1920. Charlie Johnston's company tripled the number it shipped to exactly 1,420,477 bunches. There would have been reason for the Jamaica Fruit and Shipping Company to celebrate had A.C. Goffe's upstart company not shipped exactly 741,199 bunches of bananas, itself. The battle for banana drove the price higher and higher. It was a glorious time for banana growers.

Charlie Johnston believed United Fruit had engineered the boom to drive his firm out of the market. "So much of the fruit produced in Jamaica is owned by the large Companies, and so much of it is under contract to them that the proportion of fruit left in the open market is very small and if this small quantity is reduced below a certain point it will mean that the supplies of the Jamaica Fruit and Shipping Co. Ltd will be reduced so low as to render it impossible for them to continue." It seemed, he said, all too convenient that A.C. Goffe should have begun a company when he did. "It seems peculiar that under the circumstances outlined above a new Company should be started through which our supplies of open market fruit may be reduced to such a small quantity as to render it impossible for us to continue."

When A.C. Goffe went to Baltimore in 1921 to start another new company, many of Jamaica's banana men began to grumble and ask the question: 'How is it that Freddie Goffe is starting new companies when the rest of us are fighting to stay afloat? Where is the money coming from?' Where indeed?

Still, somehow thriving while all around him were collapsing, Goffe went to the United States in August 1921 to launch the Bella Steamship Company. Fed-up paying ever rising prices for the chartering, or rental, of steamships to move his produce, he decided that purchasing purpose-built steamships were the only way to reduce costs and keep more of the profits for himself. The Bella Steamship Company's first steamer was called, appropriately, *Bella*. Next, the company purchased the *Fort Morgan* and *Fort Gaines*. Goffe's Baltimore and Jamaica Trading Company held long leases on the two ships, but figured it would be more cost effective to buy them. The steamers were hardly top of the line. The *Fort Gaines*, a Norwegian steamer, was elderly and close to retirement. It was 18 years old and, at only 1,121 tons, not a very big ship, at all. The ships had, though, been specially adapted for the fruit trade with refrigerated holds and other state of the art equipment. They'd also been re-modeled to allow for accommodation for passengers.

By the time Goffe returned to Jamaica toward the end of 1921, banana export figures for the year were available. United Fruit and Atlantic Fruit shipped pretty much what they had the year before – around two and a half million bunches each. Johnston's company shipped exactly 1,884, 812 bunches and Goffe's firm shipped exactly 1,043,793 bunches to the United States. Goffe appeared to have gained ground on Johnston. In 1920, Jamaica Fruit and Shipping had sixteen per cent of the market while the Baltimore and Jamaica Trading Company had eighteen and a half percent of it. In 1921, Johnston had almost nineteen per cent of the market and Goffe ten and a half per cent of it.

But Johnston and Goffe had become so obsessed with one another they did not notice that others had their eyes on the same chunk of the Jamaica banana market they had spent the last several years fighting each other over. In 1921, John, A.C. Goffe's older brother, gave up his post as a director of the Baltimore and Jamaica Trading Company to start a rival banana operation with, of all people, Antonio Lanasa.

Things had ended badly between the Lanasas and the Goffes in 1915 when the two families dissolved their banana company and filed lawsuits against one another. But though Alec Goffe and A.C. had filed a lawsuit claiming breach of contract against Lanasa and promised to never do business with him again, John, or 'John B' as he was known, didn't feel as strongly about the split as did his siblings. Lanasa and he kept in contact, and in 1922 John agreed to a partnership arrangement with Lanasa in which the Lanasa Fruit Corporation of Baltimore would charter fruit steamers in the United States and send them to Jamaica to collect fruit procured by John Goffe's Caribbean Fruit Company. S.C. Barham and F.S. Rutty were partners for a brief time. Lanasa took the large share of the profits because he handled the large share of the responsibilities. It was a fine arrangement and both prospered.

The news didn't please A.C. Goffe. He had felt betrayed when Alec, his younger brother joined Charlie Johnston and Joseph Di Giorgio and he felt just as betrayed now his older brother, John, had left the Baltimore and Jamaica Trading Company to join Antonio Lanasa.

Interestingly, of the six companies exporting Jamaica banana in 1922 – United, Atlantic, the Swan Hunter and Lindsay firm, the Baltimore and

Jamaica Trading Company, Jamaica Fruit, and the Caribbean Fruit Company — A.C., Alec and John Goffe helped form three of them. The three were now rivals, ready and willing to undercut or sabotage one another to be successful in the banana trade.

John Goffe Jnr, older than his brother A.C. by eight years, was the senior Justice of the Peace in St Mary and had been since his father's death in 1882, the de facto head of the family. Educated at English boarding schools, John returned home from Britain to help manage his family's mercantile business and banana estates. A popular and well liked figure around Port Maria, John chafed at the control his younger brothers, Alec and A.C., wielded over the family. Outside of St Mary it was Alec and A.C.'s names that were known, not John's. Antonio Lanasa had offered John the chance to become a banana man in his own right, and he took it.

So began a round of bad luck for A.C. Goffe in 1921. A fire gutted his wharf building in Ocho Rios, completely destroying the property and thousands of bunches of bananas laying in a warehouse ready for export to the United States. He'd allowed the insurance on the building to lapse, and only a small portion of his losses were covered. The next year he filed a lawsuit through his attorneys, Manton and Hart, to recover monies he'd given a banana agent to purchase fruit. The agent, F.A. Price, took the money, it seems, to purchase bananas, but never delivered the produce. On top of all of this, Goffe was taken ill in the United States.

He recovered, but his company was ailing. It lost one of its ships, the *Fort Gaines*, to his brother's Caribbean Fruit Company. Unable to afford its operation, the ship was sold to a Norwegian shipping company and then leased to John Goffe's and Antonio Lanasa's firm.

A.C. had considered the *Fort Gaines* the flagship of his company and was angry at being forced to sell it and having it end up in his brother and Lanasa's fleet. He was thrilled, though, when another ship he lost to his brother, the *Bella*, had an accident at sea and was forced to put into dock for long and costly repairs. Still, though the Caribbean Fruit Company had begun making large purchases of banana, orange and cocoa, it took awhile before it was fully accepted in the trade. Its name caused it to be confused with other fruit and shipping companies, like the Caribbean Steamship Company. Concerned, John Goffe sent off a letter of complaint to newspapers. "Misrepresentations are constantly being made, not only by 'our friends' but in the newspapers which are very confusing and misleading."

This aside, John's company had a good year in 1922, its first full year in the trade. It shipped exactly 414,640 bunches of bananas to Lanasa in Baltimore. The large companies did better. United Fruit and Atlantic Fruit shipped roughly three and a half million bunches of Jamaican bananas to the United States, while Charlie Johnston's company shipped 1,902,404. A.C. Goffe's firm shipped 930,726 bunches of bananas.

These figures were cause for concern for both Johnston and for Goffe. Both saw their share of the market decline by around three per cent.

The decline wasn't just because of 'John B' and Lanasa. Others, too, had come into the market. The Jamaican export market was as busy as it had ever been. Among the shippers were Swan Hunter, Globe Fruit Company, C.P.R., and Bluefields. Between them though they represented no more than one per cent of the market and shipped no more than around 150,000 bunches of bananas.

The next year, 1923, was a bad one for A.C. Goffe. While Johnston's company saw its share of the market decline another three per cent, Goffe went from shipping just over 900,000 bunches to just over 50,000. It'd been a mighty fall; from shipping nearly a million bunches of bananas to the United States to sending half its ships to the US with only a few thousand bananas in them. With such a small share of the market, A.C. Goffe liquidated his Baltimore and Jamaica Trading Company and his Bella Steamship Company in 1923, and quit the export market.

A notice appeared in the island's newspapers on 12 July, 1923. "Creditors and others having claims against the Baltimore and Jamaica Trading Company of Baltimore are requested to send particulars to Manton and Hart." H.J. Ciotti and R.N. Baer were appointed by Court No. 2 of Baltimore City to act as receivers. The same month, Antonio Lanasa arrived in Port Maria to see how the Jamaican side of his banana operations was faring. He stayed at the St. Mary home of John Goffe. It'd been almost twenty years since Lanasa had been in Jamaica. After the Lanasa and Goffe Steamship and Importing Company was dissolved in 1915, Lanasa and his family invested heavily in Cuban bananas. But political turmoil in Cuba made the banana merchant long for Jamaica. So popular was Lanasa's company in St Mary, the name 'Lanasa' and 'Lanassa' began to be given as a Christian name to children born in the parish.

Though forced to shut down his company after sustaining big losses in 1923, after a brief re-organisation and infusion of new capital A.C. Goffe was back in the banana trade in 1924. The new, improved Baltimore and Jamaica Trading Company resumed operations on 7 July 1924. But by the end of 1924, Goffe was out of the export trade again, this time for good. Ironically, though Johnston had seemed to be A.C. Goffe's chief rival, it was probably Lanasa, who increased his share year after year, who contributed most to the downfall of Goffe's company. By 1924, with less competition in the market – only United, Atlantic, Jamaica Fruit, the Philadelphia Fruit Company, the Tropical Fruit Company, and Lanasa remained – banana prices began to fall. A bunch of bananas that had once commanded as much as eight shillings in St Mary dropped by almost two-thirds in price to around three shillings per bunch.

There was more bad news for banana growers. It was around this time, too, that the variety of banana that A.C. Goffe had gotten his nickname from, the 'Gros Michel' or 'Big Michael' began dying out. Bananas had been attacked by many and various diseases over the years, but none as virulent as 'Panama Disease', a soil fungus which destroyed thousands of acres of prime banana lands in the 1920s and 1930s.

With the 'Gros Michel' banana in decline, other, hardier species of banana had to be found to replace it. Among these were the 'Sutherland 19' and the 'Walker' or 'Highgate' banana. Both had their pluses and minuses. The Sutherland was said to be completely immune to Panama Disease. But the fruit was not as large as the Gros Michel, nor as sweet as it.

The Walker banana – named after the St Mary planter and banana man, Samuel Magnus Walker – was larger and sweeter than the Sutherland, but could not claim to be wholly immune to disease. Many banana growers in St Mary and Portland adopted the Walker banana while many planters in St Catherine and Clarendon favoured the Sutherland.

What doomed both these types of banana, though, was neither traveled well. Neither the Sutherland nor the Walker was tough enough to stand the journey to the United States or Europe without suffering great damage. Though some planters did ship both the Sutherland and the Walker banana, the overwhelming majority adopted the Lacatan, a particularly hardy variety of banana which produced long and plentiful fingers from a tall growing plant. It wasn't as sweet to eat as either the Gros Michel or the Walker, but it was entirely immune to Panama Disease and traveled well in the jam-packed, refrigerated hold of a fruit steamer. The Lacatan was introduced to Jamaica from Trinidad and Tobago around 1926 by the St Catherine planter, Stanley Scudamore. Twelve of the Lacatan banana suckers brought into Jamaica by Scudamore were planted at Hope Experimental Station in Kingston. From these came the Lacatan variety of banana which took the place of the much beloved, but disease-prone Gros Michel.

Banana prices plummeting, crop disease spreading, naturally enough people began to talk about what they could do together to protect the industry. On 10 January 1924, Charlie Johnston arrived in New York City for a six-week stay. He was there to meet with Joseph Di Giorgio, whose Di Giorgio Fruit Corporation had been carrying Jamaica Fruit's bananas to the United States since 1919. Though Johnston's company was responsible for 21 bunches of every 100 bunches which left Jamaica for the United States in 1921, and though he was earning millions of pounds, he knew it couldn't last. In 1926, Jamaica Fruit's percentage of the market declined by almost 4 per cent, to just over 16 per cent. All the talk on the island in the mid 1920s was of co-operatives, for bananas and everything else.

Association

You can't go wrong if you say 'yes' to the right people, and 'no' to the rest.
Sidney Greenstreet

People in Jamaica had been talking about setting up fruit co-operatives from as far back as anyone could remember. Samuel Shephard and James Bell, two Port Antonio businessmen, set up the Portland Co-operative Fruit Company in 1878. Nine years later, in 1887, David Gideon, a Port Antonio merchant and legislator, set up the Jamaica Co-operative Fruit and Trading Company. There were other attempts. J.E. Kerr set up the Northside Fruit Company in around 1900, and A.C. Goffe set up the St Mary Fruit Growers' Association in 1901. They all faltered and failed, in part, because the big planter remained aloof and because the small grower remained sceptical. Jamaicans, it was widely believed by Jamaicans themselves, simply could not co-operate with one another long enough for any venture to succeed. Still, they tried.

In January 1919, the Council of the Jamaica Imperial Association published this notice: "At largely attended meetings of Committees of the Association within the last few weeks resolutions were passed approving of the principle of establishing co-operation in the selling of fruit and other products, through the medium of District Associations linked together in a central association."

Talk of setting up fruit co-operatives in Jamaica sent American banana companies into a panic. They'd had a free hand in Jamaica and the prospect of competing with co-operatives terrified them. The United Fruit and the

Atlantic Fruit companies demanded the American government block the entry into the United States of fruit shipped by co-operatives. The banana companies demanded the U.S. re-instate tariffs which had made it difficult for Jamaicans to bring produce into the United States during the Great War. Still, despite American threats, Jamaicans embraced the co-operative movement.

In 1925, the Jamaican government sent a delegate to a meeting of the Imperial Economic Committee in London to represent the interests of the island's banana growers. A report issued by the Committee recommended the establishment of banana co-operatives and a direct line of fruit steamers to carry Jamaican produce to England. To support these efforts, the Jamaican government gave a grant of £2,400. The United Fruit Company said Britain was interfering with the free market, free trade, and with the laws of supply and demand.

Despite American protests, in 1925 a Canada-West Indies Trade Convention was signed. Jamaican banana producers were thrilled they'd secured another market not controlled by the United and Atlantic Fruit companies. In 1925, Jamaican orange, coconut and banana growers formed the Jamaica Producer's Association, an umbrella body for agriculturalists of all sorts.

"Never has the need been felt more than today," read a circular distributed by the Association in 1925, "for joint action on the part of the island's producers." Chief among the advocates for a co-operative movement were the Presbyterian ministers, Henry Ward and Amelius Alexander Barclay of St Mary. Barclay had helped set up the Western St Mary Citizens' Association and had pressed the island's government as far back as 1917 to set up a fruit co-op to help stabilize prices and give growers a fairer share in the profits from their produce.

Though Jamaicans seemed ready at last for a co-operative, the directors of the Jamaica Producer's Association knew they needed to point to the success of co-ops elsewhere. The Association's directors pointed to successful co-operatives in Australia, New Zealand, Egypt, Norway, France, and Germany. In Denmark, co-ops had been especially successful. The 150,000 members of the country's dairy co-operative owned seventy per cent of the cattle in Denmark and handled sixty-seven per cent of its export dairy trade.

All of this was exciting news for Jamaicans. In its circulars, the Jamaica Producer's Association warned against listening to naysayers who preached against co-ops saying, "Oh Jamaica will not co-operate." John Soulette was

253

one such voice. A well-known Kingston watchmaker and frequent letter writer to the island's newspapers, Soulette said the co-operative movement was as bad as the Garvey movement and as bad as Soviet Communism. It wasn't, Soulette claimed, in the nature of Jamaicans to co-operate.

"Co-operative marketing – excellent thing but let us see whether we as a country has ever shown a desire to co-operate in any way up to now," Soulette wrote. "I defy you or anyone else to show we are but a mongrel lot to be governed with justices and prudence."

But Jamaicans defied Soulette and the other naysayers. Walter Coke-Kerr, was president of the Producer's Association, Custos of the parish of St. James, and a leading banana planter. Coke-Kerr believed the Jamaica Producers' Association offered an historic opportunity for Jamaicans to, he said, free themselves from economic slavery.

"The gathering marked an important step in the industrial history of Jamaica, an attempt that'd never been undertaken in its annals," said Coke-Kerr, a son of John Edward Kerr, one of the early shippers of Jamaica bananas to the United States. "If it failed it would be due to the fact that they were like worms, inert and careless about their affairs." Jamaicans had in the past, the Association's president said, allowed themselves to be "like dumb beasts. They had done nothing before to lift themselves from the yoke." They had a chance now, Coke-Kerr said, to break new ground for themselves and to lift the chains of industrial slavery." If Jamaicans did not unite, he warned, it would "strengthen the hands of their enemies."

The Jamaica Producers' Association's aims were bold. First, it wanted to bring all producers of fruit, big and small, together. These were the thousands of growers who had a few plants mixed with other crops on less than an acre and the handful of large planters who farmed more than 50 acres into one joint body for the purpose of joint protection and co-operative action. Second, it wanted to find ways and means of securing better production, marketing facilities, co-operative selling and ultimately better prices for producers. The Association decided to form a Central Committee whose job it was to go from parish to parish to encourage big planters and small growers to join the co-operative. "We believe that the successful outcome of this movement," a Jamaica Producers' Association circular read, "will have an important bearing on the future prosperity of the Island."

The co-operative movement had its enemies, but it had its friends, too. If anyone should have been a friend of the co-operative movement, A.C. Goffe should have been. After all, he was the founder of St Mary's first banana co-operative.

"I am the first man in the island who taught the peasantry the value of co-operation," Goffe boasted in 1901. Whether this was true, it seemed certain Goffe would be one of the loudest voices in support of the Association.

In October 1925, a big meeting to introduce the Association to St Mary was held in Port Maria. All the big planters were there, among them Sam Walker and Alec Goffe. "I came to support the movement heart, body and soul," Alec Goffe said. "I serve this country first and myself afterwards." Also at the meeting was Clifford Clemetson and A.C. Goffe. Clemetson moved that a resolution be passed saying St Mary planters would support the Association. A.C. seconded the motion, then took the floor and made a speech. He said he had formed a similar association many years before which he was sure many of them would remember. He knew, he said, something about the banana business as it was not unusual for him to ship a million bunches to the United States each year.

"We are going to be a unit," Goffe said to loud cheers, "and a powerful one at that." He did issue a warning, though. "Our people are very suspicious and unless those who are at the head are reliable and trustworthy, then bang, the dog is dead." The dog was dead for Goffe when the Producers' Association split into several smaller units – the Citrus Growers Association, the Coconut Growers Association, and in 1927, the Jamaica Banana Producers' Association. When Goffe discovered people he considered unreliable and untrustworthy – Charlie Johnston, Joseph Di Giorgio and his brother, Alec – might be placed at the head of the banana association he decided he wanted nothing to do with it. Among the 136 founding directors of the Association were Alec Goffe, Clifford Clemetson and Sam Walker A.C. Goffe's name was missing.

Once the Banana Producers' Association had been formed, its membership had to decide who would lead the organisation and which company it would employ to export and distribute its fruit abroad.

There were several proposals before the Association, among them the Direct Line scheme, which proposed ownership of a direct line of steamers to England by the Association. The money for the scheme was to be raised by the government and guaranteed by a banana tax. There was Mr. Beale's Scheme. This was put forward by an English shipping company. Under this plan, the company would build ships and market fruit on the Association's behalf in England on a profit sharing basis. There was the Bellingham and Olson Scheme which recommended the Association charter ships at a cost of £4000 per month to convey fruit to the United Kingdom and the United States.

There was also the Kerr-Robertson scheme, proposed by the president of the Jamaica Producers' Association, Walter Coke-Kerr, and by the organisation's promoter and manager, Frederick Henry Robertson. There was the MacTavish Goffe scheme, which was put forward by Clarence Goffe, A.C.'s brother. Finally, there was the Johnston-List scheme, put forward by Charlie Johnston and Sibrandt List, managers of the Jamaica Fruit and Shipping Company. There was never any doubt which scheme would be approved. The Johnston – List scheme was chosen. Johnston and List were, after all, the managing partners of the only wholly Jamaican company exporting bananas in 1927.

Johnston had been in the banana business since he was a 12 years old and Sibrandt List was a former ship's captain and manager for the United Fruit Company with extensive contacts in the United States and in Europe. Johnston and List said they could run the Producers' Association better than anyone else because they had longstanding relationships with the island's biggest planters and could convince them to give their fruit to the Association. They also, they said, had important transport and marketing contacts in the United States. Their firm, the Jamaica Fruit and Shipping Company, they said, was financially sound and they had been in the banana business longer than almost anyone in Jamaica. The island's government had the final say. It gave its blessing, as expected, to Johnston and List.

Once installed as head of the Association, Charlie Johnston arranged for Joseph Di Giorgio's company to act as the export arm of the co-operative. Di Giorgio's job was crucial. He was responsible for shipping the Association's fruit abroad, marketing it and distributing it there. It was, in essence, the same deal that Johnston, List and Di Giorgio had struck when they formed the Jamaica Fruit and Shipping Company together.

It had been a monumental task forming the Jamaica Banana Producers' Association and deciding who would lead it. It would be an even more difficult task getting banana growers in Jamaica to become members of the co-operative. Everyone had to do their part, especially the founding members of the Association. They were sent off to campaign on behalf of the co-operative in their home parishes.

Alec Goffe, Clifford Clemetson, and Sam Walker went out on the stump in St Mary. The Association set itself the task of signing 5,000 growers before April 1929, the date it planned to ship its first load of bananas to the United States. It seemed a daunting task, but wherever the Association's directors went in St Mary hundreds of growers turned out. Deliverance, the growers felt, had finally come. They would, the growers were told, get a fair deal and no longer would they have to make do with the pittance the foreign companies paid them for their produce. Hundreds signed, or put their 'X', on the dotted line. But many others were not convinced. Some doubted the motives of the 'big men,' the big planters.

Others wondered if they were giving up their independence for an uncertain reward, as a letter sent to a Jamaican newspaper in February 1928 suggested. "Do the Planters who signed these alleged Contracts understand clearly that all their lands present or future on which they may plant banana, even although not referred to in the Contract…will be irretrievably pledged to the Producers' Association." In a panic, a group of St Mary planters filed an action in Jamaica's Supreme Court to test whether or not contracts they'd signed with the Producers' Association were binding or whether they could be set aside.

The court considered the case and decided, crucially for the Association, that the contracts were binding. Indeed, legislation was passed specifically to enforce contracts signed between the Association and growers. So determined was the Jamaica government that the Association succeed, it passed a measure that made any company which bought produce a grower had already promised to the Association liable for a very hefty fine.

At an Association meeting in Wood Park, St Mary, Ken Robinson, a Jamaica Banana Producers' Association shareholder and big St Mary landowner, called those disloyal to the Association "murderers," "microbes" and "germs." Before the advent of the Association they had been, he told the growers, like "dogs at the master's table, looking for crumbs." Since they had shown their manhood like real true-hearted Jamaicans," Robinson said, "those conditions had changed. Those who had been their masters were today at their very feet begging them for fruit!"

The Jamaica Banana Producers' Association launched on April 1 1929. The next day, Alec Goffe waited at the Association's wharf, 'Producers' Wharf,' in Oracabessa, St Mary for the *S.S. Ceiba*, one of the ships made available to the Association by Joseph Di Giorgio, to arrive. The bananas had already been delivered to the Association's warehouse. Goffe had only managed to collect 5,000 bunches. It was a disappointing haul especially as so many spectators drawn by the fuss over the launch were on hand. On April 3, the Producers' ship, the *S.S. Princess May*, arrived at Oracabessa. Again the haul was small.

Though the Association had signed 6,145 growers, which was 1,145 above the figure it set for itself, few of them, for some reason, were from St Mary. Growers came to Association meetings, clapped excitedly at speeches, but were slower than those in other parishes to sign on the dotted line. As St Mary produced more bananas than any other parish in Jamaica, the Association could not be a success unless it was a success in St Mary.

Fortunately for Alec Goffe and other Association directors in St Mary, locals gave up their resistance to the Association. By December 1929, membership in the co-operative grew by another 1,700. Many of this number were new members from St Mary. By January 1930, the co-op had 80,000 acres of bananas under contract to it in Jamaica.

Coincidentally, 1929 was also the year of the Wall Street Crash and the year Jamaica ceased being the world's largest producer of bananas. It had been the top producer since 1876, but slipped to second behind Honduras. It was bad timing. Before the Association had the chance to ship one bunch of bananas, Andy Preston, boss of the United Fruit Company predicted the co-op would fail and collapse within six months. The Association lasted, but the Atlantic Fruit Company, didn't. It went bankrupt in 1930, weighed under by bad investments it'd made in Cuba. The Standard Fruit Company, owned by the Vaccaro brothers, took over what was left of Atlantic.

The biggest surprise in the banana trade that year, though, concerned Joseph Di Giorgio. He announced he was selling his interests in the banana trade and ending his arrangement with the Banana Producers' Association. Di Giorgio sold his company – ships and wharves – to the Standard Fruit Company. The New Orleans firm became the Association's new partner and took over responsibility for shipping the co-op's fruit to the United States.

Joseph Di Giorgio had decided to dedicate himself to growing fruit in California. He'd been planning this for some time. In 1919, shortly after being ousted from the presidency of the Atlantic Fruit Company, Di Giorgio began quietly buying up large blocs of land in northern California. He bought 2,000 acres in the San Joaquin Valley for around 90 dollars an acre that many thought worthless. It looked like a waste of money, but Di Giorgio knew better. His departure from the banana trade was a blow to the Association and in particular to Charlie Johnston, who'd been associated with the Italian for more than 30 years.

It was around this time, too, that Samuel Zemurray, the head of the Cuyamel Company, emerged as the most powerful figure in the international banana trade. Zemurray was a ruthless businessman willing to do anything to further his interests, even foment revolution. Angry, the president of Honduras, General Miguel Davila, refused him tax, land and transportation concessions, Zemurray arranged for two American mercenaries, Lee Christmas and Guy 'Machine Gun' Molony, to sneak into Honduras and lead a coup with the help of soldiers loyal to former president, General Manuel Bonilla. Bonilla promised Zemurray he would grant him whatever business concessions he wanted once he was returned to power.

With President Bonilla's support, Zemurray's Cuyamel Company grew to rival even United Fruit in Honduras. In 1930, Zemurray, ready to retire, sold his firm to United for $30 million in stock. But when United's stock lost nine tenths of its value in the next two years, Zemurray returned to the company. He fired the board of directors, reorganized the company and made it a profitable concern once again. In charge of United in 1932, Zemurray began to wage war against the Jamaica Banana Producers' Association. Though under enormous pressure from United Fruit, the Association managed to remain solvent, and even prosper in 1932.

The Association's troubles seemed to be behind them. Then in September 1932, Charlie Johnston, Sam Walker, Alec Goffe and the other directors of the Association were shocked to find their private business dealings exposed to public scrutiny. Their internal documents – which director was paid what – had been leaked to JAG Smith, the Legislative Council representative for Clarendon. A well-known attorney, and a big landowner himself, Smith, a black man, made his name in politics as an advocate for the common man.

Clarendon had a right to know what was going on at the Association, Smith said. Smith was right. One in three of the co-operative's members were small settlers from Clarendon. The private memoranda of the Association in his hands, Smith held a meeting in the town of Frankfield in his constituency on September 3, 1932. There he held the high and the mighty up to ridicule in front of the small growers.

Smith said the big planters who ran the Association were doing what they wished with the money earned by the co-operative. The monies paid to various directors, agents and staff of the Association was revealed in excruciating detail as were the hefty commissions paid to the agents who handled the Association's fruit. The enormous sum then of £35,000 was the yearly bill for the running of the Association's Kingston office. This did not include salary and commission the Association paid to Charlie Johnston and Sibrandt List. Smith railed against what he said were corrupt and underhanded practices. Smith suggested the reason small growers rarely received the sort of profits they believed they were entitled to was because big planters in the Association were paying themselves high salaries and large commissions. According to Smith, commission paid to Johnston and List amounted to not less than £20,000 a year. The leaders of the Association were also paid another £10,000 a year for freight and wharfage costs. The amount paid to commission agents for handling Association fruit was around £100,000. The Association could save itself between £20,000 and £30,000 a year, Smith said, if instead of bringing large amounts of bananas by rail to Kingston for shipment, it sent them from outports such as Port Antonio, Annotto Bay and Montego Bay. Smith decided to name names at the September 3, 1932 meeting in Clarendon. He cited the case of one Edwin Charles Joysey. Why, Smith asked, was Joysey, who worked on staff at Producer headquarters in Kingston, allowed to take a three months holiday in England and why did the Association pay Joysey and his family's bill while they were on holiday in Britain? Nepotism, Smith answered. There were too many individuals on the Association's payroll who were related to this one or to that one. They were given cushy, high paying jobs not because they were competent, but because they were the son, or nephew of one Association director or another.

Besides, the Association was hardly a democratic organisation. It did not operate on the one man, one vote principle. Only the big planters had a vote. People like Alec Goffe, for example, had a great deal of say while small growers had no say, at all. Was it right, JAG Smith asked, that Sam Walker and Alec Goffe, both directors and agents of the Association in St Mary, were paid commission of around 20,000 to 25,000 pounds annually. Why did they also, he asked, have the exclusive rights to the sale of produce at three railway stations and two seaports in St Mary?

"Surely the amounts paid to these agents are far too much?" Smith said. "What have they really got to do? Only to receive the fruit from members of the Jamaica Banana Producers' Association and see that they are fit for marketing." Indeed, Smith said, the real work was not being done by Goffe and Walker, but by subordinates who worked under them. "Just think at this time of depression," said the member for Clarendon, "Messrs Walker and Goffe drawing £500 a week gross for commission! The poor people and the masses want a little of the attention which we give to the bigger people."

Hailed a hero at the Frankfield meeting for exposing the 'big men' in the Association, Smith pressed the authorities to intervene in the Producers' Association, an organisation they were subsidizing. He demanded the island's Legislative Council appoint a special representative to keep watch over the Association. With many of the 'big men' in the Association also the 'big men' in the Legislative Council, Smith was not able to convince the body to investigate the Association. The Producers' Association did set up a so-called 'Vigilance Committee', made up of planters and directors of the co-operative, to investigate complaints. It didn't find much, but did report that many banana growers in the Oracabessa area in St Mary resented the influence there of Sam Walker and Alec Goffe, JBPA agents at the port. Apart from being told by the Vigilance Committee to be more circumspect in their business dealings, little changed.

The real trouble for the Producers' Association began in the final months of 1933, when the first major hurricane in years destroyed thousands of acres of bananas across the island. At the same time United Fruit raised the price of bananas so high it almost drove the Association out of the banana trade, altogether. The co-operative couldn't match the prices United Fruit was offering so thousands of growers who had agreements with the Association sold their fruit secretly to the American company. Figures show that nearly a third, 31 per cent, of Jamaica's banana growers sold their fruit to the Association in 1932. By 1934, only 19 per cent were selling their bananas to the Association. By contrast, the amount of bananas fruit growers were selling to United Fruit went up by 12 per cent. There were calls for Captain List and Charlie Johnston to resign from the leadership of the Association. No one enjoyed Johnston's difficulties more than his old adversary in St Mary.

In Oracabessa, in St Mary, enjoying Johnston's predicament and the decline in the number of fruit growers selling to the Association, was A.C. Goffe. He'd been forced out of the export trade years before because of high banana prices, the high cost of operating a fleet of steamships, and increased competition from rival fruit companies. But though he had left the banana export trade, Goffe hadn't left the banana business, altogether. He continued planting large amounts of bananas and coconuts on properties he owned in both St Mary and St Ann parishes. He could have sold his produce to the Association as other big planters did, but chose instead to sell to the Americans, to the United Fruit Company. It seemed an unusually bloody minded thing to do. His brother, Alec, and his cousin, Clifford Clemetson, were selling their produce to the Association in a fit of patriotism and because of a desire for economic independence.

"Any Producer, no matter how large or small he may be," read a Jamaica Banana Producers' Association circular, "who has his own and not the Island's welfare at heart can stand aside." A.C. Goffe didn't stand aside. Ever the contrarian, he took a very lucrative job offered by United Fruit to act as its commission agent at Oracabessa in St Mary, its most important banana port. Goffe took over as the American company's agent at Oracabessa and Rio Nuevo in June 1927. It would have been a difficult job to turn down. Besides, Goffe got a perverse satisfaction from being offered the job. Though the exact sum he earned in commission on the millions of bunches of bananas he procured for the American company is not known, it was a very hefty sum. Buying agents like Goffe were like tribal chieftains in the country parts of Jamaica. Their power and influence inspired admiration, fear and envy.

"The knowledge that one man is controlling and drawing commission on a large number of banana has bad psychological effect on the mind of the small grower." This was the view of researchers sent by the British government to Jamaica in 1935 to investigate conditions in the island's banana industry. The study the investigators produced, *The Report of the Jamaica Banana Commission*, was harsh on banana men like A.C. Goffe. Goffe didn't care. After all, his earnings from the United Fruit Company made him one of the richest men on the island.

A.C. Goffe didn't care, but others did and they said so. "There are too many Jamaican "come-betweens" in the handling of fruit on the docks," complained I.A. Peterson in *Plain Talk* newspaper in 1937. "Such people would kill their countrymen so as to get a good bonus at the end of the financial year, and a pat on the shoulder from the Company."

It wasn't A.C. Goffe alone, though, who was earning enormous sums as a buying agent. In its investigation of the Jamaican banana industry and in particular the workings of the Jamaica Banana Producers' Association, a three-man commission appointed by the British government found that large planters dominated the Association and had instituted practices designed to benefit themselves. The report criticised, for example, the practice of allowing directors to set themselves up as agents of the Association. These agents received large commissions and other special concessions while small settlers had to make do with relatively low prices for their produce.

"Wherever possible agents should be remunerated by salary and their expenses carefully controlled," the report said. "We do not think that Directors of the Association should themselves act as agents." Among the directors of the Association to set themselves up as buying agents was Alec Goffe. He and Sam Walker set up the Walker & Goffe agency. The agency purchased fruit in Port Maria, Highgate and Oracabessa on the Association's behalf. The firm employed a full staff, including two sub-agents, A.E.T. Vermont and C.L.A. Stuart to procure fruit on its behalf.

The battle for fruit in St Mary was fierce. Henry George de Lisser was agent for the United Fruit Company at Albany, Highgate, Annotto Bay, and Richmond. At Oracabessa, the most sought after port in St Mary, Sam Walker and Alec Goffe competed with the Standard Fruit Company's agents there, Magnus and Tingling, and with the United Fruit Company's agent, A.C. Goffe. It was brother against brother again, as it had so often been in the past.

Not satisfied with the enormous sums he was earning as a buying agent for United Fruit in Oracabessa, A.C. Goffe was interested in other enterprises, as well. He'd had some success in the hotel business many years before and wanted to try it again. He'd bought a large estate, Buckfield, in 1910 in St Ann and been successful with coconut and banana planting in the parish. He bought another property there, the 597-acre St Ann's Bay estate, Windsor, in the 1920s. Here he established a hotel called, appropriately enough, Windsor.

On the property was a rebuilt Great House which dated back to the 1600's. In the 1800s, Windsor became one of Jamaica's very first hotels. For all of its grand past, the Great House was in badly dilapidated condition and needed sprucing up. It was brought up to date, a roof garden erected, the property's mineral spring bath cleaned up and Windsor's famous one hundred steps renovated.

The hotel had all the modern conveniences: hot and cold running water, electric lights, a private bathing beach, a tennis court, billiard bar and room, and Buick cars and horses available for hire. The refurbished Windsor Hotel opened, officially, on 4 January, 1933. A special dance was held with music by the Thunderstorm Orchestra.

"Windsor Hotel, St Ann's Bay, Jamaica, B.W.I" read an advert for the hotel, "...situated on a hill a half mile from St Ann's Bay – commanding fine sea view; extensive grounds and gardens, hot and cold running water and electric lights throughout: mineral pool, tennis court; easy access to Fern Gully and Dunn's River."

The 1937 edition of the Tourist Trade Development Board's Guide to Jamaica shows Windsor was one of the country's larger hotels. It had room for 28 guests, which was larger even than the venerable Shaw Park Hotel in Ocho Rios, which had room only for 26 guests. The Windsor charged 20 shillings per day. Breakfast cost 3 shillings; lunch 5 shillings and dinner 8 shillings. By the 1950s, the hotel had grown considerably and now had accommodation for almost twice as many guests. A popular spot, Hollywood actor Errol Flynn, world-boxing champion Joe Louis and Nelson Rockefeller stayed at the Windsor Hotel from time to time when they were in Jamaica.

The Windsor was popular, but A.C. Goffe was not, according to a former resident of St Ann's Bay who frequented the hotel in the 1930s. "Oh, we went to things at the hotel the dances and such," explained the woman, the daughter of a well-known St Ann's Bay family. "But Freddie, Maas Mike as he was known, was not popular. I don't know if it was because he was dark or black. He was not invited to the best things, at the tennis club and so on. He was prickly, prickly like a porcupine. I think he had quite a chip on his shoulder because of his colour."

Goffe, no social butterfly, sensibly let others manage the hotel. In truth, he stayed out of sight so as not to let the many American whites who stayed at the hotel discover that a black man owned the property. He did, though, join a St Ann's parish hoteliers' association. The association, which had Flora Stuart of Shaw Park Hotel as a member, demanded the island's government improve the roads on the North Coast, develop water supplies, beautify public gardens and beaches, and install electric lights and telephones and build a small airfield to accommodate small planes. The association told the government if it did these things, they, private enterprise, would do the rest.

Still, the fruit business was Goffe's main concern. Apart from the hotel, Windsor was an enormous, 597-acre banana and coconut estate. Here, too, his reputation as a hard man followed him. "He wasn't like other planters. It was very unusual. He used to watch the men, counting each coconut as it was put into the trucks. You wouldn't have expected a man of his station to do something like that," said a planter who operated an estate nearby.

A.C. Goffe also cultivated another large property in St Ann, as well, Buckfield, in Ocho Rios. Buckfield was a 327-acre property he had bought in 1910 from T.A. Morris. No sooner had he bought the property than did the St Ann Parochial Board begin pressing him to clean up the "unsanitary" parts of the estate where water logged soil and foul smelling swamps were a breeding ground for malaria carrying mosquitoes.

Ocho Rios is today one of Jamaica's most popular tourist centres. When Goffe owned Buckfield, between 1910 and 1941, it was all agricultural land where bananas, coconuts and pimento were plentiful. Today, Buckfield, which is about five minutes from the centre of Ocho Rios in the southeastern section of the northcoast city, is a residential area where many of those who work in the local tourist industry live. It was an unusually fertile property for the parish of St Ann, and was up to 1950 the main employer of labour in the area. Working for A.C. Goffe was hard and thankless labour, said 87- year old Linton Hedge, who remembers seeing workers toiling on a large coconut estate owned by the planter.

"He used to employ women to break and grate the coconut. They would boil it everyday to get the oil from it," Linton Hedge recalled. "On Sunday the women used to say, 'we are going down to Mr. Goffe to husk coconut.' When they were not boiling oil, they would gather the coconut and put it into the barn. And when they husk and boil the oil they would send it to the wharf to go to Kingston." As to whether A.C. Goffe was popular with those he employed, Linton Hedge says diplomatically, "You are going to find that in an area it is not everybody that is going to like you," he says. "But as long as you are employing people you will find they will go with you."

The Big Tree

If you are the big tree, we are the small axe, sharpened to cut you down.

Bob Marley

By the 1930s, Old Jamaica could no longer resist the advance of New Jamaica. The planter class that A.C. Goffe and his family belonged to knew their day was all but done. The signs were many. Perhaps none so ominous as what happened at the annual general meeting of the Port Maria Tennis Club in 1935.

Alec Goffe, president of the club, gathered its members together in the pavilion at 5pm on 17 July, 1935. Goffe, the oldest member of the club, stood at the lectern with acting honorary secretary, Ken McCarthy, owner of a big real estate firm, on one side and honorary treasurer, P.R. Miller, on the other. Clifford Clemetson and wife, Elsie, were there, as were Leigh Tinling and wife, a couple of Aquarts, a Parachini, a Barham, a Demontagnac and a couple of Rudolfs. President Goffe had bad news for the group. Being select and rarified had brought them to the edge of extinction. Membership was stagnant Goffe explained. Eleven new members had been let in, but eleven others had left and a further five had been struck off the membership rolls for failing to pay their dues.

"There is no doubt that the club fails, as it is now operating, in attracting a steady attendance of members," Alec Goffe told the scant gathering. "What this is due to, I often wonder," he said, impervious to how incestuous and inbred was the group he presided over.

This was quite a collapse. It hadn't been that long ago that St Mary's tennis and country club had to turn prospective members away. Membership could not be had for love nor money in the 1920s. Back then, when Jamaica was still the largest producer of bananas in the world and banana men were making more money than they knew what to do with, St Mary's ruling class was sure of itself and of its future. Those were halcyon days for Port Maria's society set.

Unlike the gentry in other parishes, St Mary's did not have to steal away to Kingston to enjoy pleasures and entertainments. Hardly a day went by without a sparkling event of some sort. Hardly a night went by without a big dance or event of some sort. One such occasion was the opening of the silent movie theatre, one of the first on the island. When 'talkie' movies arrived years later, Port Maria was again among the first to get a cinema specially adapted for sound. Back then, in the years after the Great War, Americans called it the 'Jazz Age' or the 'Roaring Twenties,' the comings and goings of Port Maria's smart set was assiduously recorded in high society newspaper columns like "The World and His Wife".

"The opening of the new moving picture theatre was a great function, there were to be seen some wonderful creation of frocks and smart coats wending their way through town to the scene." Among those spotted at the opening of the cinema was Miss Lottie Combs, "charming in floral geor-gette," popular Mr. Prentice of Barclays Bank, and Miss Alma Walker, Sam Walker's daughter, "one of St Mary's beauties." After the movie, those who were members, or had invitations, set off for the tennis club where they danced the night away, the most daring doing the Charleston, the One Step, and the Black Bottom.

"An extremely jolly dance took place at Port Maria Tennis Club after the opening of the new Lyric Theatre," it was reported. "The music provided by the 'Hot Strutters' was a great asset. Seen dancing were Mr. and Mrs. Clifford Clemetson...Mr. and Mrs. Alex Goffe...the Misses Mary and Joyce Pullar." The society crowd partied harder than most people worked. Following the cinema opening and the bash at the tennis club, the country club put on a dance the next evening at which it boasted English royalty would be present. This turned out not to be true. The Lord and Lady in attendance were Irish, not English. They were not royalty, either, but minor aristocrats who'd taken up temporary residence in Jamaica.

"The Dance was a great success socially and financially," The World And His Wife reported. "Among those present were (Lord and Lady Athlumley), Mrs. Alan Keeling in white and silver, Mrs. Josleen in black beaded in pastel shades…Mrs. Alex Goffe in green and silver…Mrs. Betty Soutar looking charming in blue voile-de-chine."

Banana had made St Mary rich – it was the richest parish in Jamaica – and its well bred and well to do wanted the rest of the island, especially Kingston, to know it. St Mary's 'soft hand set' were tired of being referred to, patronisingly, as 'banana millionaires' by those who had made their money in sugar or coffee. They wanted people elsewhere on the island to know that life in their parish was concerned with more than planting bananas, cutting bananas, and selling bananas.

When a *Daily Gleaner* correspondent paid a visit to the parish every effort was made to convince him that St Mary people knew how to enjoy themselves. "There is no jollier crowd in the world than these St Mary people," the correspondent wrote. "They go to their lovely Clubhouse by the sea with the solid intention of thoroughly enjoying themselves; and in the course of carrying out that intention, they see to it that anyone who is lucky enough to be visiting the Club also thoroughly enjoys him or herself."

Jamaican hospitality had, the correspondent said, a worldwide reputation. St Mary outdid everywhere else on the island in its enjoyments. "There are few places in the island where that hospitality, that real old 'Club spirit' is found to greater perfection than in St Mary Country Club."

The writer wasn't exaggerating. St Mary enjoyed its sports, and was very good at them. In the eight years between 1906 and 1914, the parish won the All Jamaica Polo Cup seven times. The parish's young people were just as good as their elders when it came to a horse and mallet. They won the Junior Polo Cup on three occasions between 1908 and 1914. St Mary was on a winning streak which seemed to have no end. Banana men like Alec Goffe, who won islandwide recogniton for becoming the first man in Jamaica in the 1920s to purchase a fancy Hillman Stra 8 saloon car, were flush with cash and full of confidence in their possibilities.

Alec Goffe had already lost in a bid to win the St Mary seat in the Legislative Council in 1920, but was convinced he could win next time. He decided to try again in 1925. He was up against a churchman, and everyone knew it was notoriously difficult to defeat clerics, having as they did a ready-made pulpit and God on their side.

In 1920, Alec Goffe's opponent had been a white, Anglican minister, William Thomas Graham. In 1925, his opponent was another man of the cloth; this time a black Presbyterian, Amelius Alexander Barclay, an extraordinary social reformer. Though he was born outside St Mary in the parish of Manchester, A.A. Barclay was very popular in his adopted banana parish. The reason for this was the part he played in a pioneering land re-settlement scheme that enabled hundreds of landless peasants to purchase five and six acre lots with the help of a government loan.

The Western St Mary Citizens' Association, the group formed by Barclay, secured a large loan from the island's government and purchased two plantations, Pembroke Hall and Donnington. Plots on the estates were made available at very reasonable rates to peasants who'd never owned anything before. It was an extraordinary achievement. Peasants elsewhere on the island begun demanding the same. 'Land for the farmers, and good prices for banana,' A.A. Barclay's supporters chanted during the Reverend's 1925 election contest against Alec Goffe. Barclay was popular throughout Jamaica, not just in St Mary. The cleric also helped form the island's first islandwide fruit co-operative in 1925, the Jamaica Producers' Association. He was truly a man of the people and much more than simply a man of the cloth.

Barclay was popular with the small men and the big men, alike. The island's governor, Sir Leslie Probyn, appointed him in 1920 to a seat in the Legislative Council as a reward for his good works. But he wasn't comfortable with the appointment. He didn't want government favours. He wanted to be elected by the people. Among those who supported Barclay when he decided to run against the incumbent, W.T. Graham, was Alec Goffe.

All sides of the community in St Mary united to remove Graham, a much-disliked churchman, from office. William Graham had come to St Mary from St Catherine in 1916 to take up the post of Rector at St Cyprian's in Highgate. He was a member of a well-respected Anglican family and had been specially selected for the St Mary post by the Archbishop of Jamaica himself, Enos Nuttall. After four years in the job, Graham decided he wanted to broaden his powers. The Anglican pulpit was not sufficient for him. He won the election, but things quickly began to go wrong for the cleric. A man with a fiery temper, he feuded often with his congregation and with his constituents.

"He was a strict disciplinarian and felt that order and ethics should not be permitted to be thrown overboard and so on these grounds there arose many a feud between himself and the congregation," wrote Canon S.A. Swaby and Gwen Goffe, authors of *The Banana Church*. With his congregation in full-blown rebellion by 1925, locals were surprised when Graham announced he would seek re-election to the Council. Immediately, a movement to unseat him was launched. All sectors of the community, rich and poor, threw their support behind A.A. Barclay.

Unpopular and faced with revolt by his congregation, Graham wrote a letter to *The Gleaner* in which he claimed the Archbishop of Jamaica had told him he supported his campaign and wanted him to seek re-election. A day after Graham's letter appeared, a letter from Enos Nuttall appeared. "I have never been in favour of a clergyman of our Church serving on the Legislative Council," the Bishop wrote. It was, he said, an obvious "conflict of interest" for a clergyman to seek to serve both as a parish's spiritual leader and its political leader, as well. Defying the head of the Anglican Church, Graham refused to pull out of the race. It was no use. His campaign had been dealt a fatal blow.

Seeing his opportunity, Alec Goffe declared his intention to contest the seat the day after the Archbishop of Jamaica's letter appeared. It was a shrewd political move. Though he'd promised his support to Barclay, Goffe calculated he could take advantage of what appeared to be a backlash against clergy getting mixed up in politics. Goffe also calculated that the Presbyterian, Barclay, and the Anglican, Graham, would split the vote of the religious in the parish, leaving the way open for him.

With Wilford White, a businessman from the town of Oracabessa, his campaign manager, and excited at his prospects, Goffe published his manifesto. "The welfare of the parish of my birth is my highest ambition, and I assure that the same zeal for its betterment which has marked my career as a member of the Parochial Board for the advancement of St Mary will direct my every action in the Legislative Council, if elected."

Goffe set out on the hustings believing he had a real chance at an office that had eluded him. But in the last days of January bad news came. William Graham had decided not to seek re-election, after all. Humiliated, the clergyman quit the race and left St Mary a few weeks later to become the Rector at Harewood in St Catherine. The Rector there, Joseph Nathaniel Swaby, became Rector at St Cyprian's. This left Goffe and Barclay to fight over the Legislative Council seat.

This wasn't what Goffe wanted. He couldn't beat Barclay in a straight fight. Aside from A.A. Barclay's popularity, changes in the voting laws gave Alec Goffe little chance of victory. Though in the 1920s universal suffrage was still far off, the pool of voters on the island had been increased by the granting of the ballot to a wider segment of the population. The lowering of the income a voter was required to have in order to cast a ballot meant a greater number of Jamaicans were able to participate in elections. Women, too, got the chance to vote for the first time.

By all accounts, the presence of women voters enlivened what had been a dull election campaign. "The monotony of the proceeding was broken by fully 15 lady voters all of whom," it was reported, "voted for Rev Barclay." Though popular with women voters, Barclay was not much of a speaker on the stump. Even the cleric's supporters admitted this. A. Leo Rankin, a former member of the St Mary's Parochial Board and a onetime supporter of Alec Goffe's, said of Barclay: "he does not excel as a star in the hall of gilded eloquence."

Though the election seemed lost before it begun, Alec Goffe's followers did their best to drum up support for their candidate.

"A large crowd congregated at the Court House and as the day grew older," a newspaper reported on election day, "at one time, it is understood that a section of the Goffites assumed a threatening attitude." Nothing his supporters could do could stop Goffe from being trounced in the poll. He was well-beaten. He won only 588 votes against Barclay's 1,004 votes.

Barclay took office, but suffering from heart disease died a year later, aged only 50. H.G. de Lisser, *The Gleaner* editor, paid a fine tribute to him in his newspaper. "He will be missed. He will be missed in the Legislative Council, in his parish, in the whole colony." For some reason, Alec Goffe decided against contesting the vacant seat. It was his best chance at victory gone begging. The contestants were the planter, A.F.G. Ellis, an Englishman hardly known in the parish, and H.E. Vernon, a school teacher. Ellis had on his side that he was a founding member of the Jamaica Producers' Association. One of his chief backers was Alec Goffe. Goffe was returning a favour. Ellis had voted for him when he ran against Barclay in 1925. As for H.E. Vernon, he didn't have much at all on his side. Besides, the contest seemed, somehow, shameful and squalid, like squabbling over something the dead had left. A.F.G. Ellis won. But he, too, died in office. Vernon ran again and lost again, this time to Reverend H.B. Wolcott. A perennial loser, Vernon ran yet again and lost yet again to Wilmot Westmorland, a wealthy buffoon dismissed by one local as not simply a "dummy" but a "mummy" also.

It looked as though that would be it for H.E. Vernon. As for Alec Goffe, after losing twice in contests for national office he decided he was satisfied with being a local eminence – the longest serving member on St Mary's Parochial Board. But even his authority as a parish councillor, a post his father, and grandfather had held before him, would be challenged in time.

Alec Goffe's efforts to get into the Legislative Council had all been failures. But that did not stop another member of his clan seeking office years later. Clifford Clemetson, Goffe's cousin, made his bid for island wide office in 1934, just as the tide was turning against big men candidates. Owner of one of St Mary's largest properties, Frontier, Clemetson had attended Camperdown School in Kingston, Munro College in St Elizabeth, and Clifton College in England. He played golf at Clifton, was on the 2nd XI cricket team, and was in the school's Bisley shooting VIII. At academics, though, Clemetson was a dead loss. He didn't make it to fifth form.

In 1913, Clifford, aged 18, returned home to Jamaica and to his large estate, Frontier, which one observer described as, "a benevolent citadel over-looking the Bay and town of Port Maria." Back home, he occupied himself mostly with St Mary's social scene and with managing his property. In 1919, he was nominated to fill a vacant seat on St Mary's Parochial Board that most people said he didn't deserve. Then, in 1934, he decided he'd make a bid for an office that'd eluded his cousin, Alec. After all, his grandfather Robert Clemetson had been elected to the island's parliament in both 1841 and 1844 and his father, David, and his uncle Abraham had held seats on the Parochial Board. He felt he had the political pedigree for the job.

But it was, in part, Clifford's pedigree that was the problem with his candidacy. Clemetson's opponent for the seat in the Legislative Council, was the perennial loser, Herman Emmanuel Vernon. Now a member of St Mary's Parochial Board, Vernon had been beaten so often it seemed like abuse. If he had been a boxer he wouldn't have been allowed to fight anymore, beaten as he was on three occasions in eight years for a Legislative Council seat.

When Clemetson supporters heard Vernon was going to run yet again they were disdainful and scornful. In a fiery speech delivered at the offices of

Messrs. Goffe Bros. on Main Street in Port Maria, Henry Ward, a Presbyterian minister and member of what locals called 'The Clique' said this Vernon: "We vomited him up once. We vomited him up twice. We vomited him up thrice. Shall we swallow him now? God forbid."

Clemetson thought victory was his. He was young and rich. Vernon saw it differently. Here, he thought, was someone, at last, whom he could apply a sound beating to. When Vernon had taken on A.F.G. Ellis eight years before he had been a simple teacher, a man of little means. Since then he had become a landowner and won a seat on St Mary's Parochial Board. Against his three previous opponents – all white and wealthy – Vernon seemed overmatched and overawed.

Clifford Clemetson – though wealthier than all of Vernon's previous opponents put together – did not intimidate Vernon, at all. He was rich, yes, but Clemetson was, like Vernon, a man whose roots were in Africa not in England. He immediately went on the offensive. Vernon said Clemetson was too high born and too highfalutin. Vernon, 30 years older than Clemetson, dismissed his opponent as 'a class man' who had no understanding of the lives of working or middle class Jamaicans.

Clemetson did his best to come up with a manifesto he believed would make him attractive to the new raft of middle class voters on the rolls. He said he had a plan to eradicate 'Panama Disease,' a contagion that destroyed millions of Jamaican bananas. Clemetson also said he supported land re-settlement and outlined an initiative to break up some of the larger estates so parcels of land could be made available to small settlers. He said he wanted the government to back his banana insurance plan and another plan he put forward to shore up the shaky co-operative loan banks. He also suggested – and this was crucial for St Mary's banana industry – improvements to the parish's harbours. It was becoming clear that newer, larger ships could not dock comfortably in either Port Maria's or Annotto Bay's harbour. Clemetson wanted the harbour deepened and widened. This would, he said, preserve the banana industry in these towns and save hundreds of jobs.

He had a lot to say about the hospitals, as well. The poor ought to receive free medical care and cottage hospitals ought to be set up in the towns of Richmond and Gayle. He said major improvements needed to be made to Port Maria's hospital. It was in bad shape and needed proper lighting, better equipment and clean and comfortable accommodation for nurses.

"I feel sure that placing these particulars before you," he said, "you will realise that these are the crying Needs of this parish of Ours (St Mary)." Clemetson's manifesto seemed well thought out and well put together. For him, though, victory would not hinge on his ideas, but on his background.

Clifford Clemetson came into his fortune, ownership of the Frontier pen and banana estate and other properties in St Mary and elsewhere, because his older brother, David, was killed in action during the Great War. This made Clifford, who did not volunteer to fight, look weak, ineffectual and lucky.

Herman Vernon had to work for what he had. It was no surprise, too, that much of his support came from the so-called 'teacher class.' He had been a teacher himself, and had been educated at Mico College, employed as a teacher at Trinityville in Clarendon and at Cambridge in St James, and as a headmaster at May Pen Anglican School. Vernon gave up pedagogy for the world of the produce dealer. Cocoa was his thing, not banana, and soon he was being called the 'Cocoa King' in Annotto Bay and Richmond. Later he purchased cocoa on behalf of the British company, Rowntree, and for Lascelles DeMercado company in Kingston. A drop in cocoa prices forced him out of that trade, Vernon said, and into the banana trade.

Though he was now a man of property – he liked to talk of his homes in St Mary and in Kingston and how much land he owned – Herman Vernon insisted he was still a man of the people, especially people who were teachers.

The 'teacher class' flocked to his campaign. At a rally for him in Belfield, his hometown, B. Theo Lawson, a teacher, launched into a spirited attack on Clifford Clemetson, his rich family and his rich friends. The Port Maria man had no business representing ordinary working people, and St Mary should, Lawson said, do as other parishes had done and choose "educated men from the middle class, carefully avoiding men of great wealth and little brain."

He said Clemetson "lived a selfish life, apart from his people, secluded like a little demigod in one part of the parish." That part of the parish was, of course, Port Maria, the Goffe-Clemetson stronghold in St Mary. Another teacher, Victor Bailey, president of the Jamaica Union of Teachers, said any working or middle class person who voted for Clemetson was a traitor to their class. "A teacher would be false to his profession, yea false to Jamaica, if he supported Mr. Clemetson, if he neglected the cause of right for the cause of might," Bailey told those gathered at a political rally for H.E.Vernon.

Clearly, Clemetson would not win the vote of the middle class in the parish. Surprisingly, he did not have the support of all of the ruling class in the parish, either. Though Norman Marsh was an owner of Warwick Castle, one of St Mary's largest banana plantations, and though Marsh was married to a relative of Clemetson's, he was not a supporter of the St Mary planter. In fact, he was one of Clemetson's greatest detractors. Marsh leveled a devastating attack on Clemetson at a Vernon political rally. "What we want are brain and intelligence not wealth and riches," said Marsh, one of the richest men in St Mary. "How is it that a man living so much out of touch with the people, and so unknown, should now foist himself on the people and expect their support," Marsh asked. "It was altogether too sudden and his sudden friendliness and interest and humility was only camouflage."

It was unusually harsh language. But perhaps Marsh's antipathy to Clemetson and his lot was not so surprising. The big landowners, though they banded together to protect their financial interests in the parish most of the time, were bitter rivals the rest of the time. It'd only been a few months since Norman Marsh and Alec Goffe, both members of the Parochial Board, looked as though they would resort to fisticuffs to settle a dispute. Marsh had called on the island's government to increase spending for roads in St Mary, in his constituency in western St Mary, Retreat, in particular. Goffe, a board member for Port Maria, was outraged. "Mr. Marsh wants everything to be done in his division," Goffe complained. "Look on the agenda and you will see five motions down in his name, four of which are for improvements for roads in the Retreat Division. Retreat must have everything while the other divisions have nothing," Goffe said.

A furious Marsh countered. "That is a disgrace to you," he said pointing at Goffe. "Mr. Goffe is the oldest member on the board and during all those umpteen number of years he has been on the board he should have had the roads in the Port Maria division put in better condition than those in any other division." The members of the Board laughed and mumbled in agreement. "On the other hand," Marsh said, the roads in Port Maria are "the worse and that certainly is no credit to Mr. Goffe."

Alec Goffe had clashed, too, with H.E. Vernon, or 'Sir V' as his supporters liked to call him. Vernon suggested at a Parochial Board meeting that some of the members allowed sentimentality to affect their political decisions. Alec Goffe was infuriated. He let it be known that he made his decisions coolly and with calculation.

"I do not like the word sentiment," he roared at Vernon. "If other members vote by sentiment, A. Davidson Goffe does not."

It was just the kind of performance that had won Goffe a reputation as a blow-hard. He said Vernon was "casting aspersions" on the Parochial Board. The Board he belonged to these past 40 years "did not vote," he said fuming, "by sentiment."

Vernon wasn't intimidated. He knew most Board members didn't like Goffe and would be happy to see his inflated view of himself punctured. "Perhaps," Vernon said turning to the other members, "Mr. Goffe likes to hear his own voice sometimes." Board members fell about in laughter.

With vengeance in his heart, Alec Goffe took the opportunity later at a public meeting to cast H.E. Vernon as a wolf in sheep's clothing. He said should Vernon ever be elected to the island's parliament, it would be the end for the banana industry and for the Jamaica Banana Producers' Association. Because Vernon was employed as an agent of the Atlantic Fruit Company in St Mary, he would, Goffe said, act in the interests of that American company and against the interests of the island's banana growers and workers.

With Clifford Clemetson under attack from H.E. Vernon and his people, Alec Goffe, and his brother, Clarence, came to their cousin's aid. Clemetson's political team decided it would make issue of the fact that Vernon had been born in St James parish and not in St Mary. It was a bad idea. Vernon had been resident in the parish for more than 32 years. Besides R.P. Simmonds, W.T. Graham, A.A. Barclay, A.F.G. Ellis, and four of the five previous members for St Mary in the Legislative Council, had not been born in the parish, either. Simmonds and Ellis had been born in England, Graham in St. Catherine and Barclay in Manchester.

Clemetson's cronies knew St Mary people sometimes resented Jamaicans who came from elsewhere on the island to their parish looking for banana money. "Mr. Clemetson was a St Mary man, a man from Port Maria," said Alec Goffe at a rally in Port Maria. "His father and grandfather also being of the same town, claiming the same, and as such felt that he should get the wholehearted support of his fellow parishioners and townsfolk."

Another Clemetson supporter, T.N. Francis, took the same tack, describing Clemetson as a "true born St Mary man." But Clemetson's campaign managers made the foolish mistake of assuming their candidate was a St Mary man, born and bred. It turned out Clemetson had been born in Crescent Park, in St Ann parish. Such were the miscalculations of the Clemetson campaign.

"Mr. Clemetson who has hitherto lived in obscurity, a man of wealth – and his wealth has been inherited and there is a great difference between this and wealth earned – wants now to represent the people," Vernon said mockingly at a rally. "With such vast wealth and living as he had lived in the past it is absolutely impossible for him to come down from that height and represent you of the middle classes," he said to loud cheers. "He knows nothing, absolutely nothing of your suffering…you have tried class men for eight long years, and the result has been nothing for St Mary's."

H.E. Vernon roasted Clemetson. Clemetson's people fought back. They spread rumours that Vernon would turn off Port Maria's lighting, divert shipping from the harbour and have the wharves pulled down if he were elected.

In a veiled reference to Clemetson and to the Goffes, H.E. Vernon said, "I have no command over shipping nor do I own a Wharf, at Port Maria or anywhere else." Though he acknowledged that Clifford Clemetson had more money than he did, Vernon said the planter had nothing over him when it came to colour. They were, he said, both "dark horses." In other words, they were both black, or men of colour. In turn, Clemetson's people accused Vernon of being racist. Some of Vernon's supporters had, apparently, uttered unflattering comments about Clemetson's white wife, Elsie.

Angry, Clemetson's cronies told voters Vernon did not like East Indians. A large number of Indians whose ancestors had come to Jamaica as indentured, so-called 'coolie' labour, worked on St Mary banana plantations. Clemetson's henchmen told voters Vernon had said ugly things about Indians and did not want Indians to vote for him. Damaged by the charges, Vernon did all he could to prove he liked Indians every bit as much as he did other Jamaicans.

"If there was one race of people dear to my heart," Vernon said at a political rally, "if there was one race I had taken into my confidence, that race would be the East Indians." One race of people not dear to his heart, however, was the Chinese. Vernon complained often that Chinese merchants "crafty business practices" had forced him out of the cocoa trade in Jamaica. Such comments rarely cost politicians votes. Often they were calculated to win the votes of the many in the population who resented the Chinese for one reason or another. The Chinese were not Vernon's main target, though. The millionaire candidate, Clemetson, was. A popular ditty about Clemetson, penned by Vernon's supporters, helped make the planter a laughing stock:

> *'Clifford Clemetson hails from Frontier*
> *They say he's a young millionaire*
> *But though he's so wealthy,*
> *He won't feel so healthy*
> *When defeated by Vernon the Fair.'*

And defeat him he did. Vernon got 2,139 votes and Clemetson got just 1,297 votes. Interestingly, records were broken at the election. In an act of gross corruption, 280 people were found to have voted twice, the largest such number in Jamaican electoral history. Three hundred and seventy nine votes were spoilt. When the polls closed at 5 pm, it was expected the results would be ready before nightfall. But concerns over voter fraud delayed the process. The final results were not ready until a day later, another dubious record in Jamaican electoral history. It had never taken that long to declare a winner. The result, when it came, thrilled H.E. Vernon and his supporters. Their man had won by an almost two to one margin.

"The Happiest Man In Jamaica," is the how *The Gleaner* described Vernon after he took his seat in the Legislative Council, one of three former teachers then sitting in the parliament. His was a compelling story, the newspaper said, and one every Jamaican who had tried and not succeeded, at first, could learn from. "Yes, H.E. Vernon is a climber. He rose phoenix-like from the bottom to the top." Asked if he was happy by the reporter, he said: "You ask me if I am happy. I am certainly the happiest man to-day in Jamaica."

By contrast, Clifford Clemetson was the saddest man in Jamaica. More misery, though, for the Goffe-Clemetson clan came two years later with the defeat of Alec Goffe in St Mary's 1936 Parochial Board elections. The small axes had been sharpened and cut down a big tree.

Days before the elections, *Plain Talk*, a newspaper which advertised itself as the 'voice' of ordinary Jamaicans, bitterly criticised the state of affairs in St Mary which, it said, allowed four members of the Goffe clan: Alec, his nephew John Vincent Goffe, Sam Walker, a big landowner and father-in-law to John Vincent, and Clifford Clemetson, to hold all four seats in the Port

Maria division of the St Mary Parochial Board at one time. The family controlled a third of the seats on the board. Between them, the four held the key posts of chairman of the board, vice-chairman of the board, and chairman of the board's finance committee.

"At present the Port Maria electoral division of the district is being represented for years by…Familyism, and this goes to say – Father in Law, Son in Law, Uncle in Law, and Cousin in Law, all four in-laws representing this division," *Plain Talk* newspaper complained. It was an oft-repeated complaint, and one that John Vincent Goffe, whom everyone called 'Vin', had to tackle when he first campaigned for a seat on the Board in 1927.

"There were many Goffes already in the parish, and for the district I am standing for there was another Goffe, an uncle of mine," Vin Goffe confessed at a political rally. He told the crowd he had recently returned to Jamaica from school in England and that he had spent some time travelling to Bermuda and to Russia and felt he could make a difference in St Mary. "Only two things were beating us," Goffe said, "selfishness and favouritism."

Though he condemned favouritism, it had worked for him in his campaign for public office. Vin won a seat on the Board. Interestingly, the political interests of clan members clashed at the next election, three years later. Vin Goffe decided not to stand in 1930 when he realised if he and his cousin, Clifford, both ran the vote would be split and they would both lose.

By 1936, it really was time for a change. One of the candidates endorsed by *Plain Talk* to help break up the Goffe-Clemetson clan's stranglehold on St Mary was John Alfred Clemetson. It was a strange choice. "All eyes are now looking on…John A. Clemetson…to come forward," read an article in *Plain Talk* in 1936. "Mr. John A. Clemetson has a very large following, and is a native of Port Maria, and is a very able young man, we are sure he will be elected."

John Clemetson was elected. The only problem was he, too, was a member of the Goffe-Clemetson clan, in a way. John was a first cousin of Clifford Clemetson and a first cousin of Alec Goffe's, though both kept him at arm's length. He operated a garage in Port Maria and a car service and lived in a modest house outside the boundary of Clifford's enormous Frontier estate. Though he hadn't been educated at the fancy schools Clifford had, John was a wise, capable young man. For some reason he did not inherit the large sums of money or large pieces of property other of his relatives had.

"Oh no, we weren't part of the plantocracy," Dr Shirley Cridland, a daughter of John Clemetson said. "We weren't part of the country club, the tennis club set."

John Clemetson's inclusion in the 1936 Parochial Board elections helped pull votes from longstanding Board members like Alec Goffe, Clifford Clemetson, and Sam Walker. In a big surprise, Alec Goffe, the grand old man of St Mary politics, was defeated at the polls and driven from office after almost forty years on the board. He believed because his father and grandfather had been elected officials in St Mary that he should be a representative for life if he wished. Losing his bid for a seat in the Legislative Council in 1920 and again in 1925 was not nearly as bad as what happened to Alec Goffe in the Parochial Board elections of 1936.

Eight candidates, many of them spoilers with no chance of winning, campaigned ferociously for the four available seats in the Port Maria division. The polls opened at 7am on June 19 and closed at 12 midnight. It rained all day. This did not stop voters turning out to cast their ballot at the courthouse in Port Maria. Early in the day there was some commotion at the polling station when a voter was discovered trying to vote twice. By evening time, the polling stations were packed with onlookers desperate to know how the race for the four seats was progressing.

"What's the position?" one person asked. "Who's leading?" another asked. "Who's fourth?" yet another asked. It became clear that three of the four seats in the Port Maria division would be won by Clifford Clemetson, John Clemetson and Dr Linden Courtney Leslie, one of a new breed of black professional challenging the old order. The battle for the remaining seat was between business partners and best friends, Alec Goffe and Sam Walker, the elder statesmen on the Parochial Board.

"Everyone realised…that the battle for the fourth place was really between the old chairman and vice-chairman," *The Gleaner* reported. "It was truly interesting to hear now a murmur of applause, then a sigh of regret, as the two old horses fought for a place."

When the final count was read out at the courthouse at 11:40 pm, Alec Goffe had 307 votes and Sam Walker had 308 votes. "Mr. A.D. Goffe Loses Seat in St Mary After Nearly 40 Years' Service," is how the defeat was reported.

The four candidates with the largest number of votes were: Clifford Clemetson with 427 votes; John Clemetson with 404 votes; Dr Leslie with 350 votes; and Sam Walker with 308 votes. The also-rans were: Alec Goffe with 307; Reginald Beckford with 188 votes; Vin Goffe with 197 votes and Victor Silvera with 96 votes. Two Goffes lost their seats, an uncle and a nephew. It was a sound blow against what *Plain Talk* had called 'Familyism,' domination by a single family of the political and economic affairs of a township or a parish. Glad to have escaped the 'Familyism' backlash, Clifford Clemetson tried to steer clear of trouble. He was just glad to have been re-elected, he said.

Another of the lucky winners, Dr Leslie, had made clear in his campaign that he wanted to see an end to nepotism and the break up of the banana clique that dominated the parish's affairs. He was cheered loudly when he rose to speak. "I must take this opportunity of thanking my supporters for having rallied to the cause and seeing me through," said Leslie. "I appreciate very much all that you have done for me, and shall do all in my power for the progress and advancement, not only of the No.1 Division (Port Maria), but the parish as a whole."

Though a loser, Alec Goffe demanded and got the chance to speak. "Sorry Mr. Alec," many shouted. Though he and Sam Walker had been in a battle for the remaining seat on the Board, it was Dr Leslie, a man born in the same year Goffe first took his seat on the Parochial Board in 1898 and born elsewhere on the island, that he reserved his anger for. His parting words to Port Maria voters and to the opponent he claimed had taken votes from him by stirring up colour and class hatred were harsh and unforgiving.

"I have never experienced an election like this kind in the 40 years I have been in the Parochial Board and when a gentleman gets up and traces another gentleman from his birth, it was disgraceful," Goffe said over protests from the audience. He claimed Dr. Leslie had held a meeting in which he spewed hatred for those who had lighter skin and more money than him. "I am sorry to say it is one of the successful candidates who had said those things. I was told by a gentlemen that some of the supporters of that candidate walked out of the room – ashamed of themselves when they heard a gentleman of that kind saying such things."

Goffe wasn't done. "I was born here and have lived here over 70 years and never heard such a thing- to trace a man's character from his birth."

The audience didn't agree, and told Goffe so. "That is not true, lies. Go away, they shouted." Dr Leslie tried to get up from his seat but was forced to remain sitting. The marching band was ordered to quickly begin playing 'God Save The King' in hopes of bringing the proceedings to a close. Before the band could do this, Dr Leslie forced his way to the podium. "Ladies and Gentlemen," he said. "I should crave your indulgence for a minute in view of an aspersion that has been cast on me. I was only replying – retaliating to aspersions cast on me."

Though he blamed Linden Leslie for his defeat and for stirring up colour and class hatred, Alec Goffe did more than anyone to bring himself down when he clashed with banana workers in St Mary a year before, in 1935. Goffe, the agent for the Jamaica Banana Producers' Association at Oracabessa had no idea the tough tactics he employed to deal with stevedores in Oracabessa would lead to rioting, the calling out of armed police from Kingston, and a gun battle and siege.

After failing to convince banana workers in Oracabessa to accept seven pennies an hour to load thousands of bananas, Alec Goffe left the town for Port Maria. There he struck a deal with unemployed workers who hadn't had a day's pay in a long time. They agreed to load the JBPA ship for much less than the Oracabessa workers were willing to. They had no idea, or perhaps were too hungry to care, that they were being used by Goffe to avoid paying the Oracabessans a living wage.

There was no need for such tactics. The directors of the Jamaica Banana Producers' Association were making plenty of money and Oracabessa was one of their most lucrative ports. Besides, Goffe was making large sums of money both as a director of the JBPA and as an agent purchasing bananas on the co-operative's behalf. It was a sweetheart deal and the member of the Legislative Council for Clarendon, J.A.G. Smith, had accused Alec Goffe of double dipping.

Goffe's profits were increased if he was able to buy bananas at the lowest possible price, get banana workers to load it for the lowest possible wage and then sell it in the United States for the highest possible amount. This is why he went to Port Maria on Saturday 11 May 1935 and arranged for one hundred unemployed workers there to come to Producers' Wharf at Oracabessa the next day to load bananas for seven pennies an hour, a sum locals would not accept.

He didn't have to try very hard to convince the Port Maria workers to accept seven pennies an hour. Port Maria had once had the busiest harbour in Jamaica. But as the size of fruit steamers grew larger it became impossible for them to fit comfortably into the town's small, snug harbour. The Royal Mail Company and Standard Fruit Company stopped docking there. Standard pulled down its wharf and took the lumber away with it. The United Fruit Company did the same. Prosperity turned to poverty and the pauper rolls swelled.

Eager and happy to have work of any kind, the Port Maria workers arrived in Oracabessa bright and early on Sunday 12 May 1935. The hundred men were brought by truck the eight or so miles to the town and would be, Goffe had promised them, brought home later that night by truck once they'd loaded the ship to his satisfaction. They waited patiently at the harbour for *S.S. Asta* to arrive. Waiting there with them were Oracabessa workers Goffe had refused to pay more than seven pennies an hour. They hadn't realised there wouldn't be work for them and, at first, responded with indifference to the presence of the outsiders. It was only when the Port Maria workers alone were allowed to load the ship and they were told to leave the wharf that it became clear what had transpired.

By the time the ship was loaded late that evening, an angry crowd of around 200 Oracabessans armed with sticks, bottles, conch shells and pieces of iron piping were waiting to confront the men as they began to file into waiting trucks. "It will be hell to-night," one man was heard to say. The trucks were stoned as was the Producers' Association's buildings. The town's police arrived, but were turned back. Alec Goffe took cover in the JBPA office.

Hearing what was happening to their friends and relatives in Oracabessa, dozens of men from Port Maria set out for the town.

Unable to cope, local police pleaded with authorities in Kingston to send them as many armed officers as they could. Unable to get at the Port Maria workers, the angry Oracabessans tried to get their hands on the architect of their troubles – Alec Goffe. When they tried to enter the JBPA office, he brandished a rifle. They fled, but returned awhile later with reinforcements. In the meantime, Simeon Wright, a District Constable and Corporal Ahijah Gibbs, a soldier stationed in Oracabessa, took refuge in the Association's office. As the rioters tried to rush the building, Alec Goffe fired three shots in their direction. With one firearm between them, Goffe and Constable Wright, took turns taking potshots at the protestors until the two were rescued and calm was restored to Oracabessa. This peace was short-lived, though. *So if you are the big tree, we are the small axe, ready to cut you down, to cut you down…*

Negro Aroused

The Old World is ending; the New World has just begun.

Bob Marley

That was the year everything changed, everything. The island's government had intended to sponsor tame events featuring centenarians recalling the days of slavery, the arrival of Emancipation and how blessed the island had been these past hundred years. But all of that had to be put on hold when workers – sugar workers in Westmoreland, dockworkers in Kingston, banana workers in St Mary – went on strike. It was called a labour rebellion, but felt like a revolution.

When workers at the Frome sugar estate in Westmoreland went on strike on 29 April, 1938, the police were called. Four people, one of them a pregnant woman, died.

Next it was Kingston. Dockworkers went on strike. Agitating on their behalf, Alexander Bustamante, a moneylender turned activist, was arrested and charged with sedition and inciting unlawful assembly. Bustamante's distant cousin, Norman Manley, a respected barrister, told the governor he would set aside his legal work for a time to aid the strikers and negotiate on their behalf. But few of the owners of the large shipping companies wanted to negotiate. They wanted to re-open the docks using 'black leg' or 'scab' labour with armed soldiers as protection. One shipping company owner, though, Charlie Johnston, was more co-operative.

It had been almost 20 years since A.C. Goffe and Charlie Johnston's 'banana war' had roiled the island's fruit industry. Goffe lost that war and was forced to shut down his export firm, the Baltimore and Jamaica Trading Company. Afterward, he became the United Fruit Company's buying agent in Oracabessa. Later still, he retired to St Ann to manage two banana and coconut properties he had there and to open a hotel. By contrast, Charlie Johnston had become, by 1938, a national figure. He was head of the Jamaica Banana Producers' Association, a director of Kingston Wharves Ltd, and a leading figure in the island's shipping association, as well.

Winning a wage increase and other concessions from the shippers' association would, Norman Manley hoped, be a relatively quick and easy thing. The barrister was already on friendly terms with the association's president, Charlie Johnston. Manley had first met Johnston when the attorney was asked to help draft the Jamaica Banana Producers' Association constitution in the 1920s. He remained an acquaintance of Johnston's and was invited to go with him to New York in 1935 to negotiate with the United Fruit Company.

"C.E. Johnston...a tower of strength against force," Norman Manley wrote in the diary he kept of the events of 1938. "He sees that all wages must go up. He sees very far."

Agreement was soon reached and the strikers had all they wanted, except the release of their imprisoned leader, Bustamante. The shippers, Johnston among them, were nervous that releasing the labour leader would spark another round of demonstrations. Lawyer Manley told them they were worrying about the wrong thing. They ought, he told them, to be concerned what might happen should Bustamante not be released, and quickly. Interestingly, Johnston had once been Bustamante's employer. As a young man, the labour leader worked for a time at one of C.E. Johnston and Co.'s general stores on Jamaica's north coast. Johnston and the other shippers eventually agreed to the release of Bustamante.

Following Kingston's lead, dockworkers went on strike at St Ann's Bay later on in May. The island's most widespread and violent labour demonstrations, however, took place in St Mary in June. Thousands of workers from estates near Annotto Bay, Islington and Port Maria put down their tools and went on strike for better pay and better conditions. They were soon joined by hundreds more from Highgate and Richmond. Together they marched onto plantation after plantation taking workers' tools and demanding they join them. They blocked the main roads with boulders, trees, and tar pots and stopped scab labour replacing them. In a short time more than 6,000 labourers from various

St Mary banana estates congregated at Cenotaph Square in Port Maria. The strikers demanded to meet with the chairman of the Parochial Board, the director of the Public Works Department, and the owners of several of the area's large estates. They threatened a hunger strike. The parish in turmoil, the planters tried to regain control. Forty Justices of the Peace held an emergency meeting at the Lyric Theatre. Hoping his business would not be looted, Henry Wise Osmond, owner of a general store in Port Maria's town centre, dispersed flour, fish and meal to protestors. Hours later the Sherwood Foresters, a division of the British armed forces with a fearsome reputation, arrived from their barracks in Kingston to put down the uprising.

On their way from Kingston, too, were Alexander Bustamante and Norman Manley. Both men had grown up in rural parts and knew how hard life was there for workers who were little more than serfs tied to the land and subject to the will of the feudal lord. Manley had good reason to resent and dislike the landed gentry. He grew up, he said, as a 'Bush man' on farms in the parishes of Manchester and St Catherine. To earn pocket money, he cleaned pastures and chipped logwood. "I read with amusement writers who speak of me as if I was the product of urban conditions and pure middle class life," Manley wrote in *My Early Years – Fragment of an Autobiography*. "They do not know that I grew up with working class people in deep rural Jamaica."

Manley's father, Thomas, was a mulatto whom he described as "the illegitimate son of a woman of the people." His grandfather was a Yorkshireman who went out to Jamaica to work as a travelling tradesman. Manley's mother, Margaret, was, like her husband, a mulatto. Norman Manley described his mother, who worked as a postmistress, as "an almost pure white woman."

When Manley's father, who'd once been a prosperous produce dealer, died he left his wife and four children nearly penniless. They had lived on a large property called Roxburgh, but unable to pay the bills, Margaret Manley left her children with relatives and moved to the United States to work in the postal service. She soon returned, though, as her wages were not enough to support her or her family.

She left Manchester with her two boys and two girls and moved to a derelict property she'd inherited in the hills of St Catherine called Belmont. It was there the young Norman Manley got to know life as it was lived by most Jamaicans. Manley's mother had so little money she served as her own overseer. She made her children's clothes herself, made jellies from guava fruit and kept a small chicken farm, as well.

At night, when she had some time to herself, Margaret Manley would write letters to the few friends she had left. "Nearly all of them," Norman Manley wrote, "deserted her when she married a near black man."

So Norman Manley knew something of the harsher side of life in Jamaica. Like Manley, Bustamante knew how hard life could be in Jamaica. Though an almost white man, he enjoyed few of the privileges people of his colour usually did in Jamaica. Though Bustamante's father was white, he was poor. He made his meagre living as an overseer managing the properties of the wealthy in Hanover Parish in western Jamaica.

"We never had much for there were twelve of us," Bustamante revealed in an interview. "Sometimes we had no meat, not even herring to eat with our yam."

Impoverished, Bustamante's father could not afford to keep his son in school beyond the primary level. He had few prospects and so worked at various jobs in various parts of the island. Bustamante worked as a clerk in one of Charlie Johnston's general stores in Hanover for a time and he worked as a junior overseer – breaking horses and such – on a farm owned by his distant cousins, the Manleys.

In 1904, aged 20, he left Jamaica, as thousands of his countrymen did each year, to seek work in the United States, Panama and Cuba. While he was away from Jamaica, Bustamante claimed he was adopted by a Spanish sea captain, served as a cavalry officer in the Spanish Army in Morocco, worked as a captain in the Havana Police Force, prepared meals in a New York hospital and worked as a Wall Street investor. He returned to Jamaica aged 50 in 1934.

It is, Bustamante said, "a known fact that my name is an international one known throughout the civilised world." In Jamaica in 1934 Bustamante's name was not known, at all. Bustamante did everything he could to change this. He earned his money as a moneylender, but made his name as a political activist. Whether by chance or by design, Bustamante had returned to Jamaica at a time of great political upheaval in the Caribbean: Revolution in Cuba, sugar workers on strike in Puerto Rico, St Kitts and Guyana, land protests in St Vincent, coal carriers on strike in St Lucia, oilfield workers on strike in Trinidad, demands for trade unions in Barbados. Stirred by the upheavals, in 1936 Bustamante joined the pioneering labour leader Allan Coombs of Jamaica Workers' and Tradesmen's Union. Most people on the island found out who Bustamante was, and what his concerns were, through letters he wrote to *The Daily Gleaner*.

"The suffering of the mass of the people is intense," Bustamante wrote in one letter "They are reaching the state of desperation. Hungry women, children and men, are crying out in their humble, peaceful ways for help from their father – the Government."

With the Sherwood Forresters, a division of the British armed forces, on its way to St Mary with orders to put down the protests of banana workers, the letter writer, Bustamante, and the barrister, Manley, set off in June 1938 for St Mary, as well.

"All over the island of Jamaica today there is a certain amount of trouble because the workers of this country are asking for something more for themselves," Bustamante told the thousands of striking banana workers gathered in Port Maria's town centre. "I myself came forward and offered my services to any body of workers who were making demands for better conditions and wages because I feel there is room for improvement."

Bustamante told the strikers there was a good chance their demands would be met. Norman Manley had, he told them, met with the government's Conciliation Board before coming to Port Maria and he was optimistic a compromise could be reached on wages.

Horrified that worker's wages might be increased, conservative critics like Esther Chapman, an Englishwoman who was editor of the *West Indian Review*, protested. "It is not merely unjust to penalise one class at the expense of another, it is unwise and in the long run must defeat its own ends," Chapman said. "Sometimes even when workers suffer from the evils of underpayment, it is not because there is deliberate exploitation. Employers are often at the mercy of economic conditions."

Though Manley and Bustamante had helped quiet the strikers in Port Maria, they hadn't quieted those in Islington, a few miles east of the capital town. Protestors there clashed with armed police and four banana workers, Caleb Barrett, Archibald Franklin, Felix McLaglen and Thaddeus Smith, were shot and killed.

Violent protest also occurred in Richmond, in Highgate, in Oracabessa, at Gray's Inn, in Annotto Bay, in Guy's Hill and in Port Maria. As during slave rebellions in the 1830s, in the 1930s the landed gentry barricaded themselves on their estates, convinced they were in danger.

"The prime targets there were the big Jamaican growers and buying agents, the Lindos, Goffes, Magnuses, de Lissers and Champagnies," wrote Ken Post in his book, *Arise Ye Starvelings*. "They were the people that Quashee sought to incommode, to close down, to threaten and punish." Quashee, Post said, "struck against the rural capitalists...not as human-bearers of an inhuman system but as 'bad people' or in their role as exploiters."

Though some barricaded themselves on their estates, other members of St Mary's plantocracy tried to keep a stiff upper lip.

"The strikers are of course the chief topic of conversation here, and the fever has spread to the tennis club," the society column, *The World And His Wife*, reported. "The ball boys staged a walk out on Wednesday afternoon, with the exception of two loyal ones, who rendered yeoman service."

Among those enjoying themselves at the club while St Mary burned was Eileen Clemetson-Goffe and Lester Goffe, a neice and nephew of A.C. Goffe's. Lester, as well as being the owner of a large banana property with his brother, Maurice, was chairman of the parish's Law Abiding Society. With most of the workers from his plantation gone to join the strikers, Lester, not usually a man of action, tried to help put down the rebellion. He signed up as a member of a hastily assembled special police force, taking the title of Special Constable.

Ignoring Special Constable Goffe's likely bias, the Resident Magistrate's office placed him on the jury to judge whether the officers who shot and killed four strikers in Islington had acted lawfully. Also on the jury, and again hardly a neutral figure, was Lester's cousin, Frederick Athelstan Taylor, another plantation owner. This is how justice was meted out in St Mary. Not surprisingly, with the jury stacked with members of the plantocracy, the officers who killed the four strikers were found not guilty.

Next door to St Mary, in St Ann parish, there had been a worker rebellion, too. The strikes revealed just how bad life was for Jamaica's agricultural workers. The tasks an agricultural worker was expected to do were endless: Weeding grass, forking new lands, forking old lands, trenching new lands, trenching old lands, pruning banana, planting banana, picking and husking coconuts, cutting cordwood, chipping cordwood, chipping logwood, digging banana suckers, digging holes, working wagons, cutting banana, cutting fence posts.

A worker on the Southfield estate in St Ann, for example, was paid only ten pennies for clearing one whole square chain of banana land in very bad condition. Things weren't much better on Llandovery estate, a well-known St Ann plantation. To earn a measly shilling, a worker had to weed 20 chains of sugar cane. Coconut workers picked, husked and separated large fruit from small fruit, packed them into bags and loaded them on trucks all for just seven pence per one hundred coconuts.

There were as many women and children working the plantations as there were men. For as little as three pennies per tin, women climbed pimento trees, picked the seeds and then carried them in a basket to a delivery point miles away. Picking limes was just as poorly paid and just as demanding. Often a worker walked more than ten miles of acreage to collect two tins of lime, netting them exactly six pennies. It was not unusual to see 14-year-old girls lugging huge bunches of bananas. They were paid one penny for each bunch they delivered.

"They are not better off than slaves," wrote the *Jamaica Labour Weekly* newspaper in 1938. At Drax Hall, one of the largest and best known plantations in St Ann, copra pickers and workers at the estate's soap factory went on strike. Following their lead, so did banana workers on the neighbouring Windsor estate, which was owned by A.C. Goffe. Afraid, Goffe gave in to the striker's demands.

Even as most planters agreed to wage increases, some complained they were being held to ransom and would be bankrupted as a result. Nothing could have been further from the truth. The island's coconut industry was booming. Coconut producers like Goffe were receiving record prices for their produce. In 1937, producers handled the largest amount of coconuts in their history, more than 19 million. This was an increase of four million over 1936. In 1938, they did even better.

The island's government, afraid the labour rebellion would lead, perhaps, to revolution unless broad concessions were made, pressed employers to raise the wages of the country's workers.

The wages of dock workers, for example, including those who unloaded bananas from railway wagons, rose from five shillings and ten pence a day to six shillings and eight pence a day for loading fruit onto ships for the European market. Workers who loaded ships with fruit for the American market saw their wages increase from six shillings and eight pence to seven shillings and six pence per day. The wages of stevedores rose on average by five shillings. The wages of banana carriers, the backbone of the industry, went up, too, but not by much. Before the strikes, they were paid two shillings per hundred bunches carried. Now they would be paid only three pence more. Stackers and stalkmen also saw their wages rise. But these were just half measures.

When the social service organisation, Jamaica Welfare Limited, sent a team to St Mary shortly after the labour rebellion, the team found that the "...wish for land...is almost universal." St Mary banana workers were happy their protests had convinced the bosses to increase their pay, but what they really wanted was land. Alexander Bustamante recognised this and promised striking workers in the parish he would press the government to come up with a land re-settlement scheme.

"I cannot stand before a group of people like you and talk nonsense," Bustamante told protestors gathered in Port Maria town center. "The thing most needed is for every man to have a better opportunity to get land in this country." This is a "new dawn to Jamaica", the labour leader said, "and there is no reason why one man should have 2,000 acres of land and you have none, even to put a hut on."

Clifford Clemetson had around 2,000 acres of land, and he was not going to be forced by the government, he said, to sell one acre of his enormous property, Frontier, so peasants could own land. It had been inherited from his father, David, who had inherited it from his father, Robert, who had bought the former slave plantation in 1853 at a discount.

Frontier wasn't the largest estate in St Mary, but none was situated quite as it was with the greater part of the capital town nestled within its borders. Clemetson did, in a way, own Port Maria and he wasn't eager to give this prestige up. He wanted things to remain as they were. The way things were, poor peasants who worked on his property paid him rent to live in rundown housing in swampy sections of the estate thick with mosquitoes, without roads, without proper sanitation or drainage.

"I counted sixty in all. Frail contraptions of decaying pieces of packing cases boards, bamboo, thatch, palm leaves. Huts with unsightly, gaping holes through which I saw poverty of a revolting kind." So said the Jamaican writer, Evon Blake, who went on a tour of the Pagee section of Frontier in 1938. "Hovels. Shacks. 'Lean-to's' with scarcely elbow room to spare between them.

A mother, daughter and grand-daughter lived in one of these...Six feet long by six feet wide...This place is not fit for vermin...God! Can't somebody in this rich parish do something for them?"

The Parochial Board, of which Clemetson was a member, had tried on several occasions to do something for the people of Pagee and of Port Maria. It offered Clemetson a fair price for parcels of land so the town could be enlarged and improved and so Pagee could be drained and sold to the more than 300 peasants living there. The peasants, themselves, had approached the landlord. A deputation, led by St Mary's member in the Legislative Council, H.E. Vernon, discussed the Pagee problem with the island's governor, but could not convince him to intervene.

Interestingly, Clemetson was a churchwarden, a Boy Scout leader, and had recently been made an 'official visitor' at the public hospital. His position there gave him the power to decide who ought to receive free medical care at Port Maria Public Hospital. If he considered an individual or a family deserving, he gave them a ticket which entitled them to treatment, gratis.

Clemetson held, for some in Port Maria, the power over life and death. Still, he could not be convinced of the wisdom of allowing St Mary's landless to become landowners. Interestingly, four years before, the planter had put land re-settlement at the top of his manifesto when he made a failed bid to become St Mary's representative in the Legislative Council. Now, his hopes of high office dashed, Clemetson, who had been made chairman of the Parochial Board's Poor House Committee, said he preferred his tenants remain tenants and he remain their landlord.

Few in St Mary were surprised at Clifford Clemetson's behaviour. After all, a year before this, it was discovered their Parochial Board member was a racist. Clemetson, a light-skinned black man, showed his true colours in a confrontation he had with labour leader Alexander Bustamante in Port Maria in 1937. Bustamante had come to St Mary to convince workers there to join the Jamaica Trades and Workers' Union. Desperate for refreshments after an evening meeting, Bustamante and a few of his union colleagues headed for the only place open – the Port Maria Tennis Club. A high society dance was in progress and the parish's high and mighty were in festive mood, despite the growing worker unrest on the island.

The last person the assorted planters and their wives expected to see in their club was people's champion, Bustamante. But there he was, at the bar, ordering drinks for himself and his party. Before the labour leader's drinks could be served, the president of the club, Clemetson, a man Bustamante later described as "a tall, thin, brown skin man," stepped in.

"Are you Bustamante?" Clemetson demanded. "You are the man organising the niggers, you can't drink in my club." A hostile group, dressed in tuxedos, surrounded the labour leader. "Yes, I am Bustamante," the union leader, who always carried a pistol and wore a steel vest, said angrily. "If you folks have never seen a Wild West show, just touch me tonight and you'll see one."

The musicians stopped playing. The club went quiet. All waited to see what would happen. The first move was made by the tennis club's black bar tender. In defiance of Clemetson's orders, he served Bustamante and his colleagues the drinks they'd asked for.

"This is my country," Bustmante shouted at the tennis club president and its members. "I am going to go where I like, eat, drink and sleep where I like. Neither you nor anyone in this room is going to stop me."

Bustamante told a newspaper later that he had been shocked by the confrontation, by the "savagery" of the racist comments, especially as, he said, "most of these people in this club have no signs of being white."

Far from stopping Bustamante, Clemetson and his tennis club cronies helped spur him on. Bustamante had come to St Mary to convince banana workers to join his union. Clemetson gave him just what he needed to win their support.

"I'm going to call a meeting here in Port Maria, and tell everybody what you have said," the labour leader threatened as he left the tennis club. He kept his word. When locals attending a Bustamante rally in town the next day were told that Clemetson, their local government representative, had called them "niggers" they were in fighting mood.

Foolishly, Clemetson turned up at the meeting. He tried to make a quick exit, but Bustamante exposed him. Angry workers blocked his exit. Bustamante had to demand they let Clemetson go. Deeply affected by the confrontation and the vile racism he encountered, a few weeks later Bustamante wrote a letter to *The Gleaner* demanding Jamaicans receive "more humane treatment...hate no one for their colour or otherwise..."

Several months after the confrontation between the labour leader and the planter, Bustamante returned to Port Maria and showed he had not forgiven or forgotten. At a meeting, he denounced both Clemetson and H.E. Vernon, St Mary's representative in the Legislative Council. Bustamante said Clemetson and Vernon could not represent the working people of the parish because they were advocates of "Capital not of Labour."

Clemetson, still smarting from his past encounter with Bustamante, stayed silent. Vernon, who liked to call himself a man of the people, spoke up. He had little choice. It had gotten around that Vernon, a banana-purchasing agent for the American Standard Fruit Company, had opposed wage raises for banana workers. Fearing his chance at re-election had been wrecked by the talk, which, he said, had been circulated by Bustamante, Vernon wrote a stinging letter to *The Gleaner* in which he described the union organizer, comically, as "Alexander Bustamante, Esq, Self Constituted Labour Leader and Dictator over Jamaica and probably later on its Dependencies."

Despite Bustamante's opposition, H.E. Vernon won re-election. Interestingly, several years later, Clifford Clemetson, in a bid to protect what little power he had left in St Mary, became a member of Bustamante's Jamaica Labour Party.

Though he shared many of Clifford Clemetson's views, Alec Goffe was smarter than his cousin, much smarter. While Clifford did not see the wisdom of letting the landless become landowners, Alec did. Goffe was on his own among Port Maria plantocrats in recognising concessions would have to be made to the majority if the minority, people like him, were to retain control on the island. Alec had been a supporter of land re-settlement for many years. He figured he lost his bid in 1920 to become St Mary's representative in the Legislative Council, in part, because his platform had been too narrow and had not embraced the aspirations of the growing middle and working class in the parish. Goffe envied how A.A. Barclay, the Presbyterian churchman who helped start the Western St Mary's Association, had built an enormous base of support for himself by supporting the creation of agricultural co-operatives and by calling for the island's government to launch a land re-settlement scheme. Intending to challenge the incumbent for the parish's Legislative Council seat in 1925, Goffe set out on a tour of St Mary in 1922 to see what would appeal to voters and what would not.

"If more large properties were cut up and sold to settlers," Goffe told the Western St Mary Citizens' Association in 1922. "Jamaica would be a far more prosperous country. We would not only increase production but we would divide the wealth of the colony amongst a greater number of people. The country would be better off, he said, only when "every man in it is better off." It was radical talk, especially coming from one of St Mary's largest landowners. Unfortunately for Goffe, no one believed he was serious. Voters thought he was playing politics with them, telling them what they wanted to hear and once elected would do whatever he wanted. Hardly anyone voted for him outside his stronghold of Port Maria when he sought the Legislative Council seat in 1925.

With Parochial Board elections approaching in 1936, Alec Goffe again insisted he supported land re-settlement. It was the only way, he said, that Jamaica could both remain prosperous and reduce class antagonisms. Making everyone a landowner, giving everyone a stake in the country, he said, was morally and economically correct.

"The more land settlement, the more smallholdings paying taxes of an aggregate in excess of what the single large property would pay," he argued in 1936 at a meeting of the island's Parochial Boards in Kingston. What Goffe said next got him into trouble with planters in his parish. "The people would be better off if they were given land at reasonable and not exorbitant prices, as were charged by some in St Mary."

Unlike Alec Goffe, St Mary's landed gentry did not see the wisdom of selling off parcels of their estates so landless peasants could become landowners. The island's government did, though, and on 5 June, 1938, the Governor of Jamaica announced a scheme that would make it possible for thousands of Jamaicans to purchase their first piece of land at reasonable rates.

A few weeks later Norman Manley, who'd shelved his law practice to become a full time political leader, announced he would press the government to introduce measures that would require large landholders to allot pieces of land to permanent workers to make up for having paid them low wages.

Planters were in a panic. To resist the changes going on around them, they called an emergency meeting in Port Maria to discuss setting up a St Mary Planters' Association. Sam Walker, Henry de Lisser, A.N. White, E.A. Silvera, Vin Roche, Ken Robinson, Eileen Clemetson-Goffe, and J. Hutton Jefferson turned up. Also there was Alec Goffe, who now that he was no longer seeking a seat in the Legislative Council or on the Parochial Board, said what he truly felt about land re-settlement. He didn't agree, at all, with the compulsory re-settlement proposal put forward by Norman Manley and would, he said, fight it.

Sam Walker said he did not feel it was necessary for government to compel people like him who had given some acreage in the past to deserving peasants. But Walker, chairman of the Parochial Board, was not about to take on the government. He would, he said, do whatever the governor demanded. "If they had to bow to the inevitable," Walker said weakly, "they would have to do it."

A.N. White was fiery. He said he would not be compelled and would resist any such measure. "They should drop the compulsory business altogether," he said, "as it was out of the question."

Alec Goffe's niece, Eileen, who had recently come into possession of a large estate, said she had spoken to many of the parish's large landowners and they had told her they would not allocate one acre to labourers, no matter what the government did. She questioned which worker could rightly be considered a 'permanent worker.'

"There was no such thing as a permanent labourer, because a labourer might," she explained using tangled logic, "work on a property for four years, and if at the end of that time they wanted to get rid of that worker, you could not call that 'permanent.'" Though the gathering talked a lot about starting a planter's association, with a chapter in every township in St Mary, none was begun.

Alec Goffe didn't say as much at the planter's meeting as might have been expected. Though he was still an important person in the parish – he was a director of the Jamaica Banana Producers' Association and agent for the co-operative at Oracabessa – he was no longer a member of the Parochial Board, the body which governed the parish. He had lost his bully pulpit, and thus the opportunity to speak out and be listened to on any subject which concerned or interested him. It comforted him that after he lost his seat on the Board in 1936 the new Board passed a resolution recognizing his efforts on behalf of St Mary. H.S. Schleiffer, a firm friend, said anyone who had been on the Board for more than a few weeks knew what good stuff the planter was made of. Schleiffer said something more than words should be done to recognise Alec Goffe's 40-year tenure. A.B. Champagnie, too, said he regretted Goffe was no longer a Board member and C.L.A. Stuart said Goffe had been a "fearless and outspoken" advocate for St Mary.

The man who replaced Goffe on the Board, Dr. Linden Leslie, one of the new breed of black professionals who had been trying to dislodge the planto-crats in the parish, knew all this praise was, in part, criticism of him and those who voted for him. He and Goffe had clashed badly during the election when it was revealed Leslie had said it was time for someone who was not rich or light skinned to get a chance to serve on the Parochial Board.

As to the resolution to recognise Alec Goffe, Leslie said he hardly knew the man but would support it, anyway. Sam Walker, Goffe's partner in the Walker and Goffe banana firm and chairman of the Parochial Board, said he would miss Alec Goffe's feistiness in discussion of parish affairs and said he hoped old age — the planter was 73 — would not prevent Goffe from some day returning to the Board. That opportunity came in 1938 when Dr Leslie resigned his seat on the Board. An emergency election was called, but the deputation Alec Goffe expected would come to his home and demand he run did not arrive. His nephew, John, was selected to run, instead. A good natured but ineffectual man, Vin, whom his father-in-law dismissed as knowing nothing whatsoever about farming, didn't know much about politics, either. He was soundly beaten by accountant, Rupert Meikle, the founder of the Quill and Ink Club, a society Meikle said he hoped would help develop "the beauty, culture and art in his race."

Though no longer on the St Mary Parochial Board, Alec Goffe continued to be a subject of heated discussion and deep division for those on the parish's governing body. In July 1938, the village of Preston in St Mary held a ceremony to lay the corner stones of a new school house that Alec Goffe had worked hard to get built. He had pressed the Department of Education to put up the money and had put in a good amount of his own cash, as well, to see that the school, which was a mile or so from his home and plantation, Oxford, was completed.

Goffe was an honoured guest at the event. To open the event, Isaac Watts' splendid hymn, *O God Our Help In Ages Past*, was sung. Somehow, with all the turmoil and labour unrest everywhere on the island and especially in St Mary, the hymn seemed particularly apropos: *Our God, our help in ages past, / Our hope for years to come, / Our shelter from the stormy blast, / And our eternal home.*

The singing done, it was down to business. Several Board members invited to the event claimed not to be able to make it. Cliff Clemetson had a cold. John Clemetson had to be at court. The Custos, too, A.C. Westmoreland, begged off the event claiming important business elsewhere. H.S. Schlieffer, a Goffe loyalist, was at the event and used the occasion to chastise those from the area who had not voted for Alec Goffe in 1936. He said it was clear the people of Preston badly needed a school for had they been better educated they would not have "kicked" Alec Goffe out of office. That was, though, the kind of "thanks" men like Goffe were given for public service by the ungrateful of the parish, Schlieffer sniffed.

Bravely, Dr Leslie, Goffe's arch enemy, attended the opening of the school in Preston. Trying to diffuse the tense situation, he said Alec Goffe had a "rough exterior" but he believed he had a "genuine heart." This was greeted coolly. Abandoning the niceties, Dr Leslie challenged the idea that he had been elected and Goffe turned out of office because St Mary voters were not well educated. On the contrary, he said, it proved how well informed and enlightened they were and how keen they were for a change in the parish. Besides, he understood that they lived in a democracy and that the people had spoken and nothing else needed to be said on the subject.

To his credit, Alec Goffe said nothing on the subject. Instead, he was uncharacteristically pleasant and playful. He said once the Preston school was completed he would like to see a free lunch facility set up for the boys and girls. Learning on an empty belly was not, he suggested, an easy thing to do. He knew, he said, the young people walked miles to school and were hungry because his plantation was nearby and his orange trees had been stripped clean. He did not mind this, he said, as he had taken many a fruit from trees, too, when he had been a boy. It hardly seemed like it was Alec Goffe, at all. Had he shown this tender side of himself more often he might still have been a member of St Mary's Parochial Board.

The side of Alec Goffe most people were familiar with was on show a few months later at a meeting at Port Maria Town Hall. The meeting was to show support for Sam Walker, chairman of the Parochial Board. Walker had been under siege, accused by a rival for a seat on the Board of failing constituents and of striking a secret deal to raise water rates and taxes.

Alec Goffe, Walker's best friend and business partner, meant to shore up support for Walker when he took the floor at the Town Hall. He probably lost him votes. Goffe complained that he had lost his seat on the Board to one of a new breed of black middle class professional, people without property or pedigree who wanted to take control of the parish's affairs and push those who had run things for generations aside. He called on St Mary to reject the upstarts.

"We want men of position in the parish," he told those assembled at the

Town Hall. It was a disgrace, he said, for the new breed of candidates – teachers and doctors – to imagine they were of the same rank as "gentlemen." He told the audience if they elected one of the middle class candidates and they had to go to Kingston to meet with the governor, it was very possible the governor would not listen to them because they were not of sufficient rank. Goffe had nothing to lose – he had done running for office – so he went further. It was likely, Alec Goffe said, that a man of the middle class would not even be allowed through the door of the governor's residence at King's House. The audience was stunned. "The parish needs," Goffe barked, "men of position to lead it."

Alec Goffe was certainly not going to lead St Mary again. His diatribe made sure of that. But though Goffe lost his bully pulpit, it took much longer for other members of St Mary's elite to relinquish political power there. An angry editorial in a 1942 edition of the *New Negro Voice*, the newspaper of Marcus Garvey's Universal Negro Improvement Association, complained that the rule of the big landowners in the parish had hardly declined, at all. The *Voice* editorial complained that big planters had manipulated elections in the parish and had rigged the vote to keep the People's National Party candidate, who advocated broad social and political change, out of office.

"Intimidation, fear, and the rotten influence of wealth seeped through the entire voting structure of oppressed St Mary and rotted it from top to bottom!" the *New Negro Voice* protested: "Tenants and others dependent financially on one or another of the big clique or obligated to any organisation in which the big man's influence or that of his "tool" could be felt (e.g banana business, loan bank, etc.) were threatened with reprisals if they did not vote for the rich man's candidate. Where the small man is dependent on the big man in a parish like St Mary, political independence of thought or action spells financial suicide and economic disaster." Though balloting was supposed to be secret, the paper said, agents of the plantocracy had come up with a system which allowed them to determine who had followed their orders and voted for their candidate, and who had dared disobey them.

"These initials are a sure guarantee of a suitable and appropriate reward for proven loyalty to the clique that rules St Mary and has Highgate as its headquarters and the entire parish as its private holiday. A servile state!..such is the power of land and wealth." The 'big man's candidate', Roy Lindo, an uncle to Chris Blackwell of Island Records fame, won election to the

Legislative Council and after him Sam Walker was appointed to the Council. But it was the beginning of the end for the 'big men' in the parish, all the same. New things and new times were coming.

Hugh Burns, an advocate for change in St Mary said memorably, that those who'd been described as without position or pedigree had to "prepare to demand and seize the 'reins of Government'…that have been too long lying idle while the aged drivers lazily slept in a dying rain, dreaming of bygone days and never a thought to the future so near."

Tuff Gong and The Dowager

We no have no friend in high society.

Bob Marley

After losing his seat on the St Mary Parochial Board to a man he said had no position nor pedigree, Alec Goffe contemplated leaving St Mary for good. He couldn't, of course, as he was the agent for the Jamaica Banana Producers' Association in Oracabessa and had to be in the parish most days of the week. Still, he felt as the parish had shown it did not want nor need him anymore, he ought to show that he did not need to be in the parish all the time, either.

In a bid to broaden his world beyond St Mary, and to distance himself from the goings on there, Alec Goffe and his wife, Lesline, bought a home in St Andrew's parish on Hope Road. The house, number 56, was a short walk from several of the island's landmark properties, among them King's House, the Governor of Jamaica's official residence.

By contrast with many of the properties around it, the Hope Road house was an unimposing two-storied colonial style property without pretensions. The house, which was set back from the road behind a wall and two large iron gates, was built in 1912 as part of a new neighbourhood in St. Andrew parish called Maryfield. On the five or so acre property were an assortment of carriage houses, cottages, and servant's quarters.

After Alec and Lesline moved into the house in around 1940 it was rare that a weekend went by without a party of some sort taking place. The guest list was filled with the names of old friends from St Mary and new friends from St Andrew: DeLavante, Parachini, Ashenheim, Cahusac, Rutty.

"They lived a very amusing social life," remembered Mary Jane Todd, the couple's goddaughter. "Everybody loved Uncle Alec and Aunt Lesline and they loved that. They were always giving parties, but they could afford it."

But the parties came to an end. Lesline, her old friends complained, had fallen in with a bad lot – Christian Scientists. Some of her old crowd called her new crowd, the First Church of Christ, Science, nothing but a sophisticated modern cult, which, though it claimed to be a Christian denomination, did not believe in the existence of sin, disease nor death. Sickness and suffering exist because of a failure of belief and can be alleviated by faith, Scientists say. Members refuse medical intervention, choosing instead to rely on spiritual healing and prayer to cure disease.

Scientists had been coming to Jamaica and making a concerted effort to win hearts and minds there since the late 1920s when one speaker after another arrived in the island from the group's Boston, Massachusetts headquarters. John Randall Dunn, for example, came in 1929 and Salem Andrew Hart spoke about the faith in 1930 at Masonic Hall on Hanover Street. Hart talked at length about Mary Eddy Baker, Christian Science's founder, and how spiritual healing and inspired prayer helped cure Jamaicans of "pernicious anemia, mental instability, atrophied limbs and distressing stoppage of speech."

Christian Scientists were well organised. Their reading room, where their literature could be perused, was based at 70 Harbour Street. Their religious services were held each Wednesday and Sunday at 131 Orange Street, and their ruling body in Jamaica had its headquarters at 13 West Race Course.

When the Scientists were making their first foray into Jamaica in the 1920s, Lesline knew nothing of them. Back then she was busy on St Mary's party circuit. She was first introduced to the group, which had not yet won full-fledged religious status in Jamaica, in 1940 when she arrived in St Andrew and went with a friend to a lecture at the Ward Theatre in Kingston. The keynote speaker, Paul Harsch, a leading Scientist from the group's American headquarters, said followers of Mary Eddy Baker's teachings had lifted themselves from beds of pain and allowed those who'd lived a degraded, dishonest existence to find useful activity. Lesline knew she had not always lived a particularly useful life. She still smarted from hearing her husband's brother, Rowland, describe her as "brainless and frivolous."

Paul Harsch saw his Kingston lecture as an opportunity to build a following among upper class Jamaicans like Lesline whom he believed had some influence in the island and could win legitimacy for Christian Science there. His calculation was correct. Within a short time, Lesline had become a director of the church and one of its leading advocates in Jamaica. In July 1944, she and other Scientists applied at a sitting of the Legislative Council for the passage of a private bill that would allow them to form a Jamaican branch of the First Church of Christ, Science in Kingston.

Lesline's beliefs would be tested. Alec had been ailing for some time and looked closer to death than he was to life. Still, Lesline did not seek medical treatment for him as aggressively as some of his family members and friends from St Mary would have liked. Instead, she and other Scientists, Winston McHardy, Mercedes O'Meally, Gerald Gauntlett, and Irene Stredwick, got together at her husband's bedside and prayed forcefully for him to get better. *"There is no life, truth, intelligence, nor substance in matter. All is infinite Mind and its infinite manifestation, for God is All-in-all...Spirit is God, and man is His image and likeness. Therefore man is not material; he is spiritual.*

Alec Goffe was material. Born on 30 October, 1865, around the time of the Morant Bay Rebellion and the American Civil War, he died on 6 July, 1945, aged 79.

"DEATH OF MR. A.D. GOFFE...Noted St Mary Planter..." an obituary reads. *"The Gleaner* announces with regret the death of Mr. Alexander Davidson Goffe, J.P., noted St Mary planter, which took place early yesterday morning at his residence No. 56 Hope Road, lower St Andrew."

He was buried at St. Andrew's Parish Church. Reverend Canon Lovell, Rector of the Anglican Church, offered the last rites. It was a simple service of prayers and the reading of a scriptural lesson. After this the casket, carried by pallbearers Owen F. Wright, Commissioner of Police, Inspector E. G. Orrett, Detective Superintendent R. H. Hooker, Captain R.C.S. Rutty, owner of the Manor House Hotel, Ken Cocking, a Jockey Club stalwart and Lester Goffe, Alec's nephew, was lowered into the grave. J. J. Mills, District Grand Master, Scottish Freemansonry, led a gathering of Masons in a reading of the Masonic serivce. This done, the mound was covered in floral tokens and wreaths. Among the largest was one from the Jamaica Banana Producer's

Association and another sent by the First Church of Christ, Science. Among the mourners was A.C. Goffe. The two brothers hadn't spoken in almost 20 years. They fell out after Alec chose Charlie Johnston's Jamaica Fruit and Shipping Company over A.C.'s Baltimore and Jamaica Trading Company in 1919.

A few years after Alec's death, Lesline began cutting her ties to her husband's parish. In 1948, she tried to sell their St Mary estate, Oxford, to Emerson Bainbridge, a British born, Bermuda based millionaire whose family started the well-known British department store chain, John Lewis. The sale didn't go through so she enlisted the help of realtor Tom Mercier of Northside Estates to sell off a portion of Oxford, called 'Little Oxford', in January 1950 to Major G.I. Wilkes, a Canadian expatriate. The remainder and bulk of the estate was sold later that same year, in September, to another expatriate, Englishman E.R. Miller, a well-known banana man and racing handicapper. A good portion of the money from the sale of the 600-acre plantation was said to have gone straight into the coffers of the First Church of Christ, Science. Lesline remained a firm believer in Christian Science, but avoided proselytising. As a result, few of those that met her in later years realised she had deep religious convictions of any kind. To them she was a kindly, eccentric widow without children living out her life at 56 Hope Road. Things went on like this for much of the 1940s and 1950s. In the 1960s, she took what was thought then to be the unusual step of transforming her home into an upmarket boarding house for a bohemian set of young people living unconventional lives. Lesline, by now in her late sixties, found kinship of a sort with this generation of Jamaicans. They were far less bound by race and class prohibitions than was her own generation. All and sundry found a home away from home at 56: Jamaica's aspiring writers, its actors, its painters, its filmmakers and designers. There, too, were the children of the Jamaican upper class out on their own for the first time. There was also a sampling of English expatriates on sabbatical in Jamaica. Lesline subdivided the two-storied main house into six apartments and offered them as rentals: *56 Hope Road, Furnished -45 and 55 pounds per month* read an advert that appeared in Jamaican newspapers on 25 November 1968.

Lesline took one of the cottages on the grounds, really the servant's quarters, for herself. "It was called '56'. Everyone knew '56'," insists Winston Stona, who was both an official at the Jamaica Tourist Board and an aspiring actor when he first moved as a boarder to 56 in the 1960s. "It really was the first of its kind then."

Winston Stona is best remembered for his role as a corrupt police detective in Perry Henzell's film, *The Harder They Come*. "It was a really well known spot. A lot of people came and went." Among them was: Annabella Proudlock, owner of the Ochos Rios art gallery, Harmony Hall; Tarquin Olivier, British actor Laurence Olivier's son; and Dr Basil Keane, the well know Jamaican man about town, dentist and actor.

"Lesline loved when we gave parties. We were all young bucks then," said Winston Stona, who is today managing director of *Busha Browne*, a manufacturer and exporter of Jamaican seasonings. "When I first went there Lesline had quite a few young ladies living there like Sally Densham who married Perry Henzell. Chris Blackwell was a suitor, I think, and he was always around the place."

As the task of collecting rent from boarders and paying for the upkeep of 56 became a burden she could no longer bear, Lesline decided to sell the home where she'd lived for more than 30 years. It seemed obvious whom she would sell the place to.

Of the many young men who visited Lesline's home in the 1960s to see friends renting rooms there, Chris Blackwell, the founder of Island Records, was perhaps the most intriguing. Blackwell, a member of the Lindo clan, was born in 1937 in London but raised in Jamaica. He spent part of his time in the family home in St. Andrew and the rest on a family estate in St Mary. In 1936, aged nine, he was sent back to Britain to attend a Catholic prep school and later Harrow. After school he earned his keep as an accountant and as a professional gambler.

The music business, though, was irresistible. In 1958, Blackwell began Island Records in Jamaica. He re-launched it in London four years later, and in 1964 sold more than six million copies of Millie Small's hit song, *My Boy Lollipop*. Blackwell went on to have success with several of his rock acts before returning to his Jamaican roots and Jamaican music. In the mid 1960s, Blackwell found himself more often than not in Jamaica and more often than not at 56 Hope Road.

"The place had a magic about it," Blackwell said. "It had good memories." In around 1970, Lesline sold the house to Chris Blackwell and his business partner Dickie Jobson. But though she'd sold it, she did not leave. Lesline continued living there in a cottage on the grounds under a special arrangement even after 56 Hope Road became the busy headquarters of Island Records.

It was fitting the place should have been sold to Blackwell; after all his great uncle, Cecil Lindo, a wealthy landowner and businessman, had once owned the property. Then it had been called *Odnil*, an inversion of the name Lindo.

Lindo and his brothers had made their money in Costa Rica. They left Jamaica in the 1880s as young men and returned years later rich from their investments in bananas and railways in Central America.

When the Lindos returned to Jamaica in 1914, Cecil, the most successful of them, bought 56 Hope Road. Lindo's marriage to Agnes Dennelly was solemnized there on 4 April, 1917. In 1920, Agnes Lindo placed an ad in *The Gleaner* for a "competent and respectable coloured nurse" to care for her nine month old baby. The Lindos lived at the house until 1928 when they sold the place, which *The Gleaner* described as "one of the finest residences in lower St Andrew," to John Crook, a Kingston businessman, for £2,500.

The Lindos moved to Devon House, a grand Jamaican mansion they paid £8,000 for, a short distance away. After John Crook's tenure, 56, ended up in the possession of an English couple, F.B. Sutton, a British army sergeant, and his wife, Dorothy. They named the house *Derry* and lived there until 1942, when Dorothy Sutton, secretary of the Ladies Guild of the Sailors' Society, was killed while cycling on Hope Road. A few months later the house was sold to Alec and Lesline. It stayed in their possession for over 30 years until it became the headquarters of Island Records in Jamaica in the 1970s.

In the 1970s, 56 became the spot where record company executives, rock journalists and aspiring recording artistes could meet and greet one another. In 1971, after Island signed the Wailers, 56 became Bob Marley's favourite uptown hangout. Though Lesline had been fond of the artistic in-crowd, she could never see eye to eye with Bob Marley. Bob liked nothing better after working hard each day at Harry J's studio downtown on *Catch a Fire*, his debut recording for Island, than coming uptown to cool out, get high, and play football at 56. This was the last thing Lesline wanted, living as she still did on the grounds in a cottage. But, with *Catch a Fire* set to become a big hit and Island desperate to keep their new star happy, Chris Blackwell didn't want to rock the boat.

"It became a completely different place when he moved in," said Annabella Proudlock, who lived at 56 in the 1960s and 1970s. "People in the area were shocked at the idea of Rastas playing football in the yard and ganja smoking wasn't part of the accepted scene yet, not till much later on. I imagine that some of those who'd once lived there, in the area of Hope Road, would have been turning in their graves at what was happening at 56."

Another person who rented rooms from Lesline was Sally Henzell, owner and manager of *Jake's*, a hotel in St. Elizabeth and wife of filmmaker, Perry Henzell. "It was the first time that there was such an enclave above Cross Roads," said Henzell, referring to the accepted demarcation line between mostly posh uptown and mostly impoverished downtown.

"It was a typical macho Rasta scene, you know," she said. "The place was full of people who lived down in the ghetto and they moved up there with all of their prejudices and they found there living in their midst Mrs. Goffe."

Though Bob Marley sang about justice and racial tolerance, he didn't show the old white lady, Lesline, much of either. He was determined not to treat her any better than whites had treated black people in Jamaica.

Marley was wrestling with racial demons of his own. The son of a black Jamaican woman and a white Anglo-Jamaican man, Marley suffered the sting of rejection from wealthy white family members of his when he turned up on the doorstep of their grand home in St Andrew hoping for a loan to launch his music career in the 1960s. His white family declined to come to his aid. This kind of treatment made Marley, his wife, Rita once said, "a tortured soul."

"Sometimes he'd come across the resistance of being half-caste," Rita Marley said. "There was a problem with his counterparts: Having come through this white father caused such difficulties that he'd want to kill himself and thinking, Why am I this person? Why is my father white and not black like everybody else? What did I do wrong?"

By the time Marley arrived at 56 he was on the rise and Lesline, was on the decline. She was a rotten reminder for him of Old Jamaica. He was, for her, a dreadful sign of what was to come in the New Jamaica. They were thrown together by Chris Blackwell, who allowed them to both live there in a strange arrangement that did not work for either of them. The reggae star didn't see why he had to put up with the white widow living in the servant's quarters and the white widow didn't see why she had to put up with the reggae star living in the main house. The standoff between Marley and the white dowager continued.

"Bob found this old white lady there and he had no time for her at all," said Sally Henzell. It was ironic that the mixed-raced Marley had been thrown together with Lesline, a white woman who'd rejected her white family's racism and embraced Alec Goffe, a black man. "I remember telling Bob, you should be nice to her because she stood up for something, you know, she stood up for her Brown man, for Goffie as she called him, against her family," Henzell said.

Besides, Bob and Lesline were more alike than they knew. Both of them held unconventional religious beliefs. Bob believed Haile Selassie was God and believed black people were the descendants of the ancient Twelve Tribes of Israel and Lesline believed humans were spirits living in a material world and that death and disease did not really exist. Bob believed there was nothing that could not be cured with the wisdom weed, the immortal herb, and Lesline believed whatever ailed humans could be healed spiritually, with right thinking and inspired prayer. Still, the welfare of an old white dowager was not, understandably, of much concern to Bob back then, especially with him bubbling on the Top 100. The house, 56, was signed over officially to the reggae star by Chris Blackwell, with Lesline Goffe still living in a cottage there, on Thursday 18 December 1975.

"*ROBERT NESTA MARLEY of 56 Hope Road in the Parish of St. Andrew, Musician is now the proprietor of an estate fee simple subject to the incumbrances notified hereunder in ALL THAT parcel of land part of MARYFIELD in the Parish of SAINT ANDREW being the Lot numbered ELEVEN on the Plan of Maryfield aforesaid...*"

The property came with many encumbrances. The house's Certificate of Title says no church, school, shop, warehouse, storehouse, or place of business should be erected on the grounds, nor must any trade or business be conducted there. If a stable, kitchen or water closet was built upon the land it must not, the title says, be erected within twenty feet of the adjoining property. Somehow, Island Records and later Tuff Gong, Bob Marley's recording studio, and still later, the Bob Marley Foundation, which is now housed at 56, managed to get around these stipulations.

Marley's main encumbrance, Lesline, moved soon after the transfer of ownership to a nearby townhouse leased from an old friend, the great Jamaican sportsman, Sir Herbert MacDonald.

"Poor darling Mrs. Goffe," said Sally Henzell of Lesline. "She was just a brave, upmarket woman and was clearly flabbergasted by all that had happened."

The battle over, the house won, Bob Marley went on to make some beautiful music there. The house was, Marley biographer Timothy White said, destined to be "the spot where all curses and spells, all follies and dreams, all hopes and hungers, all hatreds and horrors, would reach their apotheosis for Robert Nesta Marley." He was right. Marley wrote and recorded some of his best music in his Tuff Gong studio there and was shot and almost killed at the house by gun-toting assassins in 1976. It could have been Lesline Goffe that Bob Marley was thinking of when he said in one of his songs, 'the old world is ending, the new world has just begun.'

Ruinate

'I didn't attend the funeral, but I sent a nice letter saying I approved of it.'
Mark Twain

One after another, the pioneers, those who'd helped make Jamaica the world's largest producer of bananas between 1876 and 1929, began to wither like fruit on the vine. United Fruit Company founders Captain Lorenzo Dow Baker, who died in 1908, and Andrew Preston, who died in 1924, did more than anyone to make Jamaican bananas popular. They also, more than anyone, ruthlessly exploited Jamaica's bananas and Jamaica's people.

Like Baker and Preston, Joseph Di Giorgio, founder of the Atlantic Fruit Company, got rich off Jamaican bananas. Unlike them, though, he helped the island's banana growers achieve a degree of independence when he agreed in 1929 to let the new co-op, the Jamaica Banana Producers' Association, use his ships to export its fruit to the United States. Di Giorgio eventually quit exporting Jamaican bananas to grow grapes, peaches, plums, pears, nectarines, and apples in northern California. By the 1940s, the Di Giorgio Corporation was the largest fruit business of its kind in America. "Di Giorgio is to farming," the *San Francisco Chronicle* said, "what Tiffany is to jewelry." Joseph Di Giorgio died in 1951.

Like Joseph Di Giorgio, Antonio Lanasa was an important figure in the development of the Jamaican banana industry. Lanasa spent more than half a century in the banana trade; more than 30 years of that buying and selling Jamaican bananas. So popular did he become in Jamaica after he and A.C.

312

Goffe formed the Lanasa and Goffe Steamship and Importing Company in 1906, people in St Mary began christening their newborn children 'Lanasa.' A street in Baltimore, Lanasa Lane, was named for Antonio Lanasa, who died aged 82 in 1953.

It was Jamaicans, though, like Charlie Johnston, who served for more than 30 years as the head of the Jamaica Banana Producers' Association, who really made the island's banana industry what it was. When he died in 1957, the *Daily Gleaner* described him as "the last of the Great Jamaicans of the Nineteenth Century, the men who crossed the Frontiers, put Jamaica beyond the pale of the primitive and brought the country into modern trade, commerce and business."

Another of those "Great Jamaicans" was A.C. Goffe. A controversial figure who both helped and hindered the Jamaican banana industry, Goffe was typical of St Mary banana men of his time, a writer said. "The St Mary banana man was never quite the same as the banana grower of other parishes...the leading planter families of the parish had a marked individuality. Their self confidence...their love of putting their opinions over, made them a power that had to be reckoned with..." But that was a long time ago. His achievements, and exploits, have been all but forgotten now. Some things linger, though. The South Transept of St Mary's Parish Church, converted into the Goffe Memorial Chapel in 1944, remains as do other mementoes of long ago and far-away.

Strangely, the town of Galina, in St Mary, where A.C. Goffe shot and killed a man who stole thirty-six coconuts from one of his estates, named one of its roads, 'Goffe Avenue', after the banana man.

Happily, though, the time when Goffe and his family treated St Mary as if it were their personal kingdom is long gone. Most of the family's grand estates have shrunk to a few acres or have been sold off entirely and now provide housing for many of the families whose ancestors laboured on their plantations. Coniston House, where A.C. and his siblings grew up in splendour in the 1860s and 1870s, now houses a busy branch of a Jamaican bank.

A.C. Goffe died aged 87 in 1951, eight weeks after Hurricane Charlie's hundred mile winds roared through Jamaica killing 154 people and making 50,000 homeless and leveling hundreds of acres of Goffe's coconut trees and beloved banana plants. Some say the hurricane killed him. Heartbroken at the devastation he witnessed, he retired to his bed and lay there, it was said, like a baby in the fetal position until he died just weeks later, struck by a massive stroke. The day he died – 27 October 1951 – was a slow news days. As no one more important died that day, his obituary made it into *The Gleaner*. This final memorial to the banana man went badly though. The paper's obituary writer got his first name wrong and called him, 'Alexander' instead of 'Alfred.'

"Mr. Alexander Constantine Goffe, planter and owner of Windsor estate and hotel, died at his home 'Rivers Dene' here this afternoon."

Today, A.C. Goffe's Windsor Hotel is a badly dilapidated government run girls' home. His beloved St Mary, which American writer Zora Neale Hurston described adoringly in a 1930s book as, "The very best place to be in all the world…everything there is perfect…St Mary's is the first parish of Jamaica" is in decay. The parish hasn't been first in anything in Jamaica since banana put it on top years ago. In 2001 and again in 2002, St Mary was ranked the country's poorest parish by the Planning Institute of Jamaica.

The banana used to be king in Jamaica. When it was King, the King Banana was a larger than life Jamaican, loved by some and loathed by many more, named Alfred Constantine Goffe.

About the Author

Leslie Gordon Goffe grew up in London listening to what he thought were tall tales about the achievements and exploits, of his great-grandfather, Alfred Constantine Goffe. He discovered, though, on journeys to Jamaica and elsewhere that the truth about his ancestor was much stranger than fiction. What begun to emerge – in conversations with family members, from Jamaica's National Archives, from Harlem's Schomburg Centre for Research in Black Culture, and from Washington D.C.'s Library of Congress – was a portrait of an extraordinary, yet deeply flawed man who helped Jamaica become, at one time, the world's largest producer of bananas.

Printed in the United States
84643LV00003B/39/A